C. P. SCOTT
1846 — 1932

C. P. SCOTT

C. P. SCOTT
1846 – 1932

*The Making of
The "Manchester Guardian"*

GREENWOOD PRESS, PUBLISHERS
WESTPORT, CONNECTICUT

Library of Congress Cataloging in Publication Data
Main entry under title:

C. P. Scott, 1846-1932; the making of the "Manchester
guardian."

Reprint of the 1946 ed. published by F. Muller,
London.
CONTENTS: Haley, Sir W. Foreword.--Nichols, H. D.
The "Guardian" before Scott.--Hammond, J. L.
C. P. Scott, 1846-1932. [etc.]
1. The Guardian, Manchester, Eng. 2. Scott,
Charles Prestwich, 1846-1932.
PN5129.M33G83 1974   072'.7'2   73-19220
ISBN 0-8371-7312-4

GRATEFUL acknowledgment must be made to Messrs. G. Bell
and Sons, Ltd., for permission to reproduce material from J. L.
Hammond's *C. P. Scott and the "Manchester Guardian"*
(1934) and, in particular, the chapter by W. P. Crozier on
" ' C.P.S.' in the Office "; and to the *Political Quarterly* for permission to print part of an essay contributed by C. P. Scott to its
pages.

First published in 1946 by Frederick Muller Ltd., London

Reprinted with the permission of The Guardian

Reprinted in 1974 by Greenwood Press
a division of Williamhouse-Regency Inc.

Library of Congress Catalog Card Number 73-19220

ISBN 0-8371-7312-4

Printed in the United States of America

PREFACE

THE centenary of the birth of C. P. Scott is an event in newspaper history that seemed worth some commemoration. When Scott joined the *Manchester Guardian* in 1871 the paper was just fifty years old; he remained its editor until eight years after it had reached its century and its governing director for another two and a half years. It was a newspaper career that has few parallels, although editorships are not infrequently long— Delane edited *The Times* for thirty-six years, J. L. Garvin the *Observer* for thirty-four, Alexander Russel the *Scotsman* for twenty-eight, Edward Russell the *Liverpool Daily Post* for fifty-one. But Scott, in a more real sense than almost any of these, made his paper. He raised a local organ, important commercially to the North-west, but negligible in national politics, into one with an international standing. It kept its local importance, but it also became perhaps the most representative voice of English Liberalism. This book is intended as a slight record of Scott's achievement. It is also an account of the history over a hundred and twenty-five years of an independent journal. Such journals are less common than they were a generation ago. English newspaper life has undergone a revolution, and the group or " chain " system of ownership and control has become widespread. But the *Manchester Guardian* has preserved its individuality intact and, as described in these pages, arrangements have been made for it to be continued (as Scott, when he became its owner, decided that it should be) as a public service and not an instrument of private profit or power. The scheme by which the controlling ownership of the Manchester Guardian and Evening News Ltd. is vested in a trust is, it may be suggested, worth attention in present discussions of the freedom of the Press.

Like the trusts in different form which govern the control of *The Times*, the *Economist*, the *Observer*, and the *News Chronicle*, the Scott Trust is an attempt to meet one of the gravest of newspaper problems, the safeguarding of a paper's independence and individuality against the encroachments of large-scale organisations. The same problem has arisen in the United States and is being approached in the same way. Adolph Ochs, who built up *The New York Times* as one of the great papers of the world, wrote in his will that he trusted his executors would so exercise their financial control of the company as

> to perpetuate *The New York Times* as an institution charged with a high public duty, and that they will carry forward and render completely effective my endeavour to maintain *The New York Times* as an independent newspaper, entirely fearless, free from ulterior influence, and unselfishly devoted to the public welfare without regard to individual advantage or ambition, the claims of party politics, or the voice of religious or personal prejudice or predilection.
>
> I trust its editorial page may continue to reflect the best informed thought of the country, honest in every line, more than fair and courteous to those who may sincerely differ with its views.
>
> I trust its news columns may continue fairly to present, without recognising friend or foe, the news of the day—" all the news that's fit to print "—and to present it impartially, reflecting all shades of opinion.
>
> I trust its business departments may continue to conform to the highest standards of business ethics and that all persons associated or connected with any of the departments of *The New York Times* organisation may be treated justly and generously.

These are high aspirations, but the words of this distinguished American journalist describe admirably the spirit in which C. P. Scott viewed the newspaper owner's responsibility towards the public, a spirit that it is the aim of his successors to maintain.

CONTENTS

ILLUSTRATIONS

9

FOREWORD

By Sir William Haley

CENTENARIES of famous figures are very often little more than melancholy acts of piety. This is especially the case when the spirit of what the man being commemorated stood for is as dead as the man himself. How far this is so is a question that should resolutely be asked at every such celebration. The answer does not necessarily invalidate the occasion. Many famous men have been purely of their time; the value of the task they were called to do was nonetheless enduring because once it was accomplished there was no necessity for a continuance of the effort. At the same time, while such men may be great benefactors of humanity and figures of absorbing historical interest, their story cannot have the same importance and sense of immediacy for us as those others whose fight, however victorious, was only one battle in an ages-long campaign; whose work, however well done, is still left for following generations to do and do again.

There is no doubt into which of the two classes C. P. Scott should be placed. While the ephemeral quality of even the best journalism is sometimes overstressed, it is in its very nature a continuing and unfinished business. For journalism is a tool as well as a task. Unendingly it has to be applied to the policies and the problems of each recurring day and each succeeding age. Every journalist taking up that tool must depend on his fore-writers for the state in which he finds it. Paramount among his responsibilities in using it is the obligation to do nothing to impair the truth and fineness of its cutting edge, its cleanness of purpose, and its precision before the time

comes to hand it on. How C. P. Scott not only observed that
obligation but improved upon it is told in this book. The
journalism that as an octogenarian he laid down was far different
from and immeasurably better than the journalism he had as a
young man in his twenties taken up. But nothing he had
conferred on it was immutable. All he had gained for it in one
generation could be dissipated and lost in the next.

C. P. S. himself was aware of this and those of us who
had the privilege of knowing him in his old age, when close
personal interest in day-to-day affairs was diminishing, and
when he looked at the broadest issues only and in a mellow and
lambent light, can recall that he talked about some aspects of
the newest journalism more than once. He appreciated many
of its qualities. He could not help wondering at what price
they were going to be bought. Increasingly through the last
fifteen years of his life he examined and re-examined the
functions of the Press. Some of his most famous writing was
given to this subject. His article on "The *Manchester Guardian's*
First Hundred Years," written on May 5th, 1921, in which he
stated his conception of the essence of true journalism, has
become a kind of Declaration of Independence for all news-
papermen. But it was not enough for him to draw up a Charter
for the Press at large. He had to ensure the preservation of his
ideals within his own paper.

It may sound too cold and impersonal to say that to this end
he fashioned two instruments and that these were his sons J. R.
and E. T. Scott. It is, in a way, a tribute. A family such as the
Scotts owning a paper such as the *Manchester Guardian* have to
take something larger than a purely personal view of life. The
elder son, John Russell Scott, had been the *Manchester
Guardian's* manager over the whole period of C. P. Scott's
complete ownership of the paper. C. P. S. was writing out of
a long and happy experience when he said, "A newspaper, to
be of value, should be a unity, and every part of it should
equally understand and respond to the purposes and ideals
which animate it. Between its two sides there should be a happy
marriage, and editor and business manager should march hand

in hand, the first, be it well understood, just an inch or two in advance." It was under J. R. Scott's management and care that the reserves of the company were slowly built up till the *Manchester Evening News* could be bought—a vital step in the progress towards economic security for the *Manchester Guardian*—and the greatly extended building in Cross Street could be completed to house the steady expansion of the two papers between the world wars. On the management side, therefore, the succession was secure. So, it seemed, was it on the editorial. C. P. Scott's younger son, Edward Taylor Scott, had gone through a long and careful apprenticeship. When in 1929 C. P. Scott, while remaining governing director, retired from the editorial chair of the *Manchester Guardian* it seemed not only in the natural order of things but thoroughly fitting that E. T. Scott should take his place. When, a little over two years later, C. P. Scott died, we in Cross Street and the world outside that is interested in such things settled down to a long reign under the two brothers—one manager, one editor—John and Ted.

It was a good partnership. C. P. Scott had the satisfaction of seeing it working well and fulfilling all his hopes before he died. He was spared by a few months the bitter pain of knowing that all the years of planning and of preparation had come to naught. For before the early summer of 1932, on the New Year's Day of which C. P. Scott had died, E. T. Scott was himself dead, drowned in a boating accident on Windermere. J. R. Scott was left alone.

It is not possible to write of the days immediately succeeding that terrible blow. One's abiding memory is of fortitude. The first thing was to carry the paper on. Judgment did not waver under stress. W. P. Crozier was appointed to the editorship. Friends of the *Manchester Guardian* outside Manchester, who knew all that the paper meant to the national life but who had no means of knowing the individual qualities of the men on its staff, had suggested, in their anxiety to perpetuate the Scott tradition, some famous and even exalted names for the post. But John Scott knew his men and through twelve of the most difficult and troubled years in history, from the rise of Nazism in 1933 to 1944, the eve of its extermination, Crozier put the *Guardian* in the van of the fight. (Scott did the same thing again when A. P. Wadsworth, the present editor, was appointed to succeed Crozier.)

But it was not enough to find a new editor. The gust of wind on Windermere had blown away the basic structure of the ownership of the *Manchester Guardian* and the *Manchester Evening News* and of the higher direction of the company. The Scott conception of the ownership of newspapers as a public trust did not accord with the fact of a single personal proprietor. Continuity of tradition was put too much in jeopardy; the preservation of all the papers stood for might be at the mercy of circumstance; a proprietor could one day come upon the scene who through stress or wish would not follow the Scott family's self-denying ordinance where the profits of papers were concerned. Faced with this dilemma John Scott, with quiet logic, divested himself of all personal beneficial interest in the papers. It was an outstanding example of the subordination of every private consideration to the public interest. The wide disparity between the earning powers of the two papers had raised certain potential complications, but on margin there was a solid profit, and both papers were substantial capital assets. There were not wanting people ready to pay handsomely for the goodwill of the *Manchester Guardian* and the revenue earning capacity of the *Manchester Evening News.* Even within the scope of the then ownership there were lucrative possibilities had the owner been other than a Scott. It was true C. P. Scott had set a tradition of taking no profits from the papers. There was nothing legally binding about it. It was open to any succeeding owner to make his own choice. In John Scott's mind there has never been any thought of choice. What his father had started voluntarily he set out to perpetuate legally. He made it sure that neither he nor his successors could derive any dividends from the papers. He renounced his personal ownership in favour of a Trust. He took into the partnership of direction a number of his colleagues on the papers, arranging for them to own and administer the Company on the basis that every pound the papers made should be applied to the papers' good. All this was not achieved easily. There is apparently in the destruction of personal beneficial interest something antipathetic to English law. But it was done in the end, unostentatiously and without any indication that something out of the ordinary was afoot. The signature that set the final seal on this remarkable act of personal sacrifice in the public interest was placed as unemotionally and undramatically as that on many a humdrum cheque. It was nonetheless an act of importance in the record of English newspaper history. Having been myself somewhat closely associated with the steps taken to bring it about I have long wished to see it made known. I think it is appropriate that it should be recorded in this centenary book of C. P. Scott. It is all the answer required to show that his spirit lives on.

It is not the only answer. Having provided the papers with a direction for the present and buttressed their absolute independence for the future, John Scott settled down to the task of guiding their reinforcement and growth. But the orbit of that guidance never included either the leader or news columns. Though the seniority of the holders of the managerial and editorial roles had been reversed since C. P. Scott's day, though no Scott was now in either editorial chair, John Scott observed the now traditional Cross Street rule of the independence and paramountcy of the editorial function. Through all the difficulties of the pre-Munich years, through the heat and stress of Munich itself he never indicated by approbation or dissent any view to his editors. Such a relationship may appear bleak. It was not. He had chosen his men; he was prepared to abide by his choice. Praise has before now been used as a method of influencing decisions as powerfully as blame. To his mind the only safe way was to eschew either. This rule was absolute. Advertisers might occasionally rage. Friends of the papers who suddenly found themselves violently at variance with one or other of their policies might deplore. It made no difference. So far as John Scott was concerned all this was kept outside the editor's door. It still is.

It may seem strange that this Foreword to a book commemor-
ating the works and achievement of one man should deal so
largely with another. But, as I have tried to show, C. P. Scott's
sons were not the least of his works. There is something fine
and reassuring in the running true of a strong and individual
strain through succeeding generations of an English family.
" Character," said C. P. Scott, " is a subtle affair and has many
shades and sides to it." But here the outline is firm from one
generation to another and it is of importance to all that C. P.
Scott strove for and to the public heritage he left in his papers
that it should be so.

" In all living things," said C. P. Scott in 1921, " there must
be a certain unity, a principle of vitality and growth. It is so
with a newspaper, and the more complete and clear this unity
the more vigorous and fruitful the growth. I ask myself what
the paper stood for when I first knew it, what it has stood for
since and stands for now." It is a question we can ask ourselves
again to-day at twenty-five years' remove. We need have no
qualms about the answer. In this centenary we are paying
tribute to a living principle as well as to a dead man. Its
essence can be summed up in that aphorism of Archbishop
Whately which John Morley liked to quote: " It makes all the
difference in the world whether we put truth in the first place
or in the second place."

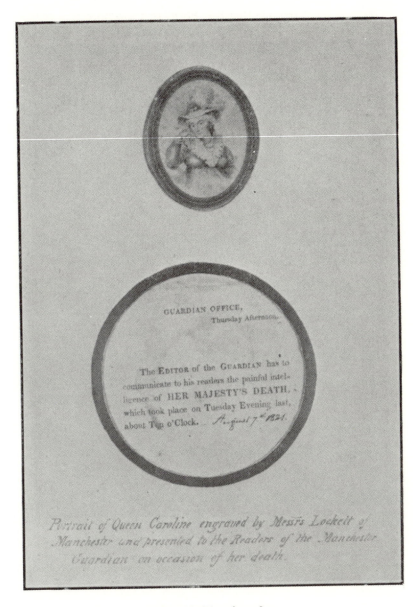

GUARDIAN OFFICE,
Thursday Afternoon.

The EDITOR of the GUARDIAN has to communicate to his readers the painful intelligence of HER MAJESTY'S DEATH, which took place on Tuesday Evening last, about Ten o'Clock. *August 7th 1821.*

Portrait of Queen Caroline engraved by Messrs Lockett of Manchester and presented to the Readers of the Manchester Guardian on occasion of her death.

AUGUST 7th, 1821
News of the death of Queen Caroline

JOHN EDWARD TAYLOR, 1791–1844
Founder and first Editor of the " Manchester Guardian "

I

THE *GUARDIAN* BEFORE SCOTT

By H. D. Nichols

WHEN C. P. Scott joined the *Manchester Guardian* on
February 8th, 1871, he was just in time to assist in
the celebrations of the paper's jubilee. For sixteen years the
Guardian had been a daily paper; before that it had been a " half-
weekly ", but it had started in 1821 as a weekly and remained so
for its first fifteen years. The founder of the paper was John
Edward Taylor, and the Taylors and Scotts were already closely
related before he married his cousin, Sophia Russell Scott, one
of whose nephews was C. P. Scott. The first John Edward
Taylor did not live to see the daily paper, though it had always
been a goal to aim at, and his publisher and first partner,
Jeremiah Garnett, achieved it. Looking back through its files
the paper seems to have taken a long time over its growing pains,
for by most counts early Victorian Manchester might have been
expected to support a daily long before 1855. Before the new
century began, Manchester already boasted itself a " commercial
capital ". By 1821 its population had quadrupled in fifty years,
and the process showed little sign of slackening.

But the taxes on knowledge, expressly designed to handicap a
popular Press, and the low level of education in all but a strictly
limited class, were to remain for many years a drag on daily
paper enterprise. A four-page paper could only be produced to
sell at sevenpence, and after five years of what was undoubtedly
good progress, the weekly circulation still stood at little more
than three thousand. As the paper had then to be printed on a
press whose output was limited to 150 an hour, it will be realised
that there were also technical obstacles to daily publication.

The new venture, which began on May 5th, 1821, at the bottom end of a Market-street whose medievalism was just beginning to be slowly and expensively " improved ", was not in itself unusual. Manchester had seen many a transient news-sheet in the past thirty years; some quickly expired, and some violently, and several remained to meet the new *Guardian's* competition, including *Wheeler's Manchester Chronicle*, to which Taylor had himself been a regular contributor for some years. But the *Guardian*, with the *Examiner* and *Courier*, both to be shortly set going, was the first of three Manchester weeklies which were to leave their competitors behind and grow into successful daily papers.

For forty years two men dominated the new paper; they had started it together and they worked on it in close partnership for twenty years. At the age of 30, John Edward Taylor was a successful Manchester merchant whose only connection with journalism had come by way of his political interests, for he was closely engaged in the Reform movement. He had some reputation as a pamphleteer, had provided London papers with their first authentic news of Peterloo, and had written the Reform party's official manifesto on that historic affair. As a writer of political broadsheets he had successfully resisted an indictment for libel at Lancaster Assizes and was already a public figure in the town when he decided to accept the offer of a number of friends to invest £1,100 to set him up with a paper of his own. The subscribers were George William Wood, Edward Baxter, George Philips, Thomas Bromiley William Sanderson, Robert Philips, Thomas Potter, William Duckworth, Thomas Wilkins, Richard Potter, Samuel Pullein, and Thomas Johnson.

Jeremiah Garnett was engaged by Taylor as his technical make-weight. He was a trained printer who had recently come to Manchester from Barnsley. He joined the *Guardian* as printer and publisher, but in the first capacity he was soon setting great quantities of his own copy as a reporter. After a few years he was playing almost as big a part in the public life of the town as Taylor himself and he survived his partner and the first of his sons to become editor of the paper.

Taylor's backers when the paper started have been described by his wife as " some of the most respectable and moderate persons in Manchester ", which suggests a Whig rather than a Radical origin for the paper. And there is no doubt that both Taylor and Garnett disappointed the expectations of the left wing of the emergent Liberal party. The paper was Whig from the start, and cautious at that. It was clearly committed to Reform, but the first instalment having been won in 1832 (by which 4,293 of Manchester's 180,798 population received political recognition) it was never among the impatient advocates of further change. Two full generations later it still distrusted the ballot. Though Taylor and Garnett were among the earliest members of the Anti-Corn Law League, they were never of the forward party in that great agitation. That battle having been won, the later extensions of Cobdenism and the policies of Bright aroused in the paper an antipathy which had once been reserved for Cobbett and the more extreme of the early Labour leaders. In municipal affairs, though the paper came down firmly and in good time on the side of the new Corporation, it was after a long period in which the Radical opponents of the Police Commissioners' regime had found little comfort in the *Guardian's* columns.

Clearly John Edward Taylor was not starting a Radical crusade when he set his new paper off on its long career. What he intended and the end that he persistently pursued from its first number was what he set out in his prospectus, the establishment of a local newspaper " promising a degree of public consideration correspondent with the wealth and intelligence of this town and of the surrounding district and their high rank in the scale of national importance." What Taylor started will seem to any reader of to-day as very unlike a modern newspaper, but it was the start of a laborious process from which the modern newspaper was to emerge. In 1821 it was not only the printing press which had a long way to go (and to go rather slowly when we consider how rapidly machinery was developing in many other fields); all modern ideas of editorial organisation and the preparation and arrangement of " copy " were still to seek. Many of them had to wait for the growth of the paper; a weekly of a few thousand circulation can support neither foreign or parliamentary services nor an adequate reporting staff, and the ordering and display of the " copy " available must, before the sub-editor was discovered, have been largely the affair of the printer.

It is perhaps the lack of any attempt at display which will first strike the modern reader of the old files. They give the impression that our great-great-grandfathers must have had better eyes than we have. (They surely cannot have read their weekly paper by lamp or candlelight or even the light from the Police Commissioners' gasworks!) As if the small type and narrow spacing were not enough, the reader is denied all visual aids to finding his way about the paper. Small and barely " leaded " headlines almost merge with the general body of the type, while leading articles and news items, courts and meeting reports and market news, and a great variety of informative " feature " paragraphs are indistinguishably blended. The unselective reader, one imagines, must have made a habit of starting at column one and going through it all. And the curious thing is that right from the start the compositor who set the advertisements was a master of display with all the arts at his command of a trade which can hardly have been ignored (it must have been despised) by the man who set the news.

For news (or should we say " intelligence "?) of foreign affairs, never neglected in the leader columns, the early *Guardian* had to depend on the London Press and at two removes; and without the telegraph it was slow to reach Manchester. Parliamentary news, too, came from London sources—a condensation for the Saturday paper up to the previous Wednesday's debate—but in its third issue the paper gave a foretaste of the grand-scale reporting for which it later became famous by producing nine and a half columns of a Commons debate on Peterloo.

Full and accurate reporting of public meetings had been one of the promises of the *Guardian's* prospectus, and no pains were spared to give effect to this policy. If there was room for improvement in the reporting standards of the early 'twenties improvements must be made. In 1830 John Harland, another printer turned reporter, was brought from Hull to Manchester to serve the *Guardian* for thirty years. He is known to the Dictionary of National Biography as a Lancashire antiquary, but to Manchester he was known as the *Guardian's* chief reporter, a fountain head through which flowed many and many-columned reports. For the greater part of the century only the grand scale was good enough for *Guardian* reporting; it was applied with a rare catholicity to a wide variety of meetings and with unusual impartiality to those which were most likely to find themselves held up to scorn or derision in the adjoining leader columns. Controversial manners were free and frank whether the paper was attacking or attacked, but if you had your say at a public meeting and were held worthy of notice you could rely on an adequate record as well as a reply.

Throughout the long struggle for the disentanglement of local government, the clearing up of the compromise system which the Police Commissioners had substituted for the simple medievalism of the Court Leet and the vestries, the *Guardian's* policy was hesitant and uncertain until it came down definitely, in the wake of Cobden, for incorporation. But its practice as a newspaper was perhaps more important than its policy in creating the conditions in which Incorporation won the day. Until Manchester got her Charter the Tory oligarchs were firmly entrenched against anything like free discussion; given the publicity which *Guardian* reporters supplied, even the unnatural alliance with the Radicals could not save them.

The generosity of the paper's reporting, of which the full bloom was to be seen at election times, was by no means confined to occasions of public dispute. Politics might come first with the *Guardian,* but other interests ran them close. The Chamber of Commerce, the Athenæum, the Medical School (which long preceded Owens College), the College itself and the earlier Mechanics' Institute, the Royal Institution, the hospitals and a score of minor local institutions could always count on the detailed reporting which came first and on the fair, if sometimes rough, handling in the leader which probably followed. The prospectus had indicated wide general interests, with the promise that no significant local activities should be neglected, and when musical festivals were organised in Manchester in 1828 and again in 1836 the reports were to be measured by pages rather than columns. In 1836 in the first Wednesday issue of the paper, as a by-product of this musical interest, over nine columns are to be found devoted to a list of the guests at a fancy dress ball.

Under both Taylor and Garnett the *Guardian* was much concerned with currency and banking questions on which great erudition was displayed both in the correspondence and leader columns. On labour questions and the " condition of the people " its economics were dominated by the dismal science of its period; its blind spots were those of " the most respectable and moderate persons " of the day. The social historian of the first half of the last century does not find much of his data in its newspaper files. They scarcely came into the recognised field of political discussion. Had they done so, and been discussed in public meetings, they would without doubt have figured more in the *Guardian's* columns. Housing and sanitation, the health and living conditions of the common man presented a picture of unrelieved misery to which the social conscience had scarcely begun to awake. This was the reality underlying the recognised controversies of the time and a reality still largely neglected in newspaper columns as in public life generally.

For the history of the early Labour movement, too, in which there was great and feverish activity throughout the 'twenties and 'thirties little of the evidence is to be found in the columns of a Whig journal. The Combination Act of 1825 had given the trade unions an existence merely and an ineffective one. Many ambitious experiments in labour organisation were made in the following years but under leaders and with an inspiration which made no appeal to the *Guardian*. Strikes which might more strictly be called lock-outs, for they were nearly all against wage reductions, were frequent in the cotton and building trades and among the engineers, and proceedings for conspiracy were a common-place of the police courts. Here again it was by reports rather than policy that the paper was justified. The trade union meetings were given reasonable space, and if one-sided justice was often seen in the courts it did not pass unrecorded. Most of the early Factory Acts, a painfully slow series culminating in the Ten Hours Act of 1847, were passed in the teeth of trade opposition, though with the powerful support of a few exceptional mill-owners. Such legislation offended against " the obvious and simple system of natural liberty ", a principle which was held to apply above all to the relations of employers and employed. The *Guardian* was not active among the reformers in this field, nor had it much sympathy for impatient and sometimes violent agitation. The early Acts were hopelessly defective on the administrative side, and the courts rarely acted effectively against defaulting employers. When this was pointed out, however, the protest received due publicity in the news, a necessary first step, if not a very long one, towards the tightening up of factory inspection.

The paper's circulation was still only a little over 2,000 after four years, but in 1835 it took over, and incorporated for a time in its title, the *Manchester Volunteer*, whereupon the sales shot up to 3,400. Three years later Jeremiah Garnett devised new methods of feeding the presses so that 1,500 pages were now put out in the hour. The Wednesday edition was started in 1836, and by the time John Edward Taylor died, in 1844, the circulation had reached about 8,000. The twice-a-week paper promised a new liveliness in production and delivery. It had come to the notice of its conductors that there were people who wished to have their paper at the breakfast table even if only for two breakfasts a week; if they would say the word it was promised that this should be arranged. The price too was down, a reduction in the stamp duty having now made it possible to put out " more than has ever been offered " for fourpence.

A leader announcing these changes laid a new emphasis on the attention to be given to local affairs and promised that the surrounding towns should not be neglected. But the paper was still appealing for such news to friends and readers, who were invited to send " authenticated communications on any events or transactions of material public concern ". With twice the space to fill there was no doubt quite enough in the home town to occupy the paper's professional reporters. In the first two numbers of the new series the musical festival and its fancy dress ball called for nearly two pages of criticism and reporting. Three days later the death and funeral of Madame Malibran took up four columns, and a meeting of the Medical School a column and a half.

By this time some advance had been made by way of make-up and the orderly arrangement of news. The whole paper was still extraordinarily tight, and headline space sternly restricted, but the reader could find his way about much more readily. It still required more than a casual glance to pick out the various features, but now some of them had been allotted more or less regular places with which subscribers might be familiar. The leader columns, announced by the paper's title and date line, followed by shoulder-heads for each article, but still unseparated from the body of the type, begin to appear at the top of a column and at the opening of an inside page. But it is not yet an organised main news-page. Two or three columns of leaders (now a strongly developed feature of the paper) will probably be followed by " Local and Provincial Intelligence "—four or five columns of solid paragraphs, mainly records of folly and misfortune from the courts, with more than an occasional " lift " from other Lancashire papers. On the next page three or four columns may go to the report of a single case at the Salford Sessions and, overleaf, under the heading " Domestic and Miscellaneous " comes about a page of pure scissors and paste extracted from a variety of periodicals or more solid publications. There is hardly a limit to the subjects covered, and most of the paragraphs suggest the correct answers to a general knowledge paper. There is less of this sort of thing in a week which happens to have provided more solid opportunities for local reporting, but it is to be some years before this old-style " Miscellany " is brought within bounds. So far the *Manchester Guardian* has established the tradition of its leading articles and its reporting, but the rest of the modern newspaper is as far away as ever.

THE CORN-LAWS.—THE BUDGET.

By a special express train which left London at ten o'clock, we have received a copy of an extraordinary edition of the *Sun* of last evening, from which we compile the following summary of the financial measure proposed last night in the house of commons by Sir ROBERT PEEL.

Sir ROBERT PEEL proposes,—

Tallow: duty to be reduced from 3s. 2d. per cwt. to 1s. 3d.

Timber (foreign): Gradual reduction to be specified on a future day.

Cotton goods: Those on which a duty of 10 per cent is now paid to be imported duty free; those on which there is a duty of 20 per cent to be subject to a duty of 10 per cent.

Woollen goods (made up): duty to be reduced from 20 per cent to 10 per cent.

Linen goods: duty to be reduced to 10 per cent.

Silk goods: duty to be reduced to 15 per cent *ad valorem.*

Paper hangings: duty reduced from 1s. the square yard to 2d. except on the most expensive kinds.

Manufactures of Metals: duty reduced from 15 per cent to 10 per cent.

Umber-lead, Hardwares, Manufacture of Hair, &c.: duty to be considerably reduced;

Carriages: duty to be reduced from 20 per cent to 10 per cent.

Candles: duty to be reduced one-half. ,

Soap (foreign): duty to be reduced one-half. Hard soap from 30s. to 26s.; soft, from 20s. to 14s.; Naples, from 20s. to 15s.

Hides (raw or dressed): duty to be repealed.

Boots and Shoes: duties to be reduced one-half.

Straw Plat: duty reduced from 7s. 6d. to 5s. and on hats from 8s. 6d. to 5s. per dozen.

Silk (dyed thrown): duty to be repealed.

Foreign spirits: duty to be reduced from 22s.10d. per gallon to 15s.

Sugar: the differential duty on foreign free-labour to be reduced 3s. 6d.; on slave-grown sugar, no alteration.

Seeds (agricultural): duty to be reduced to 5s. per cwt.

Grains (for fattening cattle): duty to be repealed.

Indian Corn: duty to be made nominal.

Buck Wheat: duty to be made nominal.

Rice Cake: to be admitted duty free.

On butter, cheese, and hops, the duties to be reduced one-half.

On cured fish, the duty to be reduced to 1s. per cwt.

On bacon, fresh beef, salt beef, fresh and salt pork, cattle, and everything of animal food, all the duties to be repealed.

On vegetables of all kinds the duties to be repealed.

THE CORN-LAWS.

WHEAT.—When the average price is under 48s. the duty to be 10s.; above 49s. duty 9s.; when 50s. and 51s. duty 7s.; above 52s. and under 53s. duty

---

THE BUDGET.

A DEFICIT OF £2,379,000 TO BE MET.

GRADUATED DEATH DUTIES.

ANOTHER PENNY ON THE INCOME TAX.

FURTHER DUTY ON SPIRITS AND BEER.

A CONCESSION TO PROPERTY OWNERS.

The House having gone into Committee of Ways and Means, Sir William Harcourt rose at five minutes to four to make his financial statement.

The CHANCELLOR of the EXCHEQUER, who was received with cheers, said: Mr. Mellor, I am sure I shall not ask in vain for the patience and indulgence of the Committee, of which I stand in need, for they are all aware that the task which is imposed upon me to-day is one of no ordinary difficulty. My first duty is to state to the Committee the financial conditions of the country during the year which has just concluded. The Committee are well acquainted with the adverse circumstances which beset that year. The rise in commerce and the general prosperity which began in 1888 and which culminated in 1890 had been in a condition of progressive decline until we hoped that it had reached its lowest point in 1893. But that unfortunate year laboured under accumulated misfortunes. The financial difficulties in America, the financial embarrassments of Australia, the disturbance of trade in India, the labour disputes at home, the general depression of agriculture, aggravated by the drought of last season, which affected the crops in the South of England—each and all of these to ordinary times might have been cause which would have adversely affected the revenue, but which in their combined effect might have been expected to produce most unhappy consequences, and a collapse of the public finance such as that which we witnessed in many foreign States in the present year; and England, from her universal trade, is more susceptible than any other country to external disturbances of the character —(Hear, hear.) Not in spite of all these adverse cause the Committee are already aware, through the usual channels of information, that the condition of the public balance-sheet is by no means an deplorable as had been anticipated some months ago —(Hear, hear.) On the contrary, I believe that that balance-sheet would show in a striking manner the abundance of your finance and the unbroken solidity of the resources of the nation.—(cheers.)

The first six months of the year were apparently disastrous, but the law of average in the end prevailed, and the second half of the year has redressed the balance, as the summer drought was succeeded by the winter rain.

CUSTOMS A SATISFACTORY ITEM.

My first business is to lay before you the yield of the revenue to the year just concluded, as compared with the Budget estimates and the yield of the preceding year. I will spare the Committee the reading of tables, and will only refer to them. The first head is that of Customs. The Budget estimate was £19,650,000. The actual receipt into the Exchequer was £19,707,000, the receipts exceeding the estimate by £67,000. I think that is a pretty accurate estimate upon a sum of nearly twenty millions. But what is more material to be observed in this case is the net receipt, which is the true comparison of the yield of revenue belonging to the several years. The Exchequer receipts of course may include sums belonging to former years. The net receipt is the actual receipt for the current year compared with the actual receipt from the different heads of revenue in the past year. The net receipt on the Customs for 1893-4 was £19,711,000, as compared with £17,619,000 for the preceding year, showing an increase of £93,000 in the last year. Under the circumstances I think we may say that in an interesting figure. The principal items I will briefly mention. In foreign spirits there is an increase of £79,000 on the whole. There is a large diminution on rum—rum drinking appears to be a capricious quantity. It prevails some years ago, and has much diminished now. But there is a still larger increase on the other kinds of foreign spirits. On tea the excess in 1893-4 over the preceding year has been £101,000—beer, hear.]—an increase of six million pounds weight, or 3 per cent upon the whole. Coffee is a constantly diminishing consumption. Tobacco shows only an increase of £7,000. It is a stagnant quantity in the last year—a good deal below

---

THE BUDGET.

NEW TAXES FOR SOCIAL PROGRESS.

LANDOWNER'S "UNEARNED INCREMENT."

HIGHER ESTATE DUTIES.

SUPERTAX ON INCOMES OVER £5,000.

ABATEMENT FOR CHILDREN.

MOTOR LEVY FOR BETTER ROADS.

TAPPING UNWORKED MINERALS

NEW SYSTEM OF LICENCE DUTIES.

SPIRIT AND TOBACCO TAXES RAISED.

£3,000,000 FROM THE SINKING FUND.

The Chancellor of the Exchequer, in introducing the Budget in the House of Commons yesterday, described it as a "war Budget"—a Budget raising money to wage warfare against poverty and squalor.

Mr. Lloyd-George's speech was much more than a review of the national finances in the past year and an announcement of the financial proposals for the coming year. It indicated the Government's plans of social reform for which money will have to be found in future years.

With fresh liabilities impending for the navy and social reform, the Chancellor deemed it the bolder and better course to examine frankly the whole financial outlook and make

---

THREE BUDGET DAY REPORTS

THE WAR.

CAPITULATION
OF THE
EMPEROR NAPOLEON
AND
MACMAHON'S ARMY.

MARSHAL MACMAHON WOUNDED.
(REUTER'S TELEGRAMS.)

BERLIN, SATURDAY.

The Queen has received the following telegram from the King:—

"DERON SEDAN, FRIDAY, 1.30 P.M.

"A capitulation, whereby the whole army at Sedan are prisoners of war, has just been concluded with General De Wimpffen, who was in command instead of the wounded Marshal Macmahon.

"The Emperor only surrendered himself to me, as he himself has no command, and left everything to the Regency in Paris. His place of residence I shall appoint after I have had an interview with him, at a rendezvous which will immediately take place.

"What a course events have assumed by God's guidance."

RECEPTION OF THE NEWS AT BERLIN.

We have received the following from our correspondent at the Prussian capital:—

BERLIN, SUNDAY, NOON.

The *Staats Anzeiger* says:—

"On the 31st of August, after a skirmish with the vanguard at Nouart, a battle began near Beaumont, in which Marshal Macmahon was driven

1870

THE WAR
IN
SOUTH AFRICA.

THE SIEGE OF LADYSMITH.

MESSAGE FROM GENERAL WHITE.

KRUGER AND THE ARREST OF A BOER SPY.

ALLEGED THREAT TO SHOOT BRITISH OFFICERS.

FUTILE BOMBARDMENT OF KIMBERLEY.

THE TROOPS AT THE CAPE.

8,000 MEN SENT TO DURBAN.

There is nothing from Natal than can be called news. A message from General White, probably of last Thursday's date, says that the bombardment continues, but practically no harm has been done. The bombardment of Kimberley has so far been a ludicrous failure.

A curious story comes from Capetown about one Nathan Mark, who was arrested as a spy in Ladysmith in the early stages of the investment.

1899

GREAT BATTLE EAST OF PARIS.

ANGLO-FRENCH ARMIES TAKE OFFENSIVE WITH SUCCESS.

GERMANS COMPELLED TO FALL BACK.

INVADERS SUFFER HEAVY LOSSES BEFORE ANTWERP.

DINANT BURNED AND CITIZENS SHOT.

great battle is being fought between Paris and the French eastern frontier fortresses. The lines stretch from the north-east of Africa. The Union has a common border

a dangerous crossing with a vigorous enemy behind. Developments seem to be preparing in South Africa.

1914

THE NEWS FROM THREE WARS

Russell Scott Taylor, the young editor who succeeded on his father's death in 1844, scarcely survived to make any deep impression on the paper. He was only in his twenty-fourth year when he was carried off by typhoid in 1848. In his four years at the office he had seen and supported the acquisition of Manchester's first public parks, the purchase of the Lord of the Manor's market rights and the end of the Court Leet, the jubilations at the repeal of the Corn Laws and the passing of the Ten Hours Act. On his death, and until his younger brother should be ripened for the task, Jeremiah Garnett carried on the office and tradition of his late partner. The 'fifties were a time of great prosperity in Manchester, now somewhat tardily recognised as a city. And in 1855 when the last of the taxes on knowledge came off, Garnett decided for a daily paper. Unlike the Liberal members for Manchester, the *Guardian* had never taken an active part in the fight to repeal the taxes on its own product. And if Cobden, now at daggers drawn with the paper, is to be credited, it was one of several established journals which looked doubtfully on the prospect of " free trade in newspapers ". The *Guardian* certainly had doubts about the character of some of the new publications which might arise but its own appearance as a daily had now become possible, if not inevitable, and any doubts that may have lingered about its financial future were soon to be settled.

With daily publication the foreign service began to develop rapidly. In 1855 the Crimean news, two or three weeks old, was quoted from various sources and both *Daily News* and *Times* correspondents were quoted from Paris; but there are already special " Our Own Correspondent " messages from Paris, from Austria and from Prussia, only four or five days old and often running over the column. A forerunner of the " London Letter " of later days began to appear as from " A Private Correspondent " who doubled the roles of London gossip writer and political correspondent when not competing, at some length, with the leading articles. The Parliamentary report would run to two columns or more. District news began to be given distinctive headlines, and the sorting out of the news became much more orderly. The second John Edward Taylor was now in the office and probably the new hand was already at work.

The daily *Guardian* started at twopence but came down to a penny in time for the general election of 1857, which it fought on a scale not before seen in English journalism. The cardinal issue of the Corn Laws now being well out of the way, the paper was free to indulge its inclination to a central Whig policy and strong support of Palmerston. At the last election, five years earlier, there had still been some doubt whether Repeal was out of danger and the *Guardian* had then qualified an otherwise wholehearted attack on everything John Bright stood for by admitting a doubt whether Manchester could afford the gesture of dismissing him. Milner Gibson might go, but a Manchester repudiation of Bright might be misinterpreted. There were no such doubts in 1857. Bright and Gibson must be sent packing and, closely linked with them, Cobden who, owing to Bright's illness and absence from the country, was coming over twice a week from the West Riding to take his place. The *Guardian* gave Cobden a rare fight and one suspects that he rather enjoyed coming over to his adopted city from the relative quiet of his Yorkshire constituency to give blow for blow.

Foreign policy was the issue of the fight and the wars with Persia and China (" the breeze of hostilities at Canton ") the centre of the argument. No quarter was given, or asked. Cobden and Gibson could have their whole page of reporting but they caught it hot and strong in the leaders, and with them the League which had been revived as a neo-Cobdenite organisation with wider interests than the Corn Laws. To the *Guardian* this election was a crusade " to rescue Manchester from the thraldom of the League " and " to end the dictatorship of Newall's Buildings." Cobden on his part was characteristically vigorous about " the vermin of your Manchester press ", which was gleefully reported as it attacked him. After the poll the paper showed the magnanimity of the victor, with a truce to hard words. Cobden and Bright had gone, with most of their friends, and before the cheering was over the paper was hoping that their talents would not long be lost to Parliament.

When the younger John Edward Taylor took over the paper on the retirement of Garnett in 1861, a new pace was set in its development. Manchester was to have at its service the resources of a Fleet-street daily. This was not an easy matter or to be had for the asking. One source of trouble was the Parliamentary report which, as Taylor found it, could scarcely be called a journalistic production. The private telegraph companies still dominated the scene and what the provincial papers got from Parliament came by way of what they called their intelligence department. It scarcely lived up to the name, was generally unreliable and sometimes incredibly bad. Taylor was one of the first to see the remedy and he helped to achieve it when the Press Association was formed, but this could not be done till 1870. Meanwhile the paper had secured a place for its descriptive writer in the Commons gallery and in the same year, 1868, it opened its own London office equipped with two private wires, now rented from the Post Office. The " Private Correspondent " in London with his all too political preoccupations gave place to the " London Letter ". Among its first contributors were Tom Taylor, the dramatist, afterwards editor of *Punch*, McCullagh Torrens, the member for Finsbury, and Tom Hughes of *Tom Brown's School Days*. The foreign service was not neglected while these changes went on and by the outbreak of the Franco-German war the *Guardian* was ready with its own staff of war correspondents. The campaign was reported for Manchester as adequately as by any of the London papers. The new editor had found much to attend to in London during these changing times and soon he was living there and largely controlling his paper from London. This was scarcely an arrangement that could last. Garnett's place as manager had been taken by a brother-in-law of Taylor's, Peter Allen, but until the appointment of C. P. Scott there seems in effect to have been only a remote control of the editorial side of the paper. In the office the editorship was often, as it were, in commission, with Richard Dowman as nominal editor, John Couper, H. M. Acton and J. M. Maclean, acting for an editor-proprietor who was never far from call but otherwise actively engaged at the London end. The second John Edward Taylor had found his role on the paper and was not coming back to the editor's room in Manchester. That was a task for which he had chosen C. P. Scott.

1821
THE LONDON "ROYAL REGULATOR"

2

C. P. SCOTT, 1846—1932

By J. L. Hammond

C. P. Scott came of stout Noncomformist stock, for his great-grandfather, John Scott, who had a small linen factory at Milborne Port in Somerset, was described as zealous "in the cause of Protestant Dissent and Civil and Religious Liberty." His grandfather, Russell Scott, who had been educated at two famous Dissenting Academies, Daventry and Homerton, was Minister of the Unitarian Church in High Street, Portsmouth, and a great figure in the life of the town. His fame as a preacher spread far and wide and his ardour for political reform, seconded by his wife, the daughter of William Hawes, founder of the Royal Humane Society, led Joseph Priestley to predict, when he left England in despair in the dark days of Pitt's repression, that Scott would soon follow him to the United States. Scott's father, also called Russell, was born in 1801, and brought up in a family school where his father educated his wife's nephews as well as his own children. He complained afterwards, as did John Stuart Mill, that his father had made him a precocious child (at the age of seven he was a theologian) and that his mind became a sort of hothouse plant. At sixteen he went into an office and at twenty-one he became partner with his uncles in Cory's coal business, doing so well that he retired before he was forty. For the rest of his life he devoted himself to his large family and to public enterprises, like the Metropolitan Association, for improving the dwellings of the industrial classes. He married in 1831 Isabella Prestwich, daughter of Joseph Prestwich, a wine merchant in South Lambeth, and sister of Joseph Prestwich, afterwards famous as a geologist. They had eight children of whom C. P. Scott was the youngest but one.

C. P. Scott was born in Bath, where his family were then living, on October 26th, 1846. Nine years later they moved to London, where they made their home in Cornwall Terrace, Regents Park. Scott was sent, like his brothers, to a school at Brighton, known as Hove House, conducted by a Unitarian minister. From there he went on to Clapham Grammar School, then in the hands of Charles Pritchard, a Fellow of St. John's College, Cambridge, well known as an educational reformer and still more famous as a scientist. He was later Savilian Professor of Astronomy at Oxford, where he achieved fame as an inventor of scientific instruments and as the author of the scheme for setting up the observatory in the Parks. Unfortunately Scott's health at this time caused some anxiety, and after two years he was taken away from this stimulating atmosphere and sent to a coach in the Isle of Wight. While there he kept up a steady correspondence with his father on public affairs and theology. His father was less radical than the Portsmouth preacher, but he was exceedingly anxious that his son should think for himself and not give too much weight to his father's opinions.

In 1865 Scott went up to Oxford. The University Act of 1854 had thrown open the Universities of Oxford and Cambridge to Nonconformists, but until 1871, when all religious tests were abolished, the several colleges could make what conditions they liked. Scott's first choice was the Queen's College and his second Christ Church, but both of them required a certificate of baptism. After a good deal of discussion, in which Jowett, then a tutor at Balliol, gave help and advice, Scott found himself at Corpus. Even there he had some trouble over attendance at Chapel, but after an interview with the Dean he agreed willingly to go to chapel regularly except on Sundays, Saints' Days or Litany Service Days. After composing his difficulties with the authorities he took an active part in introducing music into the Chapel services. Scott had a full and happy life at Oxford. He spoke at the Union, supporting, among other radical causes, the reform of the laws restricting the rights of trade unions. He

JEREMIAH GARNETT, 1793–1870

First printer of the " Manchester Guardian " and Editor 1844–1861

JOHN EDWARD TAYLOR, 1830–1905
*Editor of the " Manchester Guardian " 1861–71, and
proprietor until 1905*

took up rowing with enthusiasm and success, and he gave frequent parties. He had long discussions on religion and politics
with his friends, and as the chief of them were Churchmen like
Jacobson, the son of the Bishop of Chester, and Owen Ilbert,
son of a Devonshire parson, he got an insight into the minds
of men whose upbringing had been very different from his own.
He read hard, enjoyed the lectures of Furneaux, W. L. Newman and Bonamy Price, and though he fell into the Second
Class in Mods., he got a First in Greats. He tried, unsuccessfully,
for a Fellowship at Merton.

In the year that Scott went up to Oxford a book was published
that caused a great sensation and excited violent controversy.
This was Seeley's *Ecce Homo*. Two great religious leaders,
Shaftesbury, the Evangelical, and Pusey, the High Churchman,
condemned it. Shaftesbury called it " the most pestilential volume
ever vomited from the jaws of Hell." Pusey wrote to Gladstone,
" I have seldom been able to read much at a time, but shut the
book for pain, as I used to do with Renan." Gladstone on the
the other hand treated it with great respect, writing three long
articles on it in *Good Words* and reaching a very different conclusion, calling it " an earnest, powerful and original contribution " to the revival of Christian faith for which he hoped.
Morley, while full of respect for Gladstone's articles with " a
temper and a breadth of outlook that show no mean elements
in the composition of his greatness," remarked that Seeley's
work was " not a very effective or deeply influential book."
Whether Morley was right or wrong, the book had a decisive
influence on a young man who was destined to play an important
part in British public life. It gave Scott, as he said, the religion
by which he lived to the end of his days. Scott had at first
thought of becoming a Unitarian minister, but his speculative
beliefs were unsettled and he found in *Ecce Homo* an anchor
for his conscience and his imagination. In August 1869 he
described his state of mind in a letter to his father:

    I believe in God and his goodness partly because my heart seems
to witness to His living presence, partly because my reason tells

me that the order of the world cannot be the result of chance nor its glory of malignity. I believe in the Son of God because I see in His person a moral ideal shining with divine brightness in the midst of a dark age and constituting a revelation not only to that age but to all subsequent ones. This ideal constitutes my religion. To approach it myself and help others to approach it is the chief aim of my life.

Scott had the peace and strength of mind that come from a settled outlook and conviction on the duties and mysteries of life, and this he owed, as he said towards the end of his life, to the lasting impression made on him by *Ecce Homo*. Few men have had a sense of purpose so simple, direct, complete, and unchanging.

Scott thus left Oxford with his mind made up on fundamental questions. He left Oxford also with his career determined. His cousin John Edward Taylor, son of the founder of the *Manchester Guardian*, who had taken complete control of the paper in 1861, did not want to live in Manchester. He wished therefore to find a writer who shared his general ideas on politics with whom he could co-operate from London. It is not surprising that his mind turned to his young cousin who was making his mark at Oxford. He asked to see some of Scott's essays and was so well pleased with them that he decided to invite him to join the staff, hoping that he might blossom into an editor. Scott accepted his invitation, and after spending six months in the office of the *Scotsman*, in Edinburgh, he arrived in Manchester in February 1871, receiving a warm welcome from Peter Allen the manager, Dowman the editor, and Couper the chief sub-editor. He found good lodgings in Duncan Street, Higher Broughton. He walked to and from the office and played a good deal of tennis. His time-table, as described in a letter written to his brother in April 1871, would seem very strange to a modern journalist:

My hours are pretty much as follows: I get up at 7.30, breakfast, read the *Guardian* thoroughly, and walk into town, arriving soon after ten o'clock. I work all day and walk back for dinner about six o'clock. Read or write in the evening and go to bed soon after ten. This I find not altogether satisfactory and mean to vary by an afternoon ramble once or twice a week. I also intend to join a gymnasium and work there for half an hour or so before going home.

He soon made friends in Manchester, among the earliest being Walker, High Master of the Grammar School, and Professor Roscoe the chemist. He was also drawn into a scheme for improving the housing of the Manchester poor into which he put a great deal of enthusiasm. A society for this purpose was formed with the Bishop of Manchester and other eminent citizens as patrons, and Scott wrote to his father in December 1871, saying that he would like to give £500 of his prospective inheritance to its funds. He also proposed to spend a week canvassing for subscriptions. " The matter is so important that I feel confident that Edward will condone the temporary neglect of duty of which I shall have to be guilty."

We hear nothing about his cousin's views of this suggestion, but he cannot have been upset because in January 1872 he put Scott in to the editor's chair, two years earlier than Scott had expected. Scott was then twenty-five, and of the men to whom he had to give orders some had been on the staff before he was born. Nature had helped him by putting a good deal of authority into his face and he disguised his youth by growing a beard. He soon acquired a reputation for severity that those who only knew him outside the office found it difficult to understand. A young man holding a very responsible position was likely to be strict with his subordinates. In this case the young man had to answer for his conduct of the paper to a vigilant superior in the background, for Taylor wached over the affairs of the paper and expected to be supplied with full information on every incident and detail in the administration of its affairs. He himself kept notes of the articles and writers that pleased or displeased him as he studied each day's paper.

Scott used at first after becoming editor to spend summer week-ends at Blackpool, but the increasing popularity of that famous resort soon made this impossible. For he needed privacy for the work he took with him, and, when Blackpool was full, private rooms were not to be had at a hotel, or in lodgings. The pressure of his work and responsibilities told on him, as we know from a letter he wrote to his son Laurence who was working in Ancoats in 1904. He regretted that there were no settlements in Manchester when he was a young man. "Dull and dismal enough it was in lodgings, and I used to spend twelve hours a day I remember at the office as a refuge, a mistake, for that is the time I ought to have formed the habit of systematic reading. Only having the whole responsibility thrown on me a year after I got there I naturally took the work hardly and it cost me an illness, almost the only one of my life."

Scott escaped from all these discomforts by a very happy marriage. In October 1872 Madame Bodichon, the well-known feminist who helped to found Girton, introduced Scott's sister to Miss Rachel Cook, daughter of John Cook, Professor of Ecclesiastical History in the University of St. Andrews. Miss Cook, of whom George Eliot said that she was the most beautiful woman she had ever seen, was one of the seven original students at the Women's College at Hitchin which afterwards migrated to Cambridge to become Girton. She took the Classical Tripos at Cambridge in 1872. She had known no Latin or Greek till within a few months of going to Cambridge, but she was put into the second class, and it became known that one of her papers on Aristotle had been considered the best submitted. Scott, discovering her gifts when he made her acquaintance, enlisted her as a reviewer. In November 1873 he wrote to her from Paris thanking her for her charming little review and telling of a conversation with Gambetta and of the " hard struggle for life " that Liberty was having in France. Their friendship developed, and in May 1874 they were married in London. They found their first home in The Breeze, Kersal. In 1881 they moved to The Firs, Fallowfield, where Scott lived to the end of his life. From the time of her marriage to the breakdown of her health nearly thirty years later Mrs. Scott was a most valuable and active colleague. She shared all Scott's political interests and discussed the questions of the day with him. She was a remarkably good speaker, making a great impression in London during the Boer

War. She also contributed not a little by her æsthetic taste and literary talent to Scott's success in giving to the *Manchester Guardian* for the first time a serious standing as a critic of culture.

This was the first change that Scott made in the character of the *Manchester Guardian*. It was fortunate for him that Manchester was at that moment alive with important movements, and rich in men of intellectual distinction. The new spirit of city pride and zeal for education showed itself in the founding and development of Owens College. Manchester, while still suffering from the depression caused by the American Civil War, raised a quarter of a million to make John Owens' great benefaction an institution worthy of a great city. The College, growing gradually into a University, drew to Manchester a number of scholars, scientists and historians of the first rank. Scott moved happily and eagerly in this society, and as an editor he found at his door writers, who were masters of their subject, ready to put their knowledge and tastes at the service of his paper. As the paper acquired a reputation for distinction in this field it became easy to attract contributors who were eminent in one or other department of literature or scholarship. Among men of Scott's own age Saintsbury and A. W. Ward were writing in the seventies on literature, Dill on classical scholarship, Mandell Creighton and Bryce on history, Richard Jefferies on Nature, Comyns Carr and Walter Armstrong on art, and Arthur Evans on archaeology. Freeman and Goldwin Smith were voices from an older generation. Nowhere was the change in the paper more noticeable than in the character of its dramatic criticism. We have a picture of the earlier arrangements of the *Manchester Guardian* in a letter Scott wrote to his sister in 1871, in which he said that he thought of making himself dramatic critic. " Our head reporter does the work now but very badly. He is a somewhat dour little dissenter, and his heart is not in his work. He handled Sothern and a new play of Byron in such a way the other day that I shall be compelled to write a second notice." A. W. Ward came to the rescue, and it soon became known that anybody who brought a good play to Manchester, or who tried to raise the standard of acting, could count on finding his work discussed in the *Manchester Guardian* by a brilliant man of letters. What the paper did for the theatre in the next thirty years can be seen by a study of the pages of a little volume called *The Manchester Stage,* published in 1900, which has preserved some of the work of the four men who treated the theatre in its columns during those years, W. T. Arnold, Oliver Elton, C. E. Montague and A. N. Monkhouse.

Scott, who gave a great deal of thought and trouble to improving the range and quality of the paper as an organ of culture, paid great attention also to arrangements for improving its news service. John Edward Taylor had acquired in 1868 a London office with two private wires and these facilities made it much easier for the paper to keep in touch with the outside world and to make use of special correspondents and distant contributors. The Manchester staff did not adapt itself at once to these changes if a story of the Franco-German War is true. It is said that the news of the Sedan disaster, sent by the paper's correspondent in France, arrived as a leader-writer was leaving and that he thought it more important that he should catch his train to Altrincham than that he should take some notice of this disturbing communication. Under Scott's direction the tone and rhythm of the life of the paper were quickly changed. What he did for its dramatic and literary criticism he did also for the special correspondence of the paper, adding to its political importance by sending out men whose standing and knowledge secured for their views serious attention. In the seventies and early eighties Arthur Evans, the discoverer of the Minoan civilisation, travelled for the paper in the Balkans, where he was arrested by the Austrian police as a dangerous character. Scott gave his correspondents their independence, only asking that they should be truthful reporters. He sent J. B. Atkins to South Africa in the Boer War, although Atkins was not in complete agreement with the paper, having confidence in his integrity.

When Scott went to Manchester the *Guardian* was a moderate paper and the *Examiner* the Radical organ. In one of his earliest letters he wrote: " I have decided to be put up along with Mr.

Allen for the Reform Club. This club is at present very much in the hands of the extreme Radical party—the *Examiner* party in fact—who chiefly got it up. It is represented to me as not agreeable or desirable in any way from a strictly social point of view, but it is a political centre and I should not like not to have the entry at election times." Scott's letters at the time show how cautious and circumspect was the Liberalism that nature and training had given him. He was angry with Gladstone for suggesting in a speech on the Ballot Bill in 1870 that the franchise might be further extended, arguing that it had to be shown that a further extension would be likely to produce a better governing body, " and that I fancy it would not be easy to show." Writing in the paper on Jacob Bright's Bill for Women's Suffrage in 1871, he accepted the case for enfranchisement but urged delay until a sound education and a larger experience of life had redressed " the balance, at present so ill-adjusted, between reason and emotion." " Among women are to be found the strongest supporters of every new crochet, the most ardent enthusiasts of every ephemeral emotion which is stirred in the public mind." About Chamberlain's crusade for Disestablishment he wrote: " A great organisation, which has done more than can be calculated to elevate and to console the people of many generations, is to be torn up by the roots from the basis on which hitherto it has rested, and to be transformed into we know not what." If Scott had died in 1880 he would have accomplished his first aim of making the *Manchester Guardian* a paper worth the attention of men and women of serious culture, but the paper would not have been known as a leader of great causes or an active combatant on great issues. The change in the political character of the paper came with the titanic contest over Home Rule. Thomas Hardy, after a visit to London at this time said that the struggle into which the British people had been thrown was a struggle between the strongest impulses that can govern man. It was a new experience to Scott to find himself in such an atmosphere. At first his instincts led him to look doubtfully on Gladstone's plan. But he accepted it once it was clear to him that the only alternative was perpetual war with Ireland. Freeman wrote a series of articles on the question, treating the problem in a large historical setting, and reaching the conclusion that " either Ireland must be free or else she must be more thoroughly conquered than ever." Scott had greatly strengthened his staff in 1879 by appointing W. T. Arnold, a writer who had made his mark by a book on the Roman Imperial system. Arnold realised that what was wrong with Chamberlain was that he saw the Irish problem as something smaller than it was. Thus Scott's practical and flexible mind combined with Arnold's imaginative power to produce the strongest case for Home Rule to be found in the Press. The *Manchester Guardian* thus took a new place in public life, as the most accomplished and effective voice on the side of Home Rule in the day-to-day struggle that absorbed all the attention and excited the deepest emotions of the British people.

This experience was an education for Scott himself as well as for his public. There was something of the atmosphere of revolution in a struggle that excited hope and fear, passion and imagination on a scale unknown in politics during Scott's life. He was himself affected by it. He retained to the end of his days a judicial quality of mind that was invaluable in an editor who had to guide and control the fire and the force of gifted writers with strong individual characteristics. But inhibitions that had made him more prudent than enterprising in judging new ideas lost their hold over him at this time. This was a specially important change, for social and industrial problems were beginning to force their way to the front and the earlier Scott would have been cautious in welcoming the new ideas that were to transform Liberalism and to bring about the great reforms that are associated with the Governments of Campbell-Bannerman and Asquith. As it was the *Manchester Guardian* played a part of signal importance in this modernisation of Liberalism. Its home was in a part of England where the conflict between capital and labour had often been crude and violent, and Manchester was traditionally associated with the undiluted gospel of *laissez faire*. Scott determined to put the case for new and generous ideas before his public without considering how his public would take them. Arnold presented and defended the claims of the dockers in the great strike of 1889, Montague those of the miners in 1893, and Hobhouse those of the engineers in 1897. Montague summed up in one sentence the bad principle on which the old system rested: " The idea that wages, in other words the living, the comfort and the civilisation of the great mass of men is to be the one elastic and squeezable thing in a business has got to go." Another sentence in a leader by Hobhouse on the engineers' strike of 1897 showed how completely the *Manchester Guardian* had broken with the illusions of *laissez faire:* " The power of organised capital is the standing danger of democracy."

The outbreak of the Boer War in 1899 threw these domestic issues into the shade, and for three years the nation was absorbed in a controversy that revived in a still fiercer temper all the passions that had been excited in 1886 over Home Rule. The Liberal party was sharply divided. Its right wing followed Grey and Haldane; its left wing followed Morley, Harcourt, Bryce, Robert Reid and Lloyd George. Asquith leaned to the right from the beginning, but he was a moderating influence in the first stages. Campbell Bannerman, having just been elected leader of the party in the House of Commons in succession to Harcourt, was also a moderating influence in the first stages, though like Spencer and Ripon he leaned as clearly to the left as Asquith to the right. As the controversy grew sharper these two men diverged, and when C.B. made his famous attack on " methods of barbarism " in June 1901, the party almost split in two, Asquith, Grey, Haldane and Fowler joining to form the Liberal League, a body small in numbers but strong in wealth and influence. Behind the Liberal League was Rosebery, who, though much more critical of Milner and Chamberlain than his lieutenants, was regarded as the future leader of an Imperialist Liberal Party. The tension was acute for, when C.B. attacked farm burning, Haldane and Grey went so far on the other side as to support the proclamations that outlawed Botha and the other Boer generals in the field.

From the first Scott had been active in organising and

educating opinion against the War. He had entered the House of Commons as Member for Leigh in 1895 (after three unsuccessful attempts in North-East Manchester) and thus he had been able to watch from the centre of politics the sinister growth and unscrupulous adventures of a predatory Imperialism that had become a danger to the British Empire. The escapades of Rhodes and the Jameson Raid were the outward signs of the malignant power that J. A. Hobson described in his analysis of South African society. Hobson, whose book became a classic, had been sent to South Africa by Scott as special correspondent of the *Manchester Guardian*. It was not surprising, therefore, that Scott acted with the group in the House of Commons that followed Morley in his criticisms both of the Government's surrender to Rhodes and its forward policy in the Sudan. The Sudan conquest justified itself in history by the sequel, but Scott was suspicious with good reason of the temper that the Government displayed and the dangerous spirit with which it sought to intoxicate opinion. When hostilities seemed imminent in South Africa in the autumn of 1899, Scott persuaded Morley to speak at a great meeting in Manchester to warn the nation against war. During the war Scott was naturally a great deal in London, but he was fortunate in having two exceptionally gifted leader writers in Montague and Hobhouse, who argued the case for conciliation with consummate power. The *Manchester Guardian* made itself extremely unpopular by the course it pursued, though serious opponents recognised its force. Scott was unmoved by crude attacks like the cartoon in which he was pictured taking a bribe from Kruger, but he did on one occasion reply to a private letter that he received from a distinguished Manchester citizen, who said that, painful though it was, he was obliged to break off relations with Scott and the paper. He could only conclude from Scott's opposition to the war " either that political life has partly deprived you of reason or that you have preferred the supposed advantage of a political party to the good of the country." It is pleasant to be able to record that when a quarter of a century later Scott's admirers presented his bust by Epstein to the City of Manchester, the name of the writer of that letter appeared on the list of donors.

In spite of the unpopularity of his views, Scott kept his seat at the Khaki Election of 1900. His time and thoughts were much occupied in the next few years by anxiety over his wife's health, which broke down and made it necessary for him to take her abroad. He decided that he would leave the House of Commons at the end of the existing Parliament. In November 1905 Mrs. Scott died, and Scott lost an invaluable colleague as well as a devoted wife.

Scott was thus out of the Parliament that was returned at the great Liberal victory of 1906 to which the *Manchester Guardian* had made such an important contribution. But the election had greatly increased his personal influence, for he was in close touch with some of the leading Ministers in the new Government. Bryce, who was a very old friend, was not in office long, for in February 1907 he went to the United States as Ambassador. Churchill, who had entered the Government as Under Secretary for the Colonies, had fought and won a Manchester seat at the election (North-West Manchester) and thus he and Scott had been thrown together. But the two men with whom Scott was most intimate were Loreburn, the new Lord Chancellor, and Lloyd George, the new President of the Board of Trade. Scott had interviews and correspondence with other Ministers, including Morley, Grey, and McKenna, but he saw Loreburn and Lloyd George more constantly than any others, and they had a considerable influence on his opinions.

The Liberals who had given the new Government so huge a majority had a pretty clear vision of what they expected from it. They hoped to redress the wrong of the Boer War by giving South Africa self-government, to take a good step towards Home Rule, to cut down expenditure on the fighting services, to settle the education question and to introduce a series of large social reforms. This programme was carried out except that the Irish advance came to nothing because the Irish politicians rejected it. The *Manchester Guardian* was enthusiastic for this programme and its support was, of course, exceedingly effective. What neither the Liberal voters nor any other section of the public realised was that a revolution had taken place in British foreign policy, and a revolution of the highest importance. This had happened under the Balfour Government. Lansdowne had made an alliance with Japan and he had formed an *entente* with France which had rapidly grown into a much closer connection.

It is important to remember how this *entente* had arisen. Outwardly it was an arrangement to settle disputes that had caused friction between the two countries, and as such it was as welcome to Liberals as to Conservatives. But in fact it was much more than this, as is clear when we study its history. In 1900 and 1901 Lansdowne and Chamberlain made up their minds that isolation had become dangerous to the British Empire in a Europe which had shown a good deal of hostility in the Boer War, and where acquisitive and competitive instincts were growing in strength. They turned first to Germany, but Holstein, the most active and formidable figure in the German Foreign Office, overreached himself. He thought that Britain could never come to terms with France and Russia and he therefore demanded at once a complete and total alliance, thinking that Britain would have to take what terms Germany chose to give her. The Balfour Government then turned to France, and the *Entente* followed. The chief feature of its provisions gave Britain a free hand in Egypt in return for her recognition of a special French interest in Morocco. This *Entente* was strengthened in a very short time by the action of Germany, who began to try to bully France and to seduce Britain into dropping it. Lansdowne was naturally very uneasy at the prospect of losing the *Entente* and letting France come under the power of Germany, a prospect that did not seem remote when German bluster compelled the French Government to dismiss Delcassé, the Foreign Minister who had carried out the negotiations with Britain. He therefore promised France full support in resisting German pressure. When the Liberals took office, a conference was about to be held at Algeciras at which Britain was pledged to uphold France, and military and naval plans had been discussed by Staff Officers of the two countries.

In the next few years the *Entente* was drawn tighter and it was extended to include Russia. Here again German policy had aided and accelerated this development. For Germany pushed ahead with her big navy and would not accept any plan for a general halt. She was clearly aiming at naval as well as military supremacy in Europe. Thus under the Liberal Government Britain, already in the Continental system when Balfour resigned, though the public was entirely unaware of the fact, got more deeply into it. Grey held as strongly as Lansdowne that it was as clearly a British interest as a French interest that France should be strong enough to be independent of German pressure. Germany tried to shake the *Entente*, and only made it firmer.

The foreign policy of the Government rested on the assumption that Britain could no longer maintain her position in the world by her isolated strength. That had been the view of Lansdowne. It was the view of most of the officials who were in touch with events. But there were some important dissentients. The strongest statement of the case against Lansdowne's policy had come from Salisbury, who wrote a memorandum on the subject on May 29th, 1901. " Except during his (Napoleon's) reign we have never been in danger; and therefore it is impossible for us to judge whether the ' isolation ' under which we are supposed to suffer, does or does not contain in it any elements of peril. It would hardly be wise to incur novel and most onerous obligations, in order to guard against a danger in whose existence we have no historical reason for believing." When Salisbury wrote this memorandum the *entente* Lansdowne had in mind was an *entente* with Germany. When Lansdowne succeeded in making an *entente* with France Salisbury was dead, but the view he had taken was put strongly by Rosebery. Thus two ex-Foreign Ministers, one of them with the highest reputation enjoyed by any Foreign Minister of his time, disagreed with the underlying assumption of Britain's new foreign policy. With all that is known to-day it is difficult to believe that Germany's exorbitant pretensions in Europe could have been resisted successfully without Anglo-French co-operation, but the fact that these two experienced statesmen mistrusted the arguments that convinced Lansdowne and Grey makes it easy to understand the suspicion and hostility that the new policy excited among Liberals.

Scott's views on the subject were those expressed by Salisbury in his memorandum. He held that our unpopularity on the Continent was the result of the Boer War, and that if we abstained from imperialist adventures we should not find ourselves again in the unpleasant position we had occupied when our armies were beating down the heroic resistance of a small people. The *Manchester Guardian*, therefore, was a powerful critic of the Grey policy. That policy would have been less severely criticised if Grey had been less secretive. But the facts about German aggression were not generally known, and Grey regarded the whole subject as a departmental rather than a Cabinet matter. It happened that Loreburn, who put the case against Grey's policy to Scott in frequent conversations, was kept in ignorance of important facts, although he was Lord Chancellor. Nobody can read Scott's records of his conversations with Loreburn without seeing that too much confidence should not have been placed in his judgment. He put all the blame on Grey for our bad relations with Germany; and after the war he said to Scott that we should have averted war by co-operation with her. Few would be found to-day to agree with him on either of these points.

But Grey was to blame for Loreburn's ignorance. In January 1906, in the midst of the General Election, the Liberal Government sanctioned military and naval conversations with France, following the example of its predecessor. But this was not made known to the Cabinet. The only Ministers who knew of it at the beginning were C.B., Grey, Asquith and Haldane. It is strange that C.B., with all his experience and his good judgment, did not see the danger of leaving the Cabinet in ignorance of the facts. It was not until 1911 that the whole Cabinet knew of the intimate character of our relations with France.

In April 1911 the French sent an expedition to Fez on the plea that disorder there threatened the safety of Europeans and that they did not wish to incur the odium that the Gladstone Government had incurred from its failure to rescue Gordon. The expedition created a new situation, for Fez was outside the limits within which France held a police mandate under the agreement reached at Algeciras. Germany considered that she was entitled to some compensation, and negotiations began with that object. When discussions were in progress Germany created a crisis by sending a ship to Agadir. Grey told the German Ambassador that the British Government would expect to be consulted in any new arrangement that might be made about Morocco. This communication was made on July 3rd, and by July 21st no answer had been received from the German Government. That evening Lloyd George was to speak at the Mansion House, and on learning at the Foreign Office that the German Government was still silent, he inserted a passage into his speech, with Grey's approval, which was generally taken as a public warning to Germany; a warning that led to protests in the German Press. For some time there was acute tension, and in the middle of August Metternich, the German Ambassador, told J. A. Spender that he thought war highly probable before the end of the week. Preparations were made, and it was not until October that the crisis could be considered over. The fact of the preparations became known to Loreburn, who complained in the Cabinet in the autumn that Ministers like himself were left in ignorance about matters of supreme importance. From that time (November 1911) the whole Cabinet knew exactly how we stood with France.

Down to this time Scott's talks with Loreburn were the chief basis of his judgments on foreign policy. He did not write many leaders himself, but his sympathies were fully reflected in the criticisms and the anxieties that found expression in his paper's columns. But the Agadir crisis brought him into direct discussion with Asquith and Grey on their foreign policy. Lloyd George asked him as a personal favour not to write anything on the situation until he had seen him, and Scott went to London to see Lloyd George. He had then a series of interviews with Lloyd George, Asquith and Grey, the full records of which are included in the collection he kept of his political conversations. On his return to Manchester the *Guardian* published a leader (not written by him) of which the most important part deprecated the view that had been urged in the *Observer* and other papers that " We must stand with France at any cost against unreasonable demands, no matter of what nature." From this view the paper dissented strongly. " We should put the matter much lower, and so, we are inclined to think, would our French friends. They know that with the best intentions in the world we cannot save France from the German legions, and where Germany is concerned, she would much rather have promises of support from the armies of Russia than from the English Navy. We must take care, therefore, not to be more French than the French, and not to encourage her for motives of our self-interest in a policy which would have far more serious results for her than for us. We would suggest another formula for our policy, namely that this country should fulfil its treaty obligations and protect its own interests, and though this formula may sound less heroic, it is, we believe, fairer to France and to ourselves."

Scott was at this time President of the Manchester Liberal Federation and in January 1912 he, and other officers of the Federation, sent Grey a letter pressing this view and asking the Government to make it absolutely clear to the French Government that "we hold ourselves under no obligation either of treaty or of honour to support French diplomacy in any future controversy, by the weight of the armed forces of this country, or by any such diplomatic action as might imply such assistance in the last resort, but that this country holds itself perfectly free to take such action as it may think that the circumstances of the occasion demand when any difficulty arises."

Scott mistrusted the reasoning behind the Government's foreign policy. But he was specially distressed by its treatment of Persia. On this issue he found no support from Loreburn or from Morley, both of whom welcomed the conclusion of a

THE ELECTIONS.

No personal changes have been effected in the representation of Manchester by the polls which were taken yesterday. Mr. Jacob Bright, Sir Henry Roscoe, and Mr. Schwann have again been returned in the Liberal interest, while Mr. Balfour and Sir James Fergusson continue to represent Toryism. The statement, however, does not exhaust the interest of yesterday's vote. Mr. Balfour's majority has been reduced from 614 to 398, while Sir James Fergusson's has fallen from 1500 to 110. Sir Henry Roscoe's majority is 181, as compared with 335 in 1886; but Mr. Jacob Bright has improved his position. Six years ago he polled 111 votes in advance of his Conservative opponent; yesterday he defeated Mr. Hopkinson, a Liberal Unionist, by 148. Again, Mr. Schwann appears in augmented strength, his majority being 805, against 96 at the last general election. In Salford the Liberals have been more fortunate. In the Northern division Mr. W. H. Holland headed the poll—a clear Liberal gain,—and it is certain that but for the candidature of Mr. Hall, the Labour candidate, Mr. Forrest would have beaten Sir H. Howorth in South Salford. Sir Henry's majority was only 27, and he would certainly have sustained a severe defeat if the 553 votes wasted upon Mr. Hall had been cast in favour of the Liberal candidate. Mr. Gladstone's recent warning is here once more impressively enforced. It is with much regret that we record the fact that Mr. Benjamin Armitage has failed in West Salford. The Conservative majority was small—only 40, but in a parliamentary contest a majority of 40 is as effective as a majority of 400. In Bury Sir Henry James, who was unopposed at the last election, has won by 869 votes; while at Wigan it has been found impossible to dislodge Sir F. S. Powell. At Chester Mr. Yerburgh, a Conservative, who represented the city in the late Parliament, has held his ground, defeating his Liberal opponent by a considerable majority. Mr. Wilson has won at Middlesbrough, and the representation of the borough thus passes from a Liberal to a direct representative of Labour. Of the London elections decided yesterday not the least interesting was the contest in Battersea. There Mr. John Burns, the Labour leader, received the support of the Liberal party, the result being that he defeated his Conservative opponent by a large majority. The Liberals have gained seats in West Newington, Walworth, and Bermondsey, the majority in Newington being 1,055. Curiously enough, the Liberals have gained complete possession of the two great military ports, Portsmouth and Devonport—a fact which means a gain of four votes. There has been no change at Birmingham, and the most serious incident in connection with the Glasgow contests is the substitution of a Unionist for a Liberal in the Camlachie division, where the Liberal party has been greatly enfeebled by dissensions. Mr. Sexton, which now passes to Mr. H. O. Arnold-Forster, a Dissentient Liberal. It will be easy, of course, to find another seat for the Nationalist leader. The Liberals have done splendid work in Oldham, where Mr. Cheetham and Mr. Hibbert have been returned, displacing Mr. Elliot Lees and Mr. Maclean. This is a great triumph. The four divisions of Edinburgh voted on Tuesday, but the results were not made known until yesterday. In three divisions the Liberals have been successful; in one a Liberal Unionist, and son-in-law of Lord Salisbury, was returned. The reactionary division, West Edinburgh, has been a source of difficulty to the local Liberals ever since Mr. Gladstone put forward his Home Rule proposals. It is the "West End" of the Scottish capital, and is peopled largely by professional men and what may be described generally as the "genteel" class. In 1886 Mr. Buchanan, who was then a Unionist, was returned by a majority of 600. After a time the hon. gentleman satisfied himself that the claim of Ireland was just and ought to be conceded, and he took the manly course of resigning his seat and giving the constituency an opportunity of declaring whether or not he still possessed the confidence of the electors. The

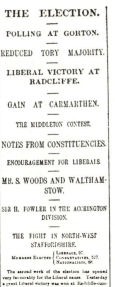

THE ELECTION.

POLLING AT GORTON.

REDUCED TORY MAJORITY.

LIBERAL VICTORY AT RADCLIFFE.

GAIN AT CARMARTHEN.

THE MIDDLETON CONTEST.

NOTES FROM CONSTITUENCIES.

ENCOURAGEMENT FOR LIBERALS.

MR. S. WOODS AND WALTHAMSTOW.

SIR H. FOWLER IN THE ACCRINGTON DIVISION.

THE FIGHT IN NORTH-WEST STAFFORDSHIRE.

LIBERALS, 97.
MEMBERS ELECTED {CONSERVATIVES, 327.
NATIONALISTS, 66.

The second week of the election has opened very favourably for the Liberal cause. Yesterday a great Liberal victory was won at Radcliffe-cum-Farnworth, where Mr. Taylor converted an adverse Conservative majority of 602 at the last election into a Liberal majority of 60. Mr. Taylor polled 5,407 votes, by far the largest number ever given to a Liberal in this division, and the Conservative poll, despite Mr. Cross's appeals to the electors to vote "for the integrity of the British Empire," presumably as personified in himself, has slightly fallen off since 1895. Thus Radcliffe is once again represented by a Liberal, as it always was before 1895. In the Gorton division, too, the Liberal and Labour candidate, Mr. Ward, did very well, though, probably for want of time to organise his campaign, he failed of complete success. As it was, he brought up the progressive vote very nearly to the standard of 1892 again, and reduced Mr. Hatch's majority from 1,664 to 570. Here again, while the Liberal poll increased largely, the Conservative poll has fallen away a little since 1895. The results in Radcliffe and Gorton will encourage Lancashire Liberals to make a good fight in the other divisions of the county which poll to-day and to-morrow. In the St. Andrews Burghs the Liberals also improved their position yesterday, bringing down Mr. H. T. Anstruther's majority from 706 to 54, and St. Andrews, it has to be remembered, has steadily returned a Unionist since 1886. A second decisive Liberal victory was gained yesterday in the Carmarthen Boroughs, where Sir John Jones Jenkins, the Conservative ex-member, was defeated by no less than 700 votes, by Mr. D. Davies. Carmarthen was, like Swansea, which Sir George Newnes recaptured last week, one of the few consistently Liberal seats in Wales that were lost in 1895, and its recovery, by so large a majority, is very welcome. Mr. Davies's poll of 2,837 is the largest recorded in the constituency since 1885.

THE ELECTION.

LIBERAL AND LABOUR VICTORIES.

CONSERVATIVE ROUT.

MR. BALFOUR DEFEATED.

MR. WINSTON CHURCHILL'S TRIUMPH.

MANCHESTER AND SALFORD SOLID.

21 LIBERAL GAINS.

The outstanding features of Saturday's polls are:—

The magnificent victories of Liberalism and Labour.

The defeat of the ex-Premier.

The triumph of Mr. Winston Churchill.

The utter rout of the Unionist party in the great constituencies of Manchester, Salford, Bradford, and Plymouth.

The gain of 21 seats by Liberal and Labour representatives.

SUMMARY OF RESULTS.

ENGLAND, WALES, AND SCOTLAND.

	L	U	Liberal gains
Friday	2	1	1
Saturday	43	10	21
	—	—	—
	45	10	22

Another striking peculiarity of the contests has been the exceptionally large number of votes recorded. So far there have been polled:—

	Votes
Liberal and Labour	239,858
Unionist	160,157

Liberal and Lab. majority   79,701

The first day at the polls has resulted in an overwhelming victory for the cause of Free Trade. The combined forces of Liberalism and Labour have achieved a triumph to which the electoral battles of the past furnish no parallel. Huge Unionist majorities have disappeared in constituencies hitherto thought impregnable to the Liberal attack, and the lesson of the by-elections of the past five years—that no majority, however great its dimensions, could be counted as safe—has

1892   1900   1906

THREE GENERAL ELECTIONS
HOW THE RESULTS WERE ANNOUNCED

ASSASSINATION

OF THE

AUSTRIAN ROYAL HEIR AND WIFE.

SHOT BY STUDENT IN BOSNIAN CAPITAL.

TWO ATTEMPTS DURING A PROCESSION.

The Archduke Francis Ferdinand of Austria, nephew of the aged Emperor and heir to the throne, was assassinated in the streets of Sarayevo, the Bosnian capital, yesterday afternoon. His wife, the Duchess of Hohenberg, was killed by the same assassin. Some reports say the Duchess was deliberately shielding her husband from the second shot when she was killed. One victim was struck in the body and the other in the face; the telegrams are contradictory about which wound the Archduke suffered and which his wife.

Two attempts were made on the Archduke's life during the day. He was in Bosnia directing the manœuvres of the Austrian Army Corps stationed in the province, and had devoted yesterday to a procession through the capital. During the morning a bomb was thrown at the Imperial motor-car, but its occupants escaped unhurt. In the afternoon in another part of the town a Serb student fired a revolver at the car, killing both the Archduke and the Duchess.

Francis Ferdinand's marriage was a morgantic alliance, and in consequence of a declaration which he made when contracting it his children do not inherit his rights to the Austrian crown. His wife was Countess Sophia Chotek when he married her in 1900. The title of Duchess was conferred on her after the wedding.

ment prevailed amongst the crowd and many people wept. Large crowds assembled all day at the scenes of the two attempts, and flags at half-mast are flying on all buildings.

Some details of the first attempt are now available. The bomb was what is called a bottle bomb. It was filled with nails and lead filings. The explosion was very violent and the iron shutters of many shops in the street were pierced by fragments of the bomb. About twenty persons were slightly injured, several women and children being among the number. In the course of the afternoon a considerable number of people reported slight injuries. An official of the local government received severe injuries in the legs from splinters of the bomb.

ASSASSIN EXPLAINS.

(REUTER'S CORRESPONDENT.)

SARAYEVO, SUNDAY, 6 P.M.

The assassin of the Archduke and his wife is a student named Gavrilo Prinzip. He is 19 years of age, and was born at Grahovo, in the district of Livno. He studied for some time in Belgrade.

On being interrogated, Prinzip declared that he had intended for a long time to kill some eminent personage from nationalist motives. He was waiting to-day for the Archduke to pass by, and made his attempt at a point where the motor-car had to slacken speed when turning into the Francis Joseph Strasse. As the Duchess was in the car he hesitated for a moment, but afterwards he quickly fired two shots. Prinzip denies having any accomplices.

JUNE 20th, 1914. THE FIRST OCCASION ON WHICH DOUBLE COLUMN HEADLINES WERE USED

Treaty with Russia which removed, as they believed, the danger of a Russian aggression on India. To give Russia a sphere in Northern Persia in return for her exclusion from Tibet and Afghanistan seemed good sense, and the reform and nationalist movement in Persia, on which Scott looked with traditional Liberal sympathy, seemed to both of them an artificial and fugitive enthusiasm. Scott felt so strongly that we were betraying Persia and countenancing Russian atrocities that he had to warn Grey that he might feel unable to take the chair at a great meeting at which Grey was to speak in the Free Trade Hall. The truth was that Russia's character for perfidy was such that she could blackmail anybody who wanted her support, and she took full advantage of her position. Scott's distress was not greater than that of our Minister at Teheran, Sir Cecil Spring Rice, who wrote " The patriots were confronted with the fact that at the very moment when they came to the fore and had a chance of saving the country, their natural ally, England, went over to the enemy and put her hand in that of the oppressors. That is the game I am playing now."

The last few years before the war were spent by Grey in making serious attempts to improve our relations with Germany, and they were so successful that at the close of the Balkan Conference in August 1913, he received public compliments from the Kaiser and from the German Chancellor. Lloyd George told Scott that Grey had kept the peace in the difficult moments of that Conference by telling Russia that Britain would not support her if she went to war. When the Sarajevo murder precipitated the crisis of July 1914, Grey hoped that he might repeat this success and he proposed a Conference, a proposal that Germany rejected. Scott was in Germany in July, having gone to Jena to consult an oculist. He returned on July 27th, on which day he saw Lloyd George, and also Illingworth, the chief Liberal Whip. He urged on Illingworth that the Government ought to make it plain from the first that if Russia and France went to war we should not be in it. To the last he was against British participation in the war, but he recognised when the history of the negotiations in the closing weeks was made known in the Government's

White Paper, that Germany had thwarted Grey's efforts for peace in rejecting his proposal for a Conference.

When war came Scott saw at once that all controversy over pre-war policy must be suspended and that we were involved in a struggle that demanded the undistracted strength of the nation. For the next four years he was in close contact with leading Ministers. In the early stages of the war he made up his mind that Lloyd George and Churchill stood out among Ministers as men of action. When the first war crisis occurred, the public anxiety and agitation over the question of supplies for the army, he was insistent in private and in public that the control of munitions should be in Lloyd George's hands. In a letter to Lloyd George of May 24th, 1915, he wrote, " It isn't Munitions alone that you will have before long to organise, I expect, but the nation for war." When Lloyd George was in this office, Scott was able to obtain for the nation the services of Dr. Chaim Weizmann, at that time Reader in Biology in the University of Manchester, who submitted to Scott a plan for manufacturing chemicals then much needed for war. The Government were anxious about the supply of acetone, an essential element in the manufacture of cordite. Acetone is produced from wood, and as Great Britain is not a great timber-producing country, we were dependent on imports from America. Dr. Weizmann discovered other ways of producing acetone. Lloyd George was always ready to listen to anybody who had a suggestion to make that might be useful, and he took up his plan. Incidentally this introduction had important political consequences, for Dr. Weizmann met Balfour and turned him into an ardent Zionist. Scott was less happy in his efforts to bring Sir John Fisher back into public life. Fisher had retired from the Admiralty in dudgeon. Scott was pertinacious in urging the Government to recall him but Scott's account of a long conversation he had with Asquith on March 8th, 1916, on this subject, showed that there were stronger grounds for their adverse decision than Scott had supposed.

In the autumn of 1916 the war was going badly in the East of Europe and the uncertainty of our military prospects produced reactions. Lansdowne prepared and submitted to the Cabinet a memorandum urging that the Allies should reconsider and restate their terms rather than continue an exhausting war for purposes that might be beyond their strength. Lloyd George, on the other hand, who held that anything that made it appear that the Allies were losing confidence would encourage Germany, proposed that a small Committee should be formed to run the war, and that Asquith should not be a member of this Committee, though he should remain Prime Minister. Scott was, of course, most anxious that Lloyd George should be able to use his power of drive and concentration to the fullest advantage. On November 28th he wrote to Hobhouse about a leader he proposed to publish.

> It was written under a growing sense of the futilities of the present conduct of affairs—witness the increasing sea-peril and the hideous disaster of Rumania—Ireland also—the fumbling half and halfness, more irritating than any resolute action, of our dealings with Greece—the long trifling with the military situation at Salonika—it is the same all round. Of course there is the question of an alternative. It must almost inevitably be Lloyd George, with Asquith possibly as Lord Chancellor and Balfour in some purely honorary office. But terms would have to be made with Ll. G.—e.g. the reinstatement of Fisher, and, in some degree at least, of Churchill, and perhaps I ought to have a heart-to-heart conversation with him before taking any decisive step. . . . Of course he has, from our point of view, great defects of temperament and outlook, but it is a question of alternatives and of the immediate use of his practical and efficient qualities for a definite purpose. I have a growing conviction that with the present men we shall *not* win the war, and that the utmost we can hope for is a draw on bad terms. Hindenburg has changed the whole aspect of affairs for the Germans, George *might* do something of the same sort for us.

This letter was written on November 28th, 1916. Within a fortnight what Scott desired had happened and Lloyd George had become Prime Minister. Scott was in constant touch with him during the discussions and negotiations that led up to this event. He saw Lloyd George on December 3rd, 4th and 5th. After that time he was laid up with a bad cold and did not see

Lloyd George again, though he wrote the leaders on this subject from his bed.

Scott spoke in his letter to Hobhouse of Lloyd George's " great defects of temperament and outlook ". During the six years of Lloyd George's term of office Scott had often to criticise him fiercely, and at one time their personal relations were strained. But he never doubted that the change of December 1916 was necessary, and on November 30th, 1918, after victory, at a time when he was sharply critical of his friend, he wrote in a leader, " He has done more than any other man in public life to win the war."

The two domestic questions that were nearest to Scott's heart in British politics during the lifetime of the C.B., Asquith and Lloyd George Governments were the questions of women's suffrage and Irish Home Rule.

The prospects for women's suffrage looked favourable in two respects when the Parliament of 1906 assembled. Four hundred Members had pledged themselves to vote for it, and the Prime Minister himself was a supporter. But this was a superficial aspect. The trouble was that no party except the Labour Party, which contained 40 Members, was agreed about it. Owing to this division neither of the older parties could take it up. Unfortunately both parties believed that their fortunes would be affected by the enfranchisement of women. Radicals believed that their prospects would be injured by a measure enfranchising a small number of women, and Conservatives that their prospects would be injured by a measure enfranchising a large. It was thus very difficult to get the House of Commons to vote in a non-party sense on this non-party question.

During the Parliament of 1906–9 two Private Members' Bills passed the House of Commons. The first, proposing to enfranchise women on the same terms as men, passed its second reading in 1908 by a majority of 179. The second, an Adult Suffrage Bill enfranchising men and women alike on a three years' residential qualification, passed its second reading in 1909 by a majority of 26.

In the new House of Commons elected in January 1910, the friends of Women's Suffrage tried to get over the difficulty that Radicals objected to one plan of enfranchisement and Conservatives to another. They formed a Committee drawn from all parties, and prepared a Bill known as the Conciliation Bill, designed to secure the maximum of support. Scott, who was active in advising the Committee and in defending its plan in his paper, described the Bill as necessarily modest in order to meet Conservative objections, but so drawn as to meet Liberal and Labour objections by giving no special advantages to property. What was perhaps most important, the Committee persuaded the militant suffragettes, whose campaign of violence had alienated many who were friendly to the cause, to declare a truce. In this atmosphere the Bill had a great success on its second reading on May 5th, 1911, gaining 257 votes to 90. Lloyd George announced that the Government would give a week to the Bill in the following session, i.e., in 1912.

Politics took a new turn in November 1911 when Asquith stated that before going out of office the Government would introduce a Reform Bill and that it would be open to the House of Commons to insert the enfranchisement of women. Scott took a hopeful view of the new prospect. Grey was to move an amendment to the Government's Franchise Bill to omit the word " male " and then three rival amendments would be moved giving votes respectively to all, to many, and to a few women. Grey and Lloyd George were to conduct a campaign in the country. " Women have waited long," Scott wrote, " for their enfranchisement; it is now at hand." " Mr. Lloyd George," he wrote in another article, " has hitherto strenuously opposed the Conciliation Bill. He has done so on the ground that a larger measure is needed and could be carried. If it is proved to him that it cannot be carried he will oppose no longer." Unfortunately Scott reckoned without the militants. They were full of suspicion and reverted to their violent methods, attacking with special fury supporters of women's suffrage. Scott himself was told that he was stupid and a coward. The renewal of disturbance on a greater scale had an immediate effect. It happened that the Conciliation Bill came on before the Government introduced its Franchise Bill, and whereas in May 1911 the second reading had been carried by 257 votes to 90, it was now defeated, the supporters having fallen to 210 and the opponents having risen to 224. Liberal opponents had increased from 35 to 74, Unionist opponents from 46 to 115, and the Irish opponents from 9 to 35. The Irish figures are easily explained. They were afraid that if women's suffrage were carried, Asquith would resign and the cause of Home Rule would suffer. But the increased opposition in the other parties was undoubtedly due in part to the revival of militant methods.

Scott was very active in seeking to allay suspicion and to remove its causes. For suspicion of the Government was widespread among suffragists. When the Government's Reform Bill passed its second reading on July 13th, with a majority of 72, rumours were spread about that Asquith would resign if the Bill were amended by the introduction of women's suffrage. These rumours were mischievous for two reasons. They were likely to turn some supporters into opponents and they excited deep suspicion among the Suffragettes. Scott saw how important it was to check them, and he wrote both to Grey and Asquith. Grey replied that for Asquith to resign would be inconsistent with the promise he had given that the Government would accept the decision of the House, and he tried to kill the rumour by sending a letter to a public meeting in Glasgow in which he said there was no truth in this report. Asquith replied in a letter to Scott that his public declarations were perfectly plain and consistent, and that he did not feel called upon to take any notice of such rumours. But all Scott's hard work in the cause came to nothing, for the Speaker astonished the House of Commons and the Government by pronouncing that a women's suffrage amendment would not be in order. The Government had relied on the precedents of the Bills of 1867 and 1884 when such amendments were allowed, but at the last moment the Speaker came to this unexpected decision. Scott's one hope now was to get Grey and Lloyd George to say that they would not enter another Liberal Government unless it put Women's Suffrage on its programme. There seemed a good chance that they might take this course. But when Parliament was dissolved women were already enfranchised. This was one of the results of the war. In February 1918, after a Speaker's Conference which reviewed the whole subject of the reform of Parliament, women's suffrage passed into law. The great part played by women in the war had convinced the majority of politicans that their exclusion from the franchise was unjust.

Fortune was less kind to Scott's other special cause. With the passing of the Parliament Act Irish Home Rule had come back into British politics. The Home Rule Bill introduced by the Asquith Government passed its third reading in January 1913 with a majority of 109; a fortnight later it was rejected by the House of Lords by 326 votes to 69. Bonar Law, who had succeeded Balfour as leader of the Opposition in November 1911, made a speech at Blenheim containing a declaration inviting Ulster to go to extremities in its efforts to defeat the Bill. " I can imagine no length of resistance to which Ulster will go in which I shall not be ready to support them." Thus encouraged, the Ulster Unionists drew up a Covenant which pledged those who signed it to " use all means that may be found necessary to defeat the present conspiracy to set up a Home Rule Parliament in Ireland." During the next two years Ulster was in violent agitation, raising an army, collecting munitions, and arranging to form a provisional Government if ever Home Rule became law. Behind the scenes the Ulster Unionists were encouraged and assisted by no less a person than the Director of Military Operations in the War Office, Sir Henry Wilson, who described in his diaries without any shame how he fomented unrest in the Army and plotted with the Ulster leaders against the Government that he was serving in a most responsible position.

Loreburn, who had retired from office in 1912, made an effort in the autumn of 1913 to avert the dangers into which the country was being drawn by these proceedings and manoeuvres.

After consultation with Scott he wrote a letter to *The Times* suggesting a conference on the Irish question. Scott supported his plea in a leading article in the *Manchester Guardian*. Encouraged by the guarded welcome that leaders on both sides gave to the idea of a negotiation Loreburn proceeded to outline his ideas for a settlement in anonymous articles in the *Manchester Guardian*. He suggested that Ulster should have a special Minister in the Irish Parliament, that no Irish Act should apply to Ulster unless it was supported by the majority of Members for the Protestant area of Ulster, and that patronage should be in the hands of a special body. Loreburn was in close touch with Lansdowne who, as a Southern Unionist, disliked the idea of separating Ulster. Scott supported the proposal and discussed it with men of all schools. But it received short shrift. Garvin wrote to Scott that the Unionist party would not look at it, and Dillon wrote to Scott that the only effect of the publication of Loreburn's articles had been to make the Ulster question much more serious; that it was like " throwing petrol on the embers of a dying fire ". As for " the dying fire ", Sir Samuel Dill wrote at the same time to Scott from Belfast describing and deploring the violence and the resolution of the Ulster Unionists. The Scott-Loreburn plan was dropped and Scott set to work on the rival scheme of excluding Ulster or part of Ulster. He had meetings with Morley, Loreburn, Garvin, Geoffrey Dawson and others, and he was in constant touch with Dillon. A study of his papers shows, what Spender brought out in his " Life " of Asquith, that the actual differences that defeated conciliation were not of great importance. But the Unionist leaders were frightened of the spirit they had raised by their reckless manoeuvres, and the Irish leaders were afraid of the rising power of Sinn Fein. So strong was this obstacle that when the leaders met at Buckingham Palace in July 1914, with the knowledge that there was a serious danger of a European War, they were unable to overcome it.

History repeated itself after the Easter Rebellion of 1916. Asquith made another effort to find a settlement and Lloyd George was sent to Ireland to negotiate. He brought back a scheme on which Redmond and Carson were agreed. But though Balfour and Bonar Law accepted it, Lansdowne and Long refused their support and the scheme was abandoned. Scott thought that Asquith should have let Lansdowne, Long and Selborne retire. On the other hand, after he had had talks with Redmond and Carson, he was not at all sure that they could have got their followers to accept their agreed plan. In May 1917, when Lloyd George was Prime Minister, the Irish question was forced again on British attention, this time by the British Ambassador in the United States, as well as by Page, the United States Ambassador in London. Page reported that President Wilson wished him to explain to Lloyd George that " only one circumstance now appears to stand in the way of perfect co-operation with Great Britain." The one circumstance was the unsettled Irish problem. Lloyd George decided to make another attempt, and at his request Scott went to see Redmond at Bath to discuss plans with him and if possible to break down his suspicions of Lloyd George. The result was an offer from Lloyd George in May 1917 either to bring the Home Rule Act into operation with the exclusion of six counties, or to set up an Irish Convention. The second alternative was suggested by Redmond. The Convention, over which Sir Horace Plunkett presided, met in July 1917, and after a chequered career presented a report in April 1918. Its work was ruined in the next twenty-four hours by a blunder on Lloyd George's part that threw into the shade all the blunders committed by the Government he had displaced. The Convention reported on April 8th; on April 9th Lloyd George, disregarding a unanimous declaration from the sub-committee of the Convention on defence, signed by Covenanters as well as by Nationalists, announced that conscription would be extended to Ireland. By the 13th, in spite of an impressive protest from Asquith, the proposal had been adopted by Parliament. Scott was of course dismayed. " All the information that reaches us," he wrote in the *Manchester Guardian,* "whether from private or public sources, goes to show that the Government are deliberately preparing catastrophe." He wrote to Dillon: " Of course I realise with you all the folly and wickedness of the course on which he (Lloyd George) appears to be embarked, and it would seem hardly credible, apart from some sinister design, did not one learn more and more every day of the almost limitless folly possible to governing men." Another sentence in his letter shows how desperate a view he took of this policy: " Of course it would be far better to overthrow this Government than to allow the policy now contemplated to go through." Thus, when the war came to an end, Lloyd George had killed the Convention and killed the Irish Parliamentary Party. To Scott, looking back to Redmond's speech at the outbreak of war and to Grey's reflection that Ireland was the one bright spot, and recalling all the hopes he had founded on Lloyd George's accession to power, this was a specially bitter catastrophe. From this time until Lloyd George was driven by the conscience of the British people to change his Irish policy, Scott was his most severe and his most effective opponent.

On November 2nd, 1918, a few days before the German armistice was signed, Lloyd George wrote to Bonar Law that he had made up his mind that a general election ought to be held as soon as possible. On the first rumour of Lloyd George's intention Scott had protested strongly against such a proceeding. " Such a Government so elected," he wrote in a leading article, " would have no real authority for the future. It would have selected a moment when the country was, as it were, disarmed, and all political parties but its own at a disadvantage and in disarray, in order to seize power." Of Lloyd George's election methods he was equally severe. " We venture to say," he wrote on December 11th, " that in no election within living memory have the issues—the really effective issues on which stress is laid and by the aid of which it is hoped that votes may be won— been so paltry, or the mode of their presentation been so reckless and vulgar." A few weeks later he took a step that was not easy for a man who had been so intimate with Lloyd George. It was proposed to make Lloyd George an honorary member of the Manchester Reform Club, with a view to making him President later. Scott wrote two articles in the paper criticising this proposal strongly, recalling the facts of the December election, and arguing that Lloyd George was not entitled to the confidence of a Liberal Club.

Scott had been one of the earliest advocates of a League of Nations, and in the autumn of 1916 the paper had published an American supplement containing articles by Bryce, Gilbert Murray, Eliot of Harvard, and ex-President Taft. In the early months of 1918, he had come to think that the hope of victory and a reasonable peace depended entirely on the United States. After the armistice he sent a message to the *New York World* in which he said that President Wilson was the only statesman of the first rank who had concerned himself to think out any policy, and that the principles he had sought to establish, if honestly applied, would give the world a peace that would compensate for the immense losses of the war. When Wilson came to England in December 1918, he visited Scott in Manchester. He asked Scott what bearing the result of the elections would have on foreign policy. Scott, whose resilient optimism was fortified, no doubt, by his desire to give Wilson encouragement, replied that it would have none; that it represented simply a passing emotion and that all the better and deeper feelings of the nation would respond to an appeal.

The results of the Peace Conference were a sad disappointment to Scott. The history of the Nazis has put those events into rather a different perspective, and the Liberals who judged the terms by the ideal standards represented by President Wilson's Fourteen Points, took perhaps in some respects too harsh a view of the Treaty. Scott was exceedingly dissatisfied. He condemned not only the irresponsible temper displayed in the treatment of Europe's grave economic problems—the defect that specially impressed Keynes—but several of the political dispositions. While the Conference was in progress he was hopeful that Lloyd George, as well as Wilson, was going to be a force on the right side, but in the end he had to admit disillusionment in respect of Wilson himself. Writing to Hobhouse about one of his articles in January 1920, he said: "I was so glad you fired off that last shot at Ll.G. and his betrayal of the League of Nations.

I had the same sort of feeling of desperate regret and disillusion when I read his reply to Asquith, as when I first realised that the whole policy of the Fourteen Points had been utterly abandoned with the connivance of its author."

The Lloyd George Government, at whose birth Scott had nursed such hopes, lasted till November 1922, when it was destroyed by the revolt of the mass of the Conservative party under Bonar Law's leadership. During 1920 and for most of the following year Scott was in bitter opposition. At one time Lloyd George spoke as if he looked forward to making a permanent party out of the Coalition. Scott warned him sternly against any such project:

How can Liberalism that is of any value ally itself permanently, let alone " fuse " itself, with elements of thought, tradition, and interest so deeply opposed to its own, and live? It is possible to divide the Liberal Party for a time and thereby gravely to injure it. It is possible by thus weakening it to drive some of its more active elements out of the party and into the ranks of Labour. It is possible to draw some of its more conservative elements into direct association, or fusion, with the Conservative Party. It is not possible to do any of these things without striking at its life. Neither is it possible for the Prime Minister, or anybody else, to do these things and yet retain for himself a Liberal following of the slightest value or permanence. It is a road to ruin, and, though the full consequences may be delayed, they are there, sure enough, and will involve personal consequences ultimately as disastrous as the political.

Still more severe were the articles Scott wrote during the evil period of the Black and Tans. The paper followed the miserable sequence of outrage and reprisal with closeness and assiduity, giving great prominence to its special correspondents' messages. On October 11th, 1920, after the sacking of Balbriggan (which had been described in the *Guardian* by the correspondent who is its present editor) Scott wrote:

Something is happening in Ireland which is new in our history—unexampled at least, for more than a hundred years—but the Ireland of to-day is not the Ireland of 1798, and the listening world is not the same world. What was tolerated then in the way of lawless violence by the forces of the Crown, though even then not without strong protest from responsible British statesmen, will not be tolerated now. . . . Englishmen are at bottom resolved to do justice to Ireland. Still more are they resolved in the process to keep their hands decently clean and their reputation in the world unsullied. That is where Mr. George is failing us.

In another article he compared Lloyd George's treatment of Ireland to the German treatment of Belgium. Day after day he returned to the attack. He put into his articles all the power that his self-control gave to his indignation, and if the Government was gradually borne down by the pressure of moral opinion, Scott's pen (with the relentless pressure of his paper's publicity) was one of the chief forces in putting an end to the terrorism of the Black and Tans. Asquith observed in a letter to a friend that the blows he received from Scott were the hardest that Lloyd George had to bear.

The year 1921 was memorable in the history of the *Manchester Guardian* for two reasons. The paper had been founded in 1821 and Scott had joined the staff in 1871. These events were noted in the Press by public men. At no time was public encouragement more welcome to Scott, for the Irish situation was at its worst and the cause that had been closest to his heart since 1886 seemed in desperate case. Encouragement came in a most impressive form for public men of all schools and newspapers of all opinions joined in tributes to his courage and sincerity and to the integrity and sense of fairness that had distinguished his treatment of political issues, however contentious the issues, and however warm his sympathies. Asquith, Curzon, Lord Cecil and many other statesmen described his great qualities and the distinction that his paper had won both at home and abroad. In Manchester a dinner was held at which Lord Derby presided, and Lord Cecil paid Scott a compliment that became memorable, saying that he had made righteousness readable. Mrs. Fawcett was present, and representatives of other causes that had had good reason to be grateful for Scott's help.

One letter, owing to an accident, did not reach Scott till the next day. It was from Lloyd George, whose policy was at that moment receiving harder blows from Scott than from any other pen in the kingdom. His letter ran:

> Pray accept my warmest felicitations. The centenary of the *Manchester Guardian*, and your own jubilee as its editor, represent a period of unexampled progress in British journalism. Your personal record is an honour to your great profession. You have maintained its noblest traditions in the great paper associated with your name, and it is highly fitting that public men representing every shade of public opinion should join in congratulating you on the splendid attainments of the past, while at the same time wishing you and the paper a career of equal brilliance and success in the future.

Scott wrote in answer:

> MY DEAR GEORGE,
>
> Your kind and welcome message, by some bungling of the hotel people has only reached me to-day and can therefore only appear in to-morrow's *Manchester Guardian*. I am sorry for that, because I should have liked the meeting to hear it, and, among all those friendly voices, it seemed in a way unnatural, after all these years, to miss yours.
>
> I wish events had not so utterly divided us. Your Irish policy breaks my heart, and what makes the thing worse is that I have the feeling that it isn't the real you that is finding expression either there or in the European policy, but that circumstances have laid a heavy hand on you. Forgive me for speaking so. I could not do it if I had not loved and admired you.
>
> Yours sincerely,
>
> C. P. SCOTT.

Lloyd George was the most unaccountable man in public life, and Scott was kept from despair by knowing that he was guided more by impulse than principle. He had taken a course in Ireland that had brought shame on the British name and had excited a volume of indignation in Britain which Lloyd George resented but could not altogether disregard. In rousing that indignation the *Manchester Guardian* had played a leading part.

In the summer Lloyd George made overtures that led up to

C. P. SCOTT
aged about 30

THE FREEDOM OF MANCHESTER
Presentation of the Scroll by the Lord Mayor, Sir Noton Barclay,
April 8th, 1930

negotiations with the Irish leaders. Scott noted and welcomed the first symptoms of a change. On July 16th he wrote:

> Consistency is sometimes a virtue, sometimes it is the opposite. No one can accuse the Prime Minister of paying it undue respect. It is as easy for him to turn his back upon himself as upon his record. If you cannot always trust him to persevere in well-doing, neither is there ever cause to despair of his willingness and capacity to redeem an error. He has an ardour of imagination which enables him to see every situation as he wishes to see it, and he finds it easy to carry others with him, because he is able first so wholeheartedly to carry himself. It is a great gift. It has led him at times into horrible lapses. At the moment it looks as though it might go far to redeem them.

Lloyd George did not disappoint these hopes. Although a few weeks earlier he had denounced Asquith's suggestion for Dominion Home Rule as " lunacy ", pictured Ireland sowing the sea with mines, and declared, " we are not going to quail before a combination of a handful of assassins ", he was soon to plunge into negotiations with the Irish leaders and to promise them very much more than Dominion Home Rule. Once embarked on this new course Lloyd George knew that he must either succeed or involve his country and himself in illimitable disaster. The Unionist leaders who went into the conference with him, Austen Chamberlain and Birkenhead, were in this respect in the same case. The negotiations were often difficult and more than once they seemed in danger of collapse. Scott, who was almost the only man who held the confidence of both sides, gave valuable help at critical moments and the Irish Treaty was signed in the early hours of the morning of December 5th, 1921. Scott, who had been constantly at Lloyd George's side during the last forty-eight hours, lunched with him on the day of the signature, and they recalled memories of the struggle for Home Rule which had played so great a part in their lives.

Scott rejoiced in the Irish achievement, but he was still most distrustful of the Government, and he was delighted when the Coalition collapsed after a crisis over Turkey in which Scott blamed Lloyd George and Mr. Churchill as reckless and

E

incapable. After the fall of the Coalition Scott hoped to see a gradual reunion of Liberals with Lloyd George now released from the bad influences that had so often misdirected his energies and his gifts during the last six years. Reunion was effected in 1923 in consequence of Baldwin's threat to Free Trade. When a Labour Government took office in 1924 Scott hoped the Liberals and the Labour parties might work together, and deal with the coal problem and other industrial questions on which he thought accommodation possible. But MacDonald was sensitive and suspicious, the Liberals were often tactless, and though the Liberal party had put the Labour Government in power, there were Liberal elements that were strongly anti-Labour. Scott bitterly regretted the Dissolution of the autumn of 1924, dividing the blame for that blunder between the progressive parties. In the ensuing general election the Conservatives raised their numbers from 258 to 415, Labour lost 41 seats and the Liberals 116, being reduced to a party of 42 Members.

Peace had been made in 1923 between the Asquith and the Lloyd George Liberals but it did not last very long. It was broken in the General Strike of 1926. The strike began on May 3rd, and the Liberal " Shadow Cabinet " met that day and decided to condemn it and to support the Government in resisting it. Asquith, Grey and Simon made speeches on these lines, but Lloyd George, who had been present at the meeting, it was noted, criticised the Government more than the strikers. When another meeting of the " Shadow Cabinet " was summoned for May 10th, Lloyd George wrote to the Chief Whip announcing his intention of absenting himself on the ground that he dissented from the line taken by " the leader of the party and others wielding great authority in the party ". He published at the same time a pessimistic article on the strike and the general situation in an American paper. Asquith sent him a letter unusually severe in its terms, breaking off relations. " It was in my judgment," he said in the course of the letter, " the primary duty of all who were responsible for Liberal policy, and certainly not least of the Chairman of the Parliamentary Party in the

House of Commons (Lloyd George's position since Asquith had gone to the Lords after his defeat at Paisley in 1924) at such a time to meet together for free and full discussion, and to contribute their counsels to the common stock. Your refusal to do so I find impossible to reconcile with my conception of the obligations of political comradeship." He went on to complain of Lloyd George's American article: " It contains a desponding though highly-coloured picture of our national straits. It depicts a long duration of the conflict and the ultimate wearing down of the steadfastness of our people through ' worry about their national trade '."

Lloyd George, on receiving the letter, decided to consult Scott before replying. Scott described what happened in a private note: " I dined with him at the Midland and went through his proposed reply to Lord O. with him. It was written with considerable acerbity. I cut out everything provocative, and left it full of mildness and dignity. He accepted the revision with complete good humour and has often joked about it since." Scott thought this was " the most serviceable thing he ever did for Ll.G." Scott was strongly on Lloyd George's side, for he believed that the danger was not that the strike would succeed, or that it would commend itself to the British people as a form of political action, but that if it were mishandled it would lead to a bitter class quarrel with lasting results. On the other hand, he told a friend that he thought Lloyd George made a mistake in writing the American article. " Of course, journalism is not his job, and he ought not to have been tempted to earn money in that way. But apart from that general objection, I don't think the American article is open to serious criticism, and his general plea for moderation is wholly to his credit."

Later in the same year Scott took the opportunity of a public dinner given to him at the National Liberal Club to celebrate his eightieth birthday to urge the Liberal and Labour parties to co-operate:

The Labour party, though it leans strongly towards a Collectivist solution of social problems and may not unfairly be described on the whole as a Socialist party, is, in fact, based almost wholly on the trade unions, which in principle are not Socialist at all, but sectional, and are accustomed to act without any particular regard to the interests of the community as a whole, regard for which is the very root principle of Socialism, rightly understood. This and the class feeling which an almost purely working-class organisation naturally engenders is perhaps the real dividing-line between Liberalism and Labour. It is important in principle, but it is a good deal less important in practice, and certainly need not prevent co-operation with the Labour party over a very wide field.

On the other hand, how profound are the sympathies which should draw the two parties together and make co-operation easy. Is not, for both of us, social justice our primary aim and the raising of the condition of the poor and the disinherited? Are we not alike the apostles of peace? Is not their patriotism, like ours, large enough to extend its view beyond our own borders and to include other nations and other civilisations in its sweep? Do we not alike place right above power and recognise that force is the appropriate instrument of a lower, not of a higher civilisation? And are not these elements of union strong enough to overcome minor differences and to enable the two parties, with reasonable good sense, to steer a common course and make real progress once more possible for the nation?

The last years of his editorship, if they brought new and difficult problems, brought also new signs of the admiration and affection with which he was regarded on all sides. He was specially delighted when his old college, Corpus, elected him to an honorary fellowship in 1923. He was a very loyal Corpus man, and he rejoiced to find himself in a select company which included among others his lifelong friend Robert Bridges. He received in May 1925 a generous compliment from Mr. Baldwin that gave him great pleasure because it came from a political opponent whom he respected who had often been criticised severely in the paper. Mr. Baldwin was speaking at the Newspaper Society's dinner, London. He said:

> While it would be an impertinence for me in my ignorance to venture to tell you how you should conduct your business, I yet feel that I cannot do wrong before I sit down to read to you the words of one of the greatest of living journalists on the ideals of your profession. Speaking on journalism and the conduct of a newspaper, he said:

" Fundamentally it implies honesty, cleanness, courage, fairness, and a sense of duty to the reader and the community. The newspaper is of necessity something of a monopoly, and its first duty is to shun the temptations of monopoly. Its primary office is the gathering of news. At the peril of its soul it must see that the supply is not tainted. Neither in what it gives, nor in what it does not give, nor in the mode of presentation, must the unclouded face of Truth suffer wrong. Comment is free, but facts are sacred. Propaganda, so called, by this means is hateful. The voice of opponents, no less than that of friends, has a right to be heard. Comment is also justly subject to a self-imposed restraint. It is well to be frank; it is even better to be fair."

Those are noble words, and it is a counsel possibly of perfection, but in them is the ideal of the higher type of English journalism, which is the highest type in the world. They are the words of Scott, of the *Manchester Guardian*. And as one who has read newspapers all his life, I can imagine no higher ideal for a great profession to live up to.

Scott thought more and more anxiously, as individual newspapers were swallowed up in syndicates, about the functions and duties of the journalist, and such a tribute to his own conduct and example was highly valued. The following year his eightieth birthday was celebrated by the presentation of his bust by Epstein to the city of Manchester, to be kept, as Lord Derby said on the occasion, " as a memorial of one who in difficult times always tried to do his duty." Manchester received the gift but all England gave it, for the subscribers included the most eminent names in politics, religion, art, and letters; three ex-Prime Ministers, the two Archbishops, the leading politicians of all parties, the Poet Laureate, and such writers as Galsworthy, Shaw, Wells, Bennett, and Barrie. Nor were the subscribers limited to Scott's fellow-countrymen; they included M. Vénisélos, Count Sforza, Dr. Breitscheid, and M. Stefannson. In the course of his speech on this occasion Scott gave in a terse form his views of the functions of a newspaper:

A newspaper has two sides to it. On the one hand, it is a business like any other business, carried on for profit and depending on profit for prosperity or existence. On the other hand, it may be described as a public-utility service, a service which may be performed well or ill, but which, on the whole, is essential to the interests of the public. These two elements in the life and purpose of a newspaper are not always in accord; they may even violently conflict. Yet on their harmony the character and usefulness of a newspaper must depend.

After a reference to the growth of newspaper syndicates, he made an allusion to his own paper which excited much enthusiasm:

> There are papers which will never be sold—which would rather suffer extinction. And it is well that it should be so. The public has its rights. The paper which has grown up in a great community, nourished by its resources, reflecting in a thousand ways its spirit and its interests, in a real sense belongs to it. How else except in the permanence of that association can it fulfil its duty or repay the benefits and the confidence it has received?

Scott took measures to prevent the paper from falling into the hands of persons who might use it as a property rather than a trust. He made it a rule that the ordinary shares of the paper should always be held by members of the family who were working on the staff. He made it a rule when he acquired the paper in 1907 to draw a modest fixed salary and never to take any profits. He treated the paper, in respect of his own personal interests as in every other respect, as if it were a great public organ, serving the community as directly as a Department of the Civil Service, with a sense of responsibility equally strong. He was able to give the paper this character because he had a steady judgment and a mind that was observant, judicial and courageous. He drew enthusiasm into his paper and then guided it. He used the impulses of impulsive men without creating an impulsive paper. The men who worked under him when he was making what had been a moderate, cautious Liberal paper into the leading moral force in Liberal journalism in Europe, brought great gifts to its service; ideas, enthusiasms, literary power, independence of the narrower spirit of party or school. All this force was guided and disciplined by a master hand. No paper could have afforded so brilliant a staff of writers had it not possessed an editor whose gifts of courage, foresight and of judgment matched their gifts of inspiration.

It was not until 1898, when Scott was over fifty, that he began to keep his own leading articles. The records show that during most of the time he was in Parliament he never wrote. Between 1906 and the outbreak of the war he wrote mostly on his special subjects which were Ireland, women's suffrage and the House of Lords. During the war he wrote a great deal. He found that he enjoyed writing more and more, and after the war he continued the practice. In the year 1919 he wrote one hundred and seventeen " long leaders ", in addition to a number of short articles, and in 1920 one hundred and twenty-three. On some critical occasions he wrote almost every night for a fortnight. He had extended his range and wrote a great deal on foreign policy and the League of Nations. The day-to-day treatment of these questions demanded the most careful and constant study, and Scott's remarkable capacity for hard work was quite unaffected by his years. At the age of eighty he was able, after a hard evening's work, to devote the next morning to the intensive study of a blue-book, and at all times he kept up a vigorous correspondence with public men on political topics. As a leader writer he excelled in presenting a case or a subject in a manner that made his readers think. In early days his leaders were often dry and too academic. In later life he developed an easy style which concealed the subtleties of his argument, and the mass of knowledge on which he drew. On occasion he could show that he was master of the most effective of all weapons, passion kept under strict control. But he liked best addressing himself to the man who used his reason, and not the man who lived in his emotions. He was probably the most persuasive of the paper's leader writers.

In July 1929, Scott decided to retire from the editorship, remaining the governing director of the *Manchester Guardian*. The news of his resignation was received in England and in foreign countries with a sympathy and interest which showed that, having found the *Manchester Guardian* a paper important to Manchester, he was leaving it a paper important to the world.

Of the tributes that were paid to him only a few can be mentioned here. The King sent a message—"For fifty-seven years you have been responsible for the conduct of a great newspaper, and his Majesty, while regretting your resignation, congratulates you on an achievement which must surely be unique in the annals of journalism." The Archbishop of York, preaching in Manchester Cathedral, prefaced his sermon with the following allusion:

> A great newspaper is a potent factor in modern life, and Manchester is justly proud both of its great journal and of its citizen who made that journal great. Alike in the selection of material that should find place in its columns and in the guidance offered to nations or cities he has made righteousness a standard of action and conscience the arbiter of policy. For such an exercise of widespread influence we should thank God.

The Prime Minister wrote of Scott's noble work to make the world a better place to live in; General Smuts wrote that Scott's work had strengthened the roots of the good life in innumerable other lives; the Swedish Minister Baron Palmstierna said that he spoke for the northern countries of Europe in regretting Scott's retirement and in acknowledging his influence in foreign lands; Signor Nitti said that Scott had made the *Manchester Guardian* the most authoritative organ of the European movement for democracy and peace. In the Press, both at home and abroad, remarkable tributes were paid to the qualities which had given a national and international reputation to a man the whole of whose journalistic work had been anonymous. When those tributes are studied, it is easy to understand what President Wilson meant when he said that Scott was one of Europe's great men, and why Nansen wrote to him when he was organising his campaign for relieving the Russian Famine in 1922: "I do not think I am overstating the case when I say that your support will make all the difference between failure and success."

It was a great delight to Scott after receiving praise and honour from all parts of the world to receive in his old age the greatest honour the city of Manchester could bestow. In April 1930, he became a freeman of the city. The presentation was made a great ceremony in which thirty Lancashire and Cheshire mayors took part, and speeches were made by the Bishop of Manchester and the Lord Mayor of Liverpool. Scott, who excelled in the kind of speaking which demands perfect taste, made a reply which was at once most appropriate and most characteristic. Manchester was a great metropolitan city known all over the world for her trade and her traders. But that was not Man‑ chester's only claim to renown. In the ancient world commerce and culture had gone hand in hand, and Manchester had fol‑ lowed that great example in founding her University and offering to her industrial people that education in the arts and sciences which had become a monopoly of the well-to-do in the ancient universities. He went on to speak of the problems that still awaited solution.

> Like all the other industrial towns which sprang up in Northern England at the time when machinery revolutionised the means of production, we suffered from the speed of an unregulated and haphazard development. The Factory Acts have remedied some of the evils thence arising; the Education Acts have remedied some of the others. But much—very much—remains to be done. To abolish the slums, to restrain overcrowding, to reduce, if so it may be, our vast canopy of smoke—to bring light to the bodies as well as the minds of the people—these are no easy tasks. . . . It is, above all, because I am convinced that the governing body of this great city has alike the power and the will to deal with them that I am proud to become an honorary freeman of Manchester.

That speech reflected the spirit of Scott's career. He was a realist with a careful eye to practical needs; a man of culture with a sense of the importance of ideas and the arts that inspire and express them; a man of action ready for bold remedies, and to the end of his life a man of faith who believed that no wrong existed which could not be set right with courage and goodwill.

Scott lived long enough to see the crisis of 1931. He took the same view as his son, who had succeeded him in the editor's chair, that the National Government was a bad blunder. He wrote to his son from Bognor: "Ll. George seems to me the only Liberal leader who has courage and insight to deal with the situation, and he, unhappily, is out of the fighting ranks." (Lloyd George was recovering from an operation.) A few days later he wrote that the party was "delivering itself bound hand and foot to the tender mercies of the Tory party, whose prime object is to plant Protection, as a permanent policy, firmly on our necks." He returned home thinking that as the paper was "breaking right away from the bulk of the party", his son might like to have him at hand for consultation.

He died in the early hours of New Year's Day 1932.

1821
A STEAM PACKET ADVERTISEMENT

3

SCOTT AS EDITOR

JOURNALIST AND EDITOR

By C. E. Montague

Scott had the prime requisites of a true journalist as distinct from a politician or trader who uses a newspaper mainly as a hoarding or mainly as a means to wealth. He believed with all his heart that, to be worth bringing out, a daily newspaper must be, all round, an instrument of civilisation. Of course no decent journalist consciously believes the opposite. But to some journalists a daily newspaper presents itself irresistibly as a space on which the placards of a party can be plastered, and not, vividly and imperiously, as anything else. Some others approach their work naturally and instinctively as a branch of commerce; they mean to be honest traders and not do dirty tricks to get a little extra money; still, the making of money by skill and quickness in giving the public, or some special part of the public, just what it wants to buy is their steadily governing aim. Others, the true journalists, feel that they fail if their paper is not, in all its parts, a faithful assistant to every man or woman who has keen interests and really wants to understand, whatever their special interests may be. Whether it pays or not, whether it furthers a party's interests or not, this, in their eyes, has got to be done, simply because it is the one thing supremely and unquestionably worth doing.

That Scott was steadily bent upon having the news services and the critical and other non-political work of his paper well done was the more to his credit because for himself politics far outweighed all other public interests. It is true that he had the serious all-round culture of the best Victorians; he had distinct likings in sculpture and painting, and was a friend and stout champion of Madox Brown in the years when, amidst much foolish censure and derision, he was painting for the Manchester Town Hall the greatest modern English mural paintings; in some forms of decorative art he had a special interest—he was a skilful judge of furniture, pottery, and jewellery. But none of these tastes amounted to a passion; he was not a collector, seldom visited a theatre, and hardly ever went to a concert except to hear some artist who, like Rosing, was a personal friend. But he desired ardently that all the civilised human interests should be discussed in his paper with knowledge and enthusiasm and without that facile complaisance towards popular rubbish which some worldly minded controllers of journals have inculcated as a piece of practical wisdom. A critic who had been severe to fashionable and much-advertised but second-rate work was always sure of Scott's loyal backing in whatever might follow. And no member of his staff was ever subjected to the iniquity of a suggestion that the winds of criticism should be tempered for some distinguished author or artist whom the editor knew. By no chief could the independence of a critical writer have been more honourably respected. He did not even demand continuity of critical policy, for he recognised that criticism can only have the highest value when it is intensely individual. It did not trouble him at all that Arthur Johnstone, the *Guardian* musical critic in the later nineties, should write from a point of view fundamentally different from that of his predecessor, Fremantle, or that Ernest Newman, in turn, should confront the paper's readers with yet a third system of critical variations. All that mattered, within the wide limits of sanity, was sincerity and power. Scott selected critical writers with extreme care, but with no reference whatever to their opinions or matters outside their subject: many of those whom he valued most were extreme Conservatives, one a Roman Catholic prelate, another an anarchist. Such things would sometimes give a little scandal to rigid-minded people. They were really the practical expression of a belief that the measure of fundamental unity between all honest intellects that are eagerly putting themselves forth upon worthy objects of effort is greater than that between the subscribers to any one set of articles of political, religious, or artistic faith. The only consistency for which Scott sought in all the critical work of his paper was that which gives a certain cohesion to the utterance of any number of different minds that love a subject and long to know and tell about it.

II

The fundamental political ideas which Scott expressed with almost no modification throughout his editorship were perhaps the last upon which a shrewd observer of the times would have thought it possible to base a career of great influence and distinction. Just when the great vogue of the rationalistic and utilitarian Liberal philosophy of a century ago was declining Scott absorbed it, and found it intensely congenial to his slowly and systematically working mind and to his distrust of unreasoned enthusiasms and mystic valuations. Not having the slightest inclination or aptitude for demagogy, he appealed only to educated men and women, and throughout his long editorship he developed the politics of his paper almost continuously in a direction opposite to that in which the politics of the educated well-to-do appeared, on the whole, to be moving.

In a Lancashire gradually moving from the Left Centre to the Right Centre Scott moved almost continuously from the Centre towards the Left, converting a Whig journal into an organ of advanced Liberalism, while a large proportion of its readers, sons and grandsons of the followers of Cobden and Bright, were pretty obviously destined to pass through the antechamber of Liberal Unionism into the Conservative household. During the whole of the pre-war generation in which nationalistic feeling was rapidly gathering strength throughout the world, and the idea of war was recovering its ancient fascination for people who had not known its realities, Scott's mind adhered completely to the internationalism of Cobden and the pacifism of Bright, the most widely and deeply unpopular ideals of the new period.

To be in a small minority, to hold some hopeless outpost against whole armies, to oppose to the practicable doctrines of successful parties some political philosophy too rigid and exacting for practice in this world—this is a passion common enough among fanatics of political asceticism and also of romanticism. Scott had no trace of this passion. He was constitutionally averse from all romantic flourishes and attitudes. And he was very sanguine. He never could believe that England, at heart, was really very far from consenting to do what he himself so absolutely believed to be her duty. In days when the office of his newspaper was guarded, against his desire, by a cordon of police to protect it and him from its readers, he was as little perturbed as he was elated when, six years later, no opponent of the views that he held could gain a Parliamentary seat within many miles round Manchester. Serene and stoical, possessed with an unquestioning belief that mankind, on the whole, was sane and good, and that any honest attempt to tell it the truth was worth while and would have some effect in the end, he was as little affected in any way by the extremes of popularity and unpopularity as any man could well be.

III

In following such a course and upholding political beliefs so far from the fashions of the day perhaps the greatest possible aid is the power of brilliant self-expression, the gift which enables a Bernard Shaw, for example, to print deeply into the minds of his readers the importance, at any rate, of ideas against which nearly all their prepossessions rebel. With this gift Scott was not endowed. He had no facility in framing new epigrams or adapting old ones. Nimble forensic dexterities in argument did not seem even to occur to his mind, or, if they did, they were rejected by some instinctive impulse towards plain dealing with his readers. It was Scott's achievement to make an unburnished and uncajoling style a powerful instrument of persuasion. The same words mean widely different things when uttered by different men. From him, this writing in which so few of the lures of fine form were employed came with a force and sincerity which made readers feel that, right or wrong, it was not negligible. The views expressed might be distasteful, but at any rate they were the real views of a real man and not a perfunctory arrangement of phrases thrown off because a paper must say something every day.

A political leading article may be any one of several things. It may be an entertainment. Done with wit and gay mischief, as it has often been done, it may be a delightful entertainment, whatever be one's views. Or it may be—quite unconsciously— an escape for vexation, in the writer and in his readers, a kind of relief for the common, rancorous partisan's irritation at being opposed when he feels so positive that he is right and that all who oppose him must simply be vicious. Or, yet again, it may be the eager and entreating protestation of one who believes, as a matter of course, that men and women of all parties are, in intention, as faithful to reason and conscience as he, and that nothing but direct and candid pleading is likely to interest or convince them. It was in this belief that Scott always addressed himself to a piece of political writing. In this work a plain and friendly gravity was his chief art, and so immense is the power of unmistakably honest seriousness upon English readers that his writing carried a weight and had traceable effects which might astonish connoisseurs of piquant literary flavours.

IV

It was only, however, in the latter part of his editorship that Scott became a regular or even frequent writer of leading articles. Until the outbreak of the war in 1914 his influence over the paper was exercised mainly by his choice of regular and temporary members of its staff and by general supervision of its editorial and business policy. For the years from 1879 to 1896 the personality which was most strongly expressed in the leader and critical columns of the *Guardian* was that of

William Arnold, whom some qualified judges believe to have been the greatest of all English journalists, certainly the greatest of all that they have known. During the decade beginning in 1895 Scott's work in Parliament and the long and ultimately fatal illness of his wife combined to make him a merely occasional writer in his paper. During the exciting general elections of 1906 and 1910 he wrote little, if anything. Only when the outbreak of the war thinned the staff of the paper did Scott become for the first time its chief regular leader-writer as well as its editor, and this he remained for many years.

Strange to say, his writing gained in these advanced years a measure of flexibility and vivacity which it had lacked during his youth. He also brought to the discussion of such questions of policy and national behaviour as arose during the war a quiet firmness and a freedom from mere rant and gush which made his comments more congenial to many distinguished soldiers than anything else in the Press. " The only decent stuff that's being written in England " was the comment of a British general in France on these sober and measured deliverances of an aged civilian. Hating war in itself, and only convinced by the German violation of Belgium that a British entry into the quarrel was obligatory, Scott's war policy was one of determination without hysteria. It was equally characteristic that he was for examining carefully, during the war, every seeming possibility of gaining a good peace by negotiation before Europe was exhausted and demoralised, and that during the black weeks of defeat in the March and April of 1918, when many hearts were failing dangerously in England, Scott's pen was one of the most heartening spurs to English hope and resolution.

His bearing in that national crisis only illustrated afresh a trait long known to Scott's intimate friends. Physically, morally, and intellectually he seemed to have an absolute incapacity for any sort of trepidation. With an angry mob howling round him he never showed a trace of agitation; he did not even seem to have any apprehensions to control. No number of falls and collisions appeared to suggest to him that for a septuagenarian blind in one eye it was risky to cycle every night through six miles of

C. P. SCOTT AT HIS DESK

PRESENTATION OF THE EPSTEIN BUST TO THE
CITY OF MANCHESTER

October 21st, 1926
Jacob Epstein: C. P. Scott: The Lord Mayor of Manchester: Lord Derby
(Sir Miles Mitchell)

Manchester traffic on the greasy Manchester setts. When the outbreak of the Boer War, and his paper's attitude towards it, converted the *Guardian's* settled prosperity, for the moment, into loss and danger of extinction and filled his own letter-box at every post with written threats, abuse, and filth, Scott seemed scarcely to notice that anything unusual was going on. His usual cheerfulness did not have to be forced; he was not in the slightest danger of falling into any attitudes of martyrdom or posing as the one just man against the world. Nor yet was there the slightest chance of his taking in any reef of his sails. After the Boer War it gradually came out, on the publication of memoirs and letters of various contemporary persons of distinction, that a large proportion of the finest and most patriotic minds of the country had, like Scott, regarded the war as dishonouring to England, both in the means by which, from the Jameson Raid onward, it was procured and in some of the methods by which it was prosecuted. Most of these critics found it possible to absolve themselves from the duty of raising their protest publicly at the time. To Scott it never occurred as a permissible course to keep this kind of comfortable and profitable silence in an evil time, and in this he was immensely aided by that constitutional inability to see dangers and menaces to himself at their full size, much less at such sizes as they assume in the eyes of the timid.

This innate fearlessness and a faculty for complete absorption in certain ideas or causes greatly lightened for him the burden of making critical decisions. He weighed conflicting considerations slowly—any kind of rapidity in thought or speech seemed impossible to him—but, when once he had formed a judgment, gave no backward glances of doubt, and threw off easily any anxiety about secondary consequences of his choice. The three chief public crises of his time, that of the Home Rule split in 1885, that of the Boer War, and that of the Great War in 1914, probably weighed upon him as little as upon any man so profoundly interested in them all; they absorbed but did not exhaust or corrode him. The same equanimity carried him unperturbed through such crises as arose in the lesser world of

journalism in his day. In the last years of the nineteenth century
that world was more or less convulsed by the discovery of a few
astute business men who had embarked in journalism. They
noted that the first stage in the organisation of universal
education in England had created a very large new reading
public, half-educated, credulous, excitable, and ready to lend
itself to neurotic joint movements, under the influence of
journalistic suggestion, like those dangerous bodily swayings
which can so easily be started in standing crowds. A nervous
impression ran through the controllers of the English Press that
the old world of daily journalism, with its relatively sober
appeals to the individual reader's reason and conscience, was
dying a natural death; that the great newspapers could retain
their influence only by ignoble concessions, by lowering their
appeals as well as their prices, by bowing to an imperious public
demand for aids and stimulants to gambling and by abandoning
serious standards of criticism in literature, drama, and the other
arts. The present writer was in frequent consultation with Scott
during this period, and cannot remember to have felt that in
Scott's opinion any big question of policy was really open. To
exploit popular ignorance, to play up to the vices or weaknesses
of half-formed characters and half-filled minds would have
seemed to him a policy no more worth considering than a policy
of living on the profits of disorderly houses. With eyes perfectly
open to the formidableness of the new forces at work in
journalism, he determined to maintain his previous course and
endeavour only the more resolutely to give the public, not what
it was currently rumoured to desire, but what he believed to be
true.

That Scott's long editorship should, after many vicissitudes,
have raised his paper to the enjoyment of the highest prestige
and prosperity attained in its whole history tells us something
alike about this most English of Englishmen (in spite of his
Border name) and about the English men and women to whom
he addressed himself. Without any glamour of beauty or wit
in writing or speech, without any skill in the study of his readers'
prejudices, with unfashionable politics and a cold side for the

strongest emotions of crowds, he pursued his own slowly chosen and frankly declared line in total indifference to what people might say about it or him. And yet the further he went the more influence did he gain over those to whom he made so few concessions: so strong is the instinctive feeling of many plain and sane minds—in England at any rate—that the friend who, in all friendliness and for no worldly motive, will withstand you to your face must be worth listening to anyhow.

1824
ADVERTISEMENT OF BALLOON ASCENTS

LIBERAL AND HUMANIST

By L. T. Hobhouse

As Delane was in his day *The Times*, so C. P. Scott was the *Manchester Guardian*, and from about 1895 onwards it is hardly too much to say that the *Manchester Guardian* was Liberalism. More and more during that period it was to the paper rather than to any personal leader that the thoughtful Liberal looked for stability of purpose. Yet in the staunchness of his Liberalism Scott was in the best sense conservative. In the country generally, and not least in Lancashire, opinion was falling away to the " Right " and to the " Left ". From 1886 the " classes " went over, at first by driblets and then in a flood, to Conservatism. From 1891 the artisans began to melt away into Socialism or Labour, and after 1896 the driblets swelled, though they hardly became a flood till the war was over. All the while Scott held firmly to the Liberal tradition. As editor and proprietor, his tenacity made his position difficult, for more and more he had his public against him, and, sanguine as he was to the last of the ultimate effect of an appeal to reason, he could not disguise from himself the losses and even the dangers to its very existence to which he exposed his paper. Of the qualities which carried him through I will try to give some impression later, but I would say here another word about Liberalism and what it meant for him. First of all, tenacious as he was of inbred conviction, he was not rigid, because it was not a rigid creed that he maintained, but Liberalism, the open mind, the value—almost the sanctity—of the " other fellow's " point of view. All that there is, or is to come, in the opening out of the human mind is Liberalism, and it was in this sense that Scott understood it. This is the reason why his own interpretation of the Liberal creed was always growing. When he became editor of the *Manchester Guardian*, in 1872, it was a Whig organ, and for several years it remained very moderate in its politics, partly, perhaps, because the young editor had incomplete control over his older and experienced subordinates, but principally, I believe, because Scott was growing and educating himself all the time. His choice of W. T. Arnold as a leader-writer in 1879 marked a new departure. The *Manchester Guardian* was to stand for something more alive than Whiggery. But the decisive moment did not arrive until 1886, when, with Arnold's brilliant aid, he threw the whole weight of the paper on to the side of Home Rule, and thereby moved decisively on to the " Left ", just as its public was going over in masses to the " Right ".

Home Rule was the logical development of the older Liberalism. It was in line with Cobdenite ideas, and Bright should never have opposed it. But a harder test was to come. Soon after 1886, markedly from the dock strike of 1889, the Labour question came to the front of domestic politics, and Liberals were once again divided. There was an individualist wing more definitely in line with the tradition of the party from Whig days, through the period of Benthamite ascendancy and the triumphant times of Cobden. If Scott's mind had been really conservative and his traditionalism rigid he would have followed that wing. It must have cost him much to move once again to the " Left " and insist on the new claims of Labour. Yet it was the movement which J. S. Mill had made twenty years earlier, and it was right and consistent, by the spirit of Liberalism, though wrong by the letter of tradition. Once again Scott encountered the wrath of his public, reading day by day with speechless indignation, almost with incredulity, apologies for strikers or advocacy of an eight-hour day. In this development Scott had the support not only of W. T. Arnold but of C. E. Montague, whose brilliant defence of the miners in 1893 first attracted the present writer to the paper. When in 1897 Scott invited this writer to join his staff the reason he gave was his belief that the relations of Liberalism and Labour must govern the future of politics, and that the problem was to find the lines on which Liberals could be brought to see that the old tradition must be expanded to yield a fuller measure of social justice, a more real equality, an industrial as well as a political liberty. In particular they had to understand that this development must involve a good deal of what was still being decried as Socialism. Of Socialism as a name Scott was never frightened. He was not easily disturbed by bogies. The essential, as he saw it, was that however Socialistic changes might be they should be such as grew out of true Liberal principles—freedom from oppression, equality of opportunity, scope for initiative, and humanity of feeling, as contrasted with either a Fabian or Marxian dictatorship. As a programme of party organisation the harmonisation of Liberalism and Labour was eventually broken down by the tactical mistake of 1918, but as a statement of ideals it has justified itself in all the main reforms of thirty years. Scott never wavered in its advocacy nor tired of ingeminating co-operation, and urging the real identity of aim as between advanced Liberalism and moderate Labour.

In the meantime Liberalism was challenged from quite another quarter by the rise of Imperialism and the allied doctrine of Protection. Here Scott took an early and a firm stand on admitted principles of Liberalism. What distinguished him was the firmness of his advocacy, which more than once brought him into direct and embittered conflict not merely with his Conservative readers but with the simple-minded, uncritical patriotism of the general public. The odium of pleading for justice and a fair hearing for miners was as nothing to the odium of urging the same plea on behalf of Boers or Germans or Indians, or, for that matter, Irish Nationalists. Indeed, the odium of pleading was not greater than the odium of publishing the bare facts, if these happened to tell on the side of the enemy. Scott faced the successive storms with unfailing serenity and with an undying belief in the ultimate reasonableness and justice of the British people. To any elements of personal danger he was by a happy constitution indifferent, and he took little more note of police protection than of the violent and sometimes filthy letters from unnamed patriots which I have seen him open at the breakfast table or have heard him mention as a jest. But though always sanguine of ultimate success, he was fully aware that he was often risking his all, and he early marked out a line which he laid down for the whole paper. No fact was to be suppressed, whether it told on one side or the other, whether it would cause a howl of execration or a shout of applause, whether it confirmed the view of the paper or told against it. But everything was to be stated and everything argued with moderation and sweet reasonableness. No conclusion, however radical, was barred, but offensiveness and over-statement in supporting it were excluded. " Nothing extenuate, nor set down aught in malice." In particular he would have no " drumming out " of the Liberal party. Here I more than once differed from him, and looking back long after the event I cannot even now admit that I was altogether wrong. I still think it would have been better on occasion if the Liberal party had definitely dissociated itself from certain eminent men and their policies, but the mistake, if mistake it was, was an error of generosity. He held that a man who professed and called himself Liberal must be taken at his word and led gently into the way of truth, while, if breach there was to be, it must come from such a man himself and not from his fellow-Liberals.

But when the victory seemed to be won and the Liberals came in with an overwhelming majority for a long spell of power Scott found himself forced into opposition on two great questions. The most acute for several years was women's suffrage, where he was not only resolute in principle, but, through the keenness of his imagination, more understanding than were most of us of the true nature of militancy. The other was the growing menace of war with Germany. He witnessed with dismay the increasing competition in armaments, and with even greater dismay the conversion of the *Entente* into an alliance and its extension to include reactionary Russia. The crisis of July 1914 came at a moment when he had barely emerged from the threat of a dangerous operation and the menace, fortunately proved vain, of a deadly disease. He threw himself into the task of rallying Liberal opinion, travelling hurriedly from one of the scattered and rather supine leaders to another, and eventually failing, as the world knows. War once declared, he recognised that the position was radically changed. We might have been wrong, as he certainly thought—and I do not know when or precisely how far he really changed this view —in entering upon it, but it was not as the Boer War, when we were doing wrong to another and weaker nation. We were up against far the greatest Power in the world. The wrong, if any, was done by our Government to our own people, and there was no going back. In the Boer War it had been a piece of silly rhetoric to suggest that our national existence was at stake and was endangered by criticism. In the War of 1914–18 it was literal truth. As between nations Scott, like most of us, believed the wrong to lie with the Germans, not with ourselves, and as keenly as any man, more so than the vast majority, he believed that the future of mankind and every principle that he held most dear were bound up with the safe maintenance of the British State in the hour of trial. He let pre-war politics alone to bury its own dead, and concentrated with all his energy on the successful pursuit of the struggle. He was in repeated communication with Ministers, acquired an intimate knowledge of the ever-changing position, and was always ingeminating the need of greater effort and radical remedies for stupidity and obstructiveness in high places. It was this side of his energies which brought him into a sympathetic contact with Lloyd George which was to become a source of chagrin to many of his political friends. The root of it was that in Lloyd George Scott found a man who opened his eyes to danger without being dismayed, who had the power of sweeping away obstructions and was no respecter of idolised but expensive generals. Scott may have been right or wrong, but it is a matter of fact that such was the impression made on him by Lloyd George, and that this was the source of an appreciation which outlasted the war and was only in part worn away by subsequent failures. Scott, who knew all the dangers, was deeply impressed by the adverse happenings of the war—particularly in the weeks before Jutland he was wrung by anxiety over the naval situation, and not without reason, as the battle was to prove. So again in the first month of the intensified submarine campaign, when it was only too clear that the handling of the danger was inadequate, and defeat was, in fact, for the first and last time upon the cards. Of ultimate success Scott was uniformly confident, and such disasters as that of St. Quentin he took, in spite of the most acute personal anxiety, with all the trust of some old Covenanter in the arm of the Lord. He stood out against dismay as firmly and finely as he had stood against the mob, and proved himself as good a patriotic leader as a statesman of humanity.

Strenuous in the prosecution of the war, he was all for the earliest opportunity of a just peace, and in the autumn of 1917, and before the Lansdowne letter appeared, was marking out lines of approach—not unobserved by the German Liberal papers. But Ludendorff decided otherwise, and peace was only to come by victory. The *Guardian* criticised the detail of the Versailles negotiations with its accustomed freedom, but it was not till the whole settlement was well before us that anyone could recognise the stupendous blunder to which we had been committed. From the moment when he grasped this Scott set himself to lessen the mischief, if that were possible. Lloyd George, a speedy yet belated penitent, was in full spate on the same side, and Scott forgave him his sins for the sake of his persistent efforts at reparation. In the Irish crisis he was again active in personal mediation between the Sinn Fein leaders and the Government, and played a man's part in bringing about the final negotiations which led to peace.

Into later and contemporary history I will not follow him, but will seek to draw together the features of character which ran through his career of noble service. Scott represented, better than any man I have known, the union of certain qualities which seldom dwell together. He had the resolution, courage, initiative, and imagination of a leader of men, and he had the humanity, considerateness, and insight of a woman. At the very root of his nature he was more a Puritan than anything else, but he was spiritually of that group of seventeenth-century Puritans who loved poetry and art and all the things of the mind, and would fain have preserved the Renaissance while carrying through the Reformation. He was what the Stoics call

" invincible ", unshaken in defeat, turning from it to plan the next victory. In the war he would not look at final disaster— " We can't be beat " was all he would say—but if defeat had come he would have turned from it to plan what was to be done next. He was, then, a man of faith, but, to be candid, his faith was in humanity as interpreted by the best of the Comtist writers as the summed conception of all that there is of justice and honour, of reason and loving-kindness in the society of mankind. Courage, I think, came more easily to him than to most, notwithstanding a sensitiveness and a power of imagination which make many brave men hesitant in dangers. It was one expression of a perfectly balanced constitution—the healthy mind in healthy body. Again, there are idealists who are not practical, and practical men who are very far from idealists. Scott was an idealist who cared nothing about the abstract, but sought day by day to find practical expression for high aims— seldom speaking of them as such, but showing how the denial of them worked out. Some great humanitarians occupied with all mankind are little concerned with individuals. Scott could always see the personal point of view. " I find an odd kind of considerateness in Scott's business arrangements," said a journalist who came into casual relations with the *Manchester Guardian,* as though this would be a novelty to one who had worked with Scott for years. Lastly, and perhaps above all, Scott lived outside himself in his work. In his eighties he still sat down immediately after a breakfast of raw fruit to the masses of his correspondence; was at it all day, but for an hour on his bicycle in the afternoon; spent the evening in editorial work at the office; and would be home by car—night-bicycling on greasy Manchester streets was suppressed by an intensive campaign of his relations at seventy-eight—and at eleven o'clock sit down to a late supper, also mostly of raw fruit. I never knew a happier man.

"C.P.S." IN THE OFFICE

By W. P. Crozier

For many years "C.P.S." arrived at the *Guardian* office at 6 p.m., latterly by car, before that on the famous bicycle. Mounting the stairs to his room with a purposive air, he thrust the door to with a vigorous left-hand push without looking behind him. The bang announced the presence to his staff. A few moments later, having unpacked and handed over to a Messenger two eggs, salt wrapped up in a screw of paper, milk and, sometimes, an apple, all of which he had brought from home,[1] he spread out the evening papers on his desk and was ready for all comers. No interruption, no visitor, no office conference was allowed to delay the sacred task of fixing for the night the subject of "the Long". This was the Long Leader, prime instrument of policy, the voice, persuasive or protestant, for whose utterance, more than for any other single purpose, he believed the paper to exist. Suddenly, murmuring "I must see about the Leader," he would hurry from the room, and the resumption of the conference depended on the conversation demanded by the Long. Whether in the leader-writer's room or in "C.P.'s," the discussion was not hustled. Chief reporters, chief sub-editors, editorial writers who desired to see him, might kick their heels: no matter; other joinery must wait while the Ark of the Covenant was planned. It waited still more if "C.P." himself wrote the Leader. The writers of the Long were, by sanctity of office, protected from disturbance, but practice invaded tradition according to the standing of the writer. "C.P." was not disturbed without strong reason. He began early, made notes, perhaps sent for one of his big volumes of

---

[1] In earlier days he sent out for three brown scones and a pot of cream. He kept a butter-jar on a little ledge which he had had constructed outside the window of his room.

cuttings, or scurried off, sometimes almost running, to get one of his men to remove or confirm a doubt; back in his room, he settled to work intently. Usually he wrote in ink, and then, like others, when he corrected he wrote over the line; when he used pencil, he would open the right-hand top drawer of his desk, extract a big piece of india-rubber, efface the offending passage, replace the india-rubber, shut the drawer, all with great briskness, and then carefully substitute the amended words.

The Leader finished, he turned to letters and memoranda. On some of these he had written initials, whose owners he now summoned or visited in order to make a suggestion, offer a criticism or ask for explanation. Then he dictated letters or wrote them in his own hand, as to the last he often did; in consenting to have letters typed he had yielded only to necessity, through the compulsion of an injured right hand and after the failure of an obstinate attempt to teach himself to use his left. By this time the proofs of the Leader had come down, and again he was absorbed. He went warily over what he had written, tightening an argument, expressing with finer exactitude the desired shade of meaning, rewriting whole passages. Occasionally he asked someone to read over his Leader. " See if I've got the facts right," he would say, or " See if you think I've been too violent." If it were a matter of tone, of undue severity, of possible obscurity, he was quick to be convinced. Saying "That's what I was rather doubtful about," he would take the pen of correction. Proofs sent up, he worked again at correspondence or paid more visits or, gathering up his letters, which he girded into a stout bundle with an india-rubber band, he stuffed them into a coat pocket and rapidly disappeared. He had no fixed time for leaving. His cheerful " Good night, Charlie!"[1] or " Good night, Ted! "[2] as he looked into the room next to his own was the signal to those within range that he was going. Sometimes, to a subordinate who had failed to catch him unoccupied, it was a signal for pursuit. He did not allow such interviews to be prolonged, but he was seldom impatient. When he had gone to bed, so that he could no longer be reached on the tele-

[1] C. E. Montague.   [2] E. T. Scott.

phone, it might be found that an inaccuracy had crept into his leader or had been created in it by the arrival of later news. In that case, whoever was " in charge " corrected the error and sent him an explanation. Unless plain error was discovered it was well to resist suggestions that " C.P.'s " words should be improved. It is known that Homer nodded, but not what Homer said when he was told about it. For reasonable corrections " C.P." sent down a note of thanks. " I'm glad you did," he would say, " very stupid of me! " He had phrases for situations, and " stupid " was his word for himself when he desired to make confession.

When " C.P." revised Leaders he allowed great freedom of treatment to his writers, but much more on subjects in which he was not personally expert than on others, like domestic politics, about which he felt strongly. He desired diversity of individual thought but, since it had to be consistent with the moral and political unity which the paper through him represented, he modified, rewrote, and sometimes " spiked " the work of others to the satisfaction of his conscience. The process of amendment or of destruction was left by the tradition of the office, to convey its bleak lesson to the original writer. So, also, he encouraged the individuality of foreign correspondents. They had the large liberties of independent thinking within the bounds of the spirit of the paper's policies. Except within the same frontiers outside contributors, even the famous, were not welcome. " C.P." was chary of asking Bernard Shaw or Dean Inge for contributions because " when we got them we might not like them."

If " C.P." was " taking Shorts " (revising Short Leaders) he drew his subjects from the events of the night, from the cuttings which some member of the staff had left in the morning at his house, and from other cuttings which were put on his desk in the early evening. These cuttings presented a field of adventure uncharted, unchartable, and, for the staff, alarming. " C.P." had the good journalist's capacity for being interested in many subjects and of coming to each of them, whether it was new or only new to him, with fresh excitement. His mental excitations, which he assumed his staff to share, were thought by some to be extreme. The novice who was asked to discuss the influence of breast-feeding on the dentition of the young, soon learned to fend off the terrible unknown by spontaneous suggestion; infantile dentition, though he might hastily concede to " C.P." its social and scientific importance, might be repelled by the offer of a Short on the poor spirit of Londoners who did not even own their gas and water, or the Marbles Championship of the Middle West, or perhaps (a certain winner) Miss Violet Douglas-Pennant. But " C.P." was difficult to evade. To a reluctant writer professing inadequate knowledge he said, " Well, but, my dear fellow, ask questions about it; say we want to know," or, " Well, at any rate you seem to know more about it than anyone else, so—if you could manage a short one? " and then he was gone. He was gentle, with a formidable gentleness. So many things stirred him that by the end of the evening he often had far more Shorts than could be used. The superfluous perished, like infants exposed, without recognition outside the family.

In the whole field of writing and of editorship the liberty of treatment which " C.P." allowed was conditioned by moral principles which he applied with great fidelity. A Long Leader by any other of the prophets would have begun with " The word of the Lord that came to . . ." " C.P.", without revelation, had the same direct conviction of what was right and wrong. By this he guided himself among the maze of questions which, since no man can be master of all subjects, he did not profess to understand in detail. By this more than all he impressed his personality, as sincere in purpose as it was independent in thought, on the instrument by which he moved opinion. He rated moral earnestness most highly in his staff. Of an invaluable colleague it was rumoured that there had at one time been grave doubts how he would turn out: had not " C.P." said that he was " a little lacking in moral earnestness "? He was amused but not displeased when he heard that two of his men had been described as—the " twin Galsworthies of the *Guardian* office."[1] In his

---

[1] Before Mr. Galsworthy got the " O.M."

rightness about principle he would not compromise. His view of that new phenomenon, the giant sweepstake, he expressed with simplicity. He thought it dangerously demoralising, and " the most unfortunate people," he said, " are those who win the prizes." When a discussion raged about a fundamental question, when he thought that anyone was proposing to palter with principle, then the eyes flashed and the beard shook and the Commandments came down again in thunder and lightning. He was a poor speaker, but in writing he had a voice whose sound was like the sea.

In the actual business of composition " C.P." stood for argumentative, reasonable moderation. If he looked into a room and said, " I like your leader—very persuasive," he gave his highest praise. He disliked intemperance of speech. His occasional vehemence in conversation misled the unwary, who, having engaged with him in mutual severities against an offence or an offender, sat down and wrote with equal passion, only to find that " C.P.", revising, had eliminated from the argument all trace of violence. " A fine article," he said once, referring to a man of strong views—" a fine article: X holding himself in." He liked people to feel deeply, think clearly, and hold themselves in. It was only towards the end, when his grip was at last relaxing, that he passed intemperate utterance. He approved of a man who grappled with the strongest points of an opponent's case; " there has been no one like him," he said of a fine journalist who was leaving the paper, " for getting to the heart of a subject." He liked plain, muscular work. " Clear and vigorous " was one of his phrases of approval. Provided that a writer, having something to say, said it well, he thought the niceties of style unimportant. The flamboyant and the rhetorical offended him; when an enthusiastic reader sent him a scream of delight about an article in the paper, he cut it out and sent it to one of his staff with the comment, " I don't agree; much too rich." He made war on woolliness. He once gave a man the proofs of an overgrown leader. " Would you take a quarter of a column out of this thing by X," he said, " I have to go early and it's turned out much too long." " Any particular part that I should go for,

Mr Scott?" "Oh," he said, "it doesn't matter; you can get it out almost anywhere." As a sub-editor he got rid of the redundant and the turgid with the conscientiousness of a machine that presses the superfluous moisture out of yarn. The man who passed " seaward journey to the great metropolis," and when the " copy " came back to him, found written in firm blue pencil " voyage to London " knew what sort of English " C.P." liked. Once, when an article in type was shown to him because a certain sentence expressed a doubtful judgment, he noticed that the English was slovenly, amended it, and then, being drawn on from sentence to sentence and becoming more and more dissatisfied, he made innumerable minute corrections until at last, having made a complete mess of the proof, he looked up and said gently, " Dear X; of course, he's not a trained sub-editor."

Thinking as he did of his function and that of his paper, he spared others as little as himself. An autocrat, he would have said that it was " the good of the paper," not he, that made supreme demands. When he was told, as occasionally happened, that someone had left the *Guardian* for one of the great dailies, he was amused. " Really? " he said, throwing his head back as at a joke; after all, not everyone could be expected to understand the privilege of door-keeping in the Temple. He hardly realised that individuals, although devoted to the paper, might not always be able to submerge their personal view. When it was suggested to him that a senior of ability might not like being turned into an assistant to a junior on a new piece of work, he said with severity, " I don't think he will object if it is for the good of the paper." When one of his best men, on leaving, mentioned to him that he had resented the elevation of a junior over his head to a distinguished position where no suggestion of superior merit could be made, " C.P." said simply, with great sincerity, " It never occurred to me." His demands on those whom he trusted were ruthless. " By the way," he once said, " will you take part of X's work next week, He wants to have a week's holiday. He says he's tired. Why are these young men tired? You and I are never tired." He once, from his house, rang up the same man, whose hours were then from about 5.0 p.m. to 3.0 a.m., and said, " Old Blank is staying with me and we want to get out a pamphlet on the Persian question. I thought you'd like to help. We mustn't lose any time, so would you be here by ten o'clock? We could make an early start, have lunch and get on in the afternoon before we go down to the office." This lasted for some days. At the finish he remarked, " I should think you've always liked hard work." Having with difficulty collected about him men whom he trusted, he desired them to be available, by which he meant at their desks; the system of sending members of the indoors staff occasionally out of doors, whether at home or abroad, in order to increase their experience might, he admitted, have its value, but it was, he thought, " very inconvenient." He did not practise it. He thought that his staff should be kept well occupied. "What exactly," he said once, " does X do? " naming an important person. " Yes," he said, on hearing the answer, " but that can't take him long." It was, perhaps, not unconnected with the inquiry that X was shortly afterwards reported to be missing his last tram home.

He would let no one increase holidays, which ran from Saturday to Saturday, by adding to them the Friday before or the Sunday after, even if the holiday-maker was entitled to it as a legitimate " day-off " according to the rules. When he discovered that one experimenter, full of ignorance or of art, was proposing to split his holidays into four separate weeks and add a lawful Sunday " off " to each of them, his indignation was profound. In practice he often conceded what in principle he refused, adding, " Don't tell anyone; it mustn't be a precedent."

Since he regarded the paper more as an influence than as a news-sheet, " C.P." was not interested in circulation as a counting of heads nor in advertisements as a means of profit. He desired more readers in order that his ideas might be, if not accepted, intelligently discussed; he sought the circulation that brought the advertisements that provided the revenue that improved the paper as an engine for the moving of opinion. He neither courted the advertiser nor without reason offended him.

G

If there were reason, it was a pity. He watched the advertisements lest anything unseemly or unsightly should creep in, and he used to say that the less the editorial and the advertisement departments had to do with each other the better for the paper. When a rash young man remarked to him that it must be difficult to conduct a certain feature without yielding to pressure from advertisers, "C.P." said to a senior, "I felt like kicking him downstairs."

He desired circulation but not at the cost of the character of the paper. When circulation figures were good he liked to give the credit to the quality of the leader-columns; when they were not so good, he turned a questioning eye on the news departments. About new ideas he was willing but slow to be convinced. Realising the tough conservatism of the loyal subscriber, he frowned on "jumpiness"; but he was willing to consider any change that might confirm old readers or bring new ones. He would consider with detachment the adoption of a serial story or regular verse or caricatures, but at the close there was the same formula—" of course they would have to be very good." Many warm debates ended, like a Cabinet meeting, in indecision; who could say how much of the masses might be won over by the " very good " at 2d.? Such discussions had surprises for " C.P.", who knew nothing about the suburbs of literature. Someone suggested facetiously that a serial story might be procured from Allen Raine or Ruby M. Ayres. "C.P." repeated the names slowly, thought, and said firmly, " I never heard of either of them." When verse was discussed, Wilhelmina Stitch was mentioned. " What a funny name! " said " C.P." " I never heard of her—who is she? " It was explained that she was a great " puller " of circulation. " Well," said " C.P." briskly, " that sounds promising, doesn't it? " On further illumination about popular verse he passed to another subject. After the conference was over he went to one of those who had taken part and said, " I want to know—do you really think that more verse might bring more circulation? Of course we could only have the best."

As the years went on, he introduced into the paper new features to meet new tastes. To some of them he would have assented long before had it not been for the Old Guard. To the repeated suggestions that the time had come when the paper ought to " notice " films, " C.P." having consulted the Old Guard, replied that it could not be done because, " if we did, they are so bad we should have to attack them," which, indeed, eventually " we " did, thereby moving angry managers to withdraw their advertisements. When it was proposed that particulars should be given of important books which were about to be published, he was advised that either such notes would express an opinion about the books, in which case they would amount to an additional review, or they would not, and then they would be merely publishers' " puffs ". It was not " C.P." who, when new features attractive to women were advocated, sternly hoped that there was " going to be something in them to interest an intelligent woman," nor was it he who, when the greater use of photographs was discussed, exclaimed, " Good God! Must we come to photographs of weddings? " He was ready to modernise the paper, consistently with its character, in order to increase its usefulness. He did not despair of leading Philistines up to the City of Zion. He never feared that they might weaken the fibre of the paper; he was too confident that he could weaken theirs. He would go firmly as far as he was persuaded was necessary on a long view, but no further. It was urged on him that the building should bear the name of the paper in an illuminated sky-sign. At last he agreed. " Very well," he said, " have it—but don't let it wink, John."[1]

Since the paper was critical, independent, and in frequent opposition to popular opinion, he felt that everything should be done to make it clear to the average man and woman. It was to appeal to the intelligent rather than to the erudite. He tried to keep out of it the pedantic and obscure, pretence and ostentation. He liked plain English, holding that everything in a foreign language, living or dead, that crept into the paper could have been said as well or better in English. (" Why do they say ' portfolio ' when they mean an English ' Ministry '? ")

[1] J. R. Scott.

He constantly asked the question, " What does it mean? " or
" What does he mean? " If a man who had allowed something
unintelligible to appear in the paper said " I thought it meant
so-and-so," " C.P." would forgive the greatest stupidity, but to
insert anything without having a clear opinion, however wrong,
about its meaning, was a serious offence. " But, my dear fellow,
if you didn't think you knew what it meant, you shouldn't have
let it in." He would go bustling into a room, waving a cutting
or a proof, in which was an obscure phrase, a preciosity or an
Americanism. " What does he mean by this? He talks about a
' final showdown '? An Americanism, I suppose. What does
it mean? Generally known? . . . I don't know it. Taken from
cards? I never heard of it." He resented, except in a few cases,
the use of initials, especially in headlines, to represent some body
with which the journalist might be familiar and the public not.
He carried this objection far. For a long time after the railway
amalgamations he would not allow L.M.S. to appear in a headline. He had found it at the top of a Short Leader. He came in,
according to his custom,[1] bristling. " These letters L.M.S.," he
said, " What do they mean? " The amalgamations were
recalled to him. " May be," he said, " but what do the letters
stand for? " " A combination, Mr. Scott, of the London North-
Western . . ." " Ah," he said, relaxing, " That explains it. I
always went North-Western and I can never think of it by any
other name." What was intended to be intelligible to the public,
in a leader, a report, a telegram, or a poster, must be intelligible
to him, an admirable standard of measure since he never
pretended to be a know-all but was unsurpassed in clear thinking
and expression.

The slovenliness in language which, partly because of loose
thinking, partly because of mere misuse of words, threatens to
infest a newspaper, roused him. " Look at this," he said.
" Blank died literally in harness. He didn't." Or " This man
says that we shall have to pay literally through the nose. He
knows we shan't." He protested almost passionately against a
witness at an inquest who described himself as having been

---

[1] " More suo " not permitted.

"only too willing" to save a woman from drowning. "He doesn't mean that, you know," said "C.P." "Then why does he say it?" He watched for and cut out of the paper false usages and vulgarisms. He sent the cutting sometimes to the culprit, more often to one of his assistants for what he called the "little collection". He would not allow misuses in reports and contributions to be justified by the distinction of either Cabinet rank or a University Chair. Drawing attention to a lapse by a well-known master of letters, he said, "Even the great can stumble—but it should have been altered." He demanded a certain precision and dignity of language; all parts of the paper, reports and letters to editor included, had to conform to it. He was fastidious about translations, especially from the French, a language to which he gave exact attention. He was impatient with writers of letters who complained when English grammar was forcibly imposed on them. "They ought to be grateful to us," he said, "as speakers should be to reporters." His vigilance extended to the smallest points. If Mr. Lloyd George was "Mr. George" in the leader-columns, that was the precision of "C.P." not, as Mr. George is reported to have said, the malice of Labour men gathered on the *Guardian* staff.

"C.P." demanded correct English in the common words and phrases. Someone had said "the extremists have now neither the money, backing, or confidence to launch a new programme." "Should be 'nor'," wrote "C.P.", "but wrong even so, as 'neither' implies only two alternatives." He had a nose for outrages on the participle. Cutting out a paragraph which said: "An aeroplane made a forced landing on the Goodwin Sands yesterday, the pilot and two passengers being picked up by a passing steamer," he noted "'Being' here implies some relation of cause and effect and there is none." He never ceased to point out the improper use of the personal pronoun, as in "I can vouch for them being uncomfortable." "Should be 'their'," he said curtly. "He agreed to them being removed to Australia;" "Should be 'their'," he wrote. "Lord Rosebery's remark about it being easy to talk when one had a contempt for one's audience "—" Should be ' its ', " he said, and so on through a hundred other vulgar errors like " very gratified," " some form or another," " equally . . . as," " cruel or otherwise." As the errors had all been committed by some individual in the editorial departments, " C.P." was puzzled. He desired to bring the niceties of correct usage to the general notice, but not to do anything which might pillory an individual. " Could one suggest," he asked, " any easy method by which correction of the ' little errors' could be made generally available without offence? " A method was possible, and he agreed to it, as the statesmen say, in principle. But, like them, he did nothing. He could be stern in his private rebukes; a Chief Reader, summoned to an interview on misprints and recommended by a friend not to defend the indefensible, went away murmuring, " He's a hard man if you give in to him." But " C.P." shied from the instruction which, if made " generally available ", might here and there be read as a public censure. To the end he continued to send the little notes, pinning the cutting at the top of a scrap of paper. But he never wrote, much less circulated, a Book of Leviticus. Sometimes he held a nightly inquisition into misprints, which led a shocked conference to discover that the correction of a comma is the root of much typographical evil. Thereupon battle. Did commas matter? Yes, but did they " really " matter? Should one regulate them by grammar or by rude common sense, fight for each jot and tittle of a punctuative creed or take what one was given in fear of a worse fate? It became a war of exhaustion, broken by the armistice of summer holidays, and not renewed.

In many small ways " C.P." took pains to spare the personal feelings of others. Once, having given someone charge of an important feature, he decided that the experiment was unsuccessful. He sent to a senior the original " copy " which showed the changes made by the reviser, with the comment " Miles better in the original." Then, although he put someone else in charge, the dispossessed received from him a note which gave no sign of dissatisfaction. He thought that this was a promising young man who should not be discouraged. To individuals except to those with whom he came in close contact he rarely gave direct commendation for a good piece of work. He thought of work as its own reward (but journalists are human), so that although he noticed and in conversation spoke of good performance, he seldom conveyed his praise to those who sometimes wondered, without cause, whether their work was appreciated by him. Some of his commendations, for their rarity, entered the office traditions. On ceremonial occasions, anxious to thank the editorial departments for their common effort, he could not conceal his view of the gulf which separated the writer, the creator of opinion, from the purveyor of news; if all the writers were suddenly missing, he more than once said, " Even the sub-editors would be able to knock up some sort of a leader."

He was slow to give his confidence and had a long memory for disappointments. Whether it was the case of a new man coming for trial as a writer or of anyone in the office being appointed to a new duty, he followed his work from day to day and plied him with comment and criticism. If, finally, he ever reached the phrase " Oh, you can say—" or " You can do what you like about it," the recipient knew that even if " C.P." did not mean quite that, he was completely trusted. It has been said that he chose men well. Certainly he almost always chose them with great caution. When a vacancy had to be filled without delay, he weighed specimens of work, records, and personal impressions and called subordinates into council. He liked specimens; he thought that from even one or two you could generally get an idea of a man's quality, whereas an interview, though necessary, was treacherous; it might leave you with a wrong impression or, annoyingly, with none at all. Of candidates for the writing staff he held that it did not matter how long a vacancy was kept open provided that, at the finish, it was rightly filled. If a valuable man was lost to the staff, his work could be divided out among the remainder until a suitable successor had been discovered, tested, and finally confirmed. It was unfortunate, no doubt, for the remainder, if the time was long, but that was irrelevant; it might be years, and on one occasion was. Of all alike he said,

" You see, we have to be careful, because we can't get rid of them." He was behind the times of easy-come and easy-go. He expected letters of recommendation to be serious, and he weighed them seriously. They did not always help the applicant. He read out one, pausing over each paragraph and sometimes commenting, until he came to the sentence " and he is a brilliant conversationalist." " I think," said " C.P.", " that we have enough of them already."

He held the strictest views about the function of editor. For him the Editor was the personality, controlling, directing, harmonising, which gave unity of purpose and of character to the paper. He was not equally interested in all parts; he left the Commercial to the commercial; he rarely looked at the sports pages; news never excited him like an idea, but he felt so strongly that the organism, if it was to be a consistent whole, must reflect a single personality, that he objected not only to the existence of self-sufficing departments but also to the conferment of the title of " Editor ", either by day or by night, on anybody charged with a feature or a department. " Night-editor? " he said wonderingly, having at that time himself been night-editor as well as Editor for nearly fifty years. " Ah, but of course, we don't have that system here." He wrote " London Manager ", not " London Editor " for the head of the London Office. He would say " my assistant ", but not " assistant editor ". He referred not to " sports editor " but to " sports sub-editor ". When a list of all the " editors " on a great New York daily was read out to him, he was much amused, and said, " I wonder what on earth they all find to do." His rule was that all letters written by members of the staff must be signed on behalf of the Editor with their initials only. He rejected the suggestion that a reference should be given at the head of letters which would bring the answer direct to the right person; the reply should be addressed to the Editor and find its way to its personal destination through normal, even though devious, office channels. There is but one God, and Allah is his prophet. " C.P.'s " idea of an editor was that he had both functions.

The news which he despised was that which resounds without significance. When a paragraph appeared in the paper saying that the Honourable Somebody had been operated on for appendicitis by Sir Frederick Treves, he sent a cross note saying that it should not have been given because "(i) The Honourable Somebody is nobody; (ii) All those people have appendicitis nowadays; (iii) Sir Frederick Treves operates on all of them." He was displeased with the sentimental gush about the Queen's Dolls House. He appreciated, without himself pursuing, the journalistic "scoop"; some time after a large "scoop" had been fortuitously obtained, he remarked that it would be "very useful" to the news columns if we could have another. He kept "copy" late on his desk to the distraction of the sub-editors, and, apologising when at last he released it, did the same next night. On most modern papers he would have been "sacked" repeatedly, he had such ideas about news-values. There was an evening when it was announced that *The Times* had come down to a penny. E. T. Scott, who was then his secretary, went to see the news editor. "My father wants to know how much we are giving about *The Times* at a penny." "I thought about a quarter of a column," was the reply. "E.T.S." looked gloomy. "I don't think he will regard that as enough." In a few moments the news editor was summoned to "C.P.S.", who was sitting magisterially. "Oh, X," he said, "how much are we giving about *The Times* coming down to a penny?" "A quarter of a column, Mr. Scott." He shook his beard. "It's not nearly enough," he said. "We ought to have at least a column. If the news had come in earlier it would have been the subject for 'the Long'." When he said, as he sometimes did, "Now what can we do to strengthen ourselves against *The Times*?" his news editor could have made a suggestion to him. But it would have made no difference, for he was magnanimous.

Some editors, it is said, get news for their papers; a man may be a Dinner Editor, so that what goes into his tentacular ears comes out in his paper next morning. "C.P." kept his paper and his private information distinct. He scarcely ever gave his own paper a piece of news; rarely would he allow it even to prepare for something he had heard was about to happen. He would not use any information which had come to him as a private person for the purposes of his paper. He made men despair. One night he came abruptly into a room. "Have we anything ready," he said, "about J. L. Paton?"[1] "No, Mr. Scott—is he dead?" "No, no. He's resigned the High Mastership. I knew a fortnight ago." Sometimes he overreached himself. Once he brought along the usual cutting; it referred to a public man in Manchester who had been the subject of controversy for years. "Why did we criticise him like this?" he said, looking vexed. "Well but, Mr. Scott, we've said pretty much the same thing about him for two or three years." "I know, I know," he said, "but I've spent the last three months trying to get him round to a better frame of mind and I had just succeeded." Sometimes he went to London to see Personages. When he came back he might mention some of the things that had been said to him, and occasionally it seemed to his listeners, who were impartial men, that something in the information might even have been intended by the Personage to see the morning light. The comedy had a set form. "Don't you think, Mr. Scott, that something of this ought to be indicated in the news columns—I mean in order to give it its proper importance— or perhaps in the London Letter?" "C.P." would appear to think over this suggestion. After a time he would say, "I think, perhaps, on the whole, it had better be kept for the Leader. I'm just going to write." Then he wrote the Leader, and the profane, seizing the First Edition to see what he had done, would swear that neither Personage nor public would ever find the embedded news. During the war he often went to London. There was one week-end when he went on the Friday and returned on the Monday. On Monday morning a full summary of an exciting document appeared in a London paper. In the evening this was shown to him. He pored over it with recognition and named a well-known journalist. "That's X," he said. "When I went to see Z yesterday"—he named a Personage—"X was just coming out of his room. He had a copy of this report under his arm." Beaming on his outraged assistants he added, "I had a

---

[1] High Master of the Manchester Grammar School.

copy too." Personages must have wept at his loyalty to confidence.

He sought for solid quality in the matter that went into the paper. Being thrifty and determined to have reasonable value for money, he tried to catch contributors young, before others had detected their quality and their prices had risen. He watched the reviews which the paper printed, took notice of new, promising authors, and instructed his staff to draw his attention to any new contributor who ought to be encouraged. The system, which grew up in the newspapers during the war, of paying popular novelists large sums to pronounce on any question, shocked him. When he was told that one of them was paid forty guineas an article he said with great energy " But he's not worth it!" The most popular contributor did not attract him if the contribution did not. A famous man of letters offered for a bagatelle some signed speculations on post-war Europe. "C.P.", not liking their trend, rejected them, and the great man wrote pleasantly saying that he had placed them elsewhere for a hundred guineas. In administration he had Gladstone's hate of waste. Someone at a conference referred to the prevalence of waste in the office. "Waste, waste!" said "C.P.", looking like Jove when all Olympus trembled at his nod, "how can there be waste?" He threw his head back, brushing his beard up and up from beneath and darting sideways glances at the other. "Waste of stationery," was suggested. "Waste of stationery!" he repeated with indignation. "But where?" He turned to the editorial hierarchs. "What is the system by which we get our stationery?" He was mollified when assured that one could scarcely get a postcard without filling up a form.

While "C.P." watched the "feeders" that led from without to the features of the paper, he stimulated his staff with suggestions from his widely-ranging mind. He must have sent down to them tens of thousands of notes, crisp and shrewd, on the topics of the day or the day after, from the threepenny bit to the bicycle, from whatnots to salaries for wives, from home-baking to Yugoslavia and food-rationing by ticket:

June 11th, 1911

This estimate relating to home-baking from stone-milled flour seems rather important. I wonder if we could get someone to write with knowledge on the extent to which home-baking is still carried on among the poor and as to the instruction of girls at the technical schools in baking. Home-baking is certainly very much commoner in the north of England than in the south. I never had a cook yet who could not bake and didn't expect to do so; whereas in the south my friends tell me it is practically a lost art. The whole thing would make a good back-pager if we could get the right person to do it.

January 11th, 1917

It is a large order to break up the Austrian Empire and to reconstruct the fragments. We shall have pretty carefully to count the cost as well as the practical gain. Would a Southern Slav State, I wonder, hold together? These smaller Slavonic nationalities seem to have a wonderful capacity for fighting each other.

February 5th, 1917

In view of the possible imminence of " rationing " how would it be for someone to write an article giving the most precise information obtainable as to its working in Germany and Austria-Hungary? I believe the system of tickets to be entirely unsuited to our needs and that the rationing could be far better done by a system of local committees to whom a pretty free hand as to methods should be given and with some discretionary power. If everyone were obliged to select a particular butcher, or baker, or grocer, and the tradesmen had to keep a strict account, the whole business could be done without the intolerable nuisance of tickets or queues.

If occasionally he was excited on discovering things which were not new, it was one side of a cardinal journalistic virtue, but sometimes he insisted that the discovery should be immediately shared by his readers. The announcement that the Manchester Corporation, determined to abate the smoke-nuisance, was now hiring out gas-cookers to ratepayers had to be delicately transmuted into a sketch of the progress made by a long-established piece of municipal machinery up to the point which was now triumphantly disclosed, and after " C.P." had paid an enthusiastic but belated visit to " the dogs ", the paper indulged itself in grave appreciation of the æsthetic beauties of a scene which, as a sordid stimulant of gambling, it had for some time damned.

" C.P." encouraged the use of maps in the news-columns. He looked out for the Pointer and the Scale, compared the distances in the news-columns with those in the map, though it might be a small map of a large country, and wrote a note if he thought there was anything wrong. If a Leader contained much geography he might have a map specially drawn and inserted somewhere else. When it was suggested that a one-column map might just as well be dropped into the actual Leader, he smiled without warmth; one should not jig about the Ark. He grew to be fond of illustrations. In their early days they had been regarded as a comforter for baby-readers, as a little " cheap "; hence, for self-respect, drawings were used rather than half-tone photographs. Later, in a changed world " C.P." would agree, for the joke, that some readers might even look at the illustrations before the Leaders; why, he did it himself in the case of *The Times* but, of course, that was different. He watched the pictures jealously because they were " so prominent ". He did not like photographs of " disasters ". Whereas, thirty years ago, he had printed hunting articles to interest hunting people, his views had changed so much that at the end he would not give a photograph of a meet, however good. He disliked the conventional in photography. " All these football pictures," he said, " are exactly alike." He complained that if photographers " took " a golfer when driving, they always showed the end instead of the beginning of the swing. They must, he said, be told to change their ways; but he yielded when assured that a photographer clicking his camera just when one of the most sensitive creatures was about to drive would be as good as dead. To caricatures he never fully reconciled himself. For a special purpose, for a short time, as at an election, they might be tolerable, but since as he said, " they hit you in the face ", he suspected them. The sense of proportion which he prized they lacked.

To his staff he was courteous and suave, with an absolute

authority. Those under his eye he ruled with an almost military discipline but he did not like it said so. To men occupying new posts he made clear his desire that the machine should run without friction, and what he desired he assumed. He directed by tone as much as by word. If he said " It is important that there should be no friction . . ." it was enough. As he grew old he could not tolerate the loud and truculent; he protected himself against them by not seeing them. He welcomed criticism, the threshing of ideas, the opposition of independent minds. " X is weak," he said. " He proposes something and, when you object, agrees with all you say." He believed so much in the goodness of human nature that he could be taken in by private and public humbugs. When the Germans first dropped bombs on undefended places he would not believe it; on the ground that there must be defences of which the Germans knew, he sent people to look for them.

He had a stock of euphemisms. Acts of insubordination were " irregular ", the worst " most irregular ". A person with whom nothing could be done " had to go ". He told of a colleague who, in the 1870's, would not produce reports as the young " C.P.", the new editor, wanted them. " Eventually," he summed up brightly, " he had to go." He never completely trusted anyone whom he had once detected by sight, sound, or smell, to have taken alcohol in excess. One night when he was in the room of a junior, the door opened stealthily and in the aperture appeared a large flushed face, whose owner,[1] looking fixedly for some seconds at " C.P.", said with solemnity, " It's all right, Mr. Scott." " C.P." regarded him without speaking. The intruder, his face bathed in benevolence, repeated, " It's all right, Mr. Scott," and as stealthily withdrew. " C.P.", his head thrust forward and bristling like a well-bred dog, glared at the closed door. Then he said, " He's been drinking. He'll have to go." To " have to go " was the regular verb in which he conjugated the ultimate sentence. Later the culprit " went ", though another reason was given him. No one could despatch the silken bow-string with more courtesy than " C.P."

[1] Now dead.

Letter-writing was to him a subtle instrument through which to convey the nicest shades of purpose. He was a master of the art, from silences to plainest speech. He worked on an important letter as on a leader or a review, seeking the just word, demanding a subordinate's criticism, looking like a chess-player to the moves beyond the next, drafting and redrafting. No one wrote with more intention. A novice pointed out to him, when he had written a careful reply to an important letter, that he had not answered one of the principal paragraphs. " Well, no," he said with a smile, " you see, that is the answer. He'll understand." He could convey a warning in an ambiguity and by silence procure a resignation. He preferred the flexibility of letters to the brusqueness of the telegram. He desired others to write as he did, to the point. He could not do with wordy letters or memoranda, and often he did not read them. " Another long screed from X!" he would say, " let me know what he says "— and " Would you read this for me and tell me if I ought to answer personally." It was alleged that one man had fought a winning battle against " C.P.'s " critical notes by a counter-bombardment with lengthy memoranda.

Himself scrupulous in answering letters, " C.P." expected his staff to be so. If anyone wrote complaining that an earlier letter had not been adequately treated, " But it was, of course, acknowledged? " he asked. The only letters which he ignored were those which he called "ill-conditioned" and "impossible". He would send a letter on with a note " An ill-conditioned screed! Read and destroy!" or " An impossible fellow! Better just file." He was generous to all who had a reasonable point of view to put forward in the correspondence columns; newspapers being almost a monopoly, the public must be granted its voice. But he would not allow the display of ill-temper which the correspondence columns of a newspaper attract. For this reason he was slow to ventilate theological and ecclesiastical questions. He feared the ill-temper of the bickering sects, some of whom, though he always kept the balance even between them, complained each that he favoured another. There were those who, if a paragraph were dropped in the nightly scurry out of a 24-page paper, thought that he was conspiring against their faith, if faith it was. He was patient, but he abstained from giving them occasions. He rejected more than once a suggestion that the paper should have a series of articles summarising the recent course of the Higher Criticism at home and abroad. " They " would be up in arms. " But, Mr. Scott, if the writer only described the theories of the critics without pronouncing on them, they could not well protest." " Oh, yes," he said, " they would. They would want to know why we were doing it." In religious discussion, like that of the Prayer Book, he kept the writing in his own hands. He was surprised, as well as pleased, when at last he found a substitute on the staff to satisfy him.

Those who knew " C.P." only in his later years spoke of his defective memory. But it had always been so, nor was it defective so much as capricious. One day a subordinate reported himself on return from holiday. " Ah, my dear fellow," said " C.P.", " back from holiday? Have you had a good time? " " Yes, thank you, Mr. Scott." " Where have you been? " " I've been down in Kent." " Among the hop-fields? " " Right in the middle of them." " And did you do any hopping? " On the next night, at the same time, the subordinate waited on " C.P." " Ah, my dear fellow," he said cordially, " back from holiday? Have you had a good time? " " Yes, thank you, Mr. Scott." " Where have you been? " " I've been down in Kent." " Among the hop-fields? " and so on to the end of the kind interrogation, with no ripple from yesterday's existence troubling his serenity. That was when he was at the height of his powers. He forgot names and faces easily. " Who is that? " he said when a man who had been two or three years in the office passed him. " X? Ah, a newcomer, I suppose. I think I haven't come across him yet." His forgetfulness was, perhaps, partly self-protective. He remembered what mattered by forgetting what did not. If no one knew what he might forget, no one was certain what he would not remember, nor did lapses of memory impede the powerful working of his mind.

There was a character on a famous football field who, when he made an assertion, confirmed it solemnly by saying " an' no

W. T. ARNOLD, 1852–1904

C. P. SCOTT

*From the painting by T. C. Dugdale, R.A., presented to the
Manchester Press Club by K. R. Brady*

bettin'." "C.P." was an editor "an' no bettin'." He thought of the paper as possessing, in whole and in part, a character which nothing must diminish. The character safe, anything might be changed. He himself read slowly, wrote slowly, made up his mind slowly, but he was tremendously right when his mind was made up. Serene in spirit, he strengthened any who were rudely shaken by the inevitable mishaps of newspaper work. Courage and composure did not fail him. He was, as the Teutons said of the Romans, "invincible, not to be overcome by any blow." As such a man he is remembered by the generations of those who gladly served him, from the days of his prime to the later years when, white and bowed, but still with fresh, clear mind, still inspiring and directing with the old fire, he hurried with quick shuffling steps along the corridors, and so to the last months when sometimes, his son absent, he " took Leaders " and sat long over the fire, holding some piece of " copy " in his hand, his mind far away but trying still to respond to each new call on his attention, grave and cheerful, firm and courteous, a greater journalist and a greater man than his staff had known or will know.

1825
ADVERTISING AN ARDWICK SEMINARY

SCOTT'S LIEUTENANTS

By H. D. Nichols

W. T. ARNOLD

W. T. ARNOLD, the first chief leader writer of C. P. Scott's own appointing, was a grandson of Arnold of Rugby. Matthew Arnold was his uncle and Mrs. Humphry Ward his sister. In 1879 when Scott brought him from Oxford to try his hand at journalism in Manchester he had just won the Arnold Prize (awarded in memory of his grandfather) with an essay on Roman Provincial Administration. It was recognised as much beyond the usual prize essay in merit and its subject and historical period were to remain an absorbing interest of its author's life. History gave Arnold to journalism and journalism took the gift at history's expense. For though he continued to work at his chosen period during his seventeen years on the *Guardian*, doubling the task with that presented by his new career to the sad detriment of leisure, his success in history was that of an influence rather than an achievement and little was left to show for it.

Arnold believed, however, that the two disciplines of scientific history and day-to-day journalism were complementary, and so far as his journalism was concerned those who knew him best felt that he had proved his case. At the age of forty-four he was struck down by a " rheumatism " which proved to be a more serious spinal complaint and had to retire from the paper, but not before he had established a reputation among those who knew as one of the great journalists of his day. " Those who knew " were not many and, though he had made Manchester the centre of his interests from the day of his arrival in the city, Manchester scarcely knew him. His role was anonymous; his pen was that of the paper to which he gave himself, it has been

said, " as a Jesuit to the order." " There is no limit " he himself
would sometimes quote, " to what a man can do when he does
not care who gains the credit for it." Quoting for the benefit of
another he might have, but did not, make the application to
himself. Arnold played the full part in shaping the paper which
is only possible when first-rate intellectual power and force of
character are allied with the aptitude and zest for their full
exercise under the exacting conditions of newspaper production. " He wrote," as the greatest of his contemporaries has
said, " by choice, on far more things than most men of fair
mental power and alacrity can discuss at call without becoming
mere thinkers by proxy and re-arrangers of unfelt phrases."

In politics Arnold was guided by two strong influences, an
intense interest in human individuality and a strong respect for
authority in things intellectual. But he disliked the practice
common in the journalism of his day of concentrating all the
writing strength of a paper on politics. It was criticism, he maintained, that stamped a paper more than anything, and he himself
wrote particularly of painting and the theatre with unusual
reserves of relevant knowledge. Roman history has been called
the " trade wind " of his intellectual life but he was widely
and deeply read in many subjects. He had the true journalist's
universal curiosity; no mere inquisitiveness but a passion for
thoroughness of inquiry. Where he was not an expert he
generally knew what the experts were at and would reveal himself surprisingly abreast of the times in a galaxy of subjects. His
seventeen years were all too short but they left a tradition in the
office which is not to be ignored.

C. E. MONTAGUE

C. E. Montague who came to the paper as a young man from
Balliol in 1890, became chief writer when ill-health compelled
Arnold's retirement six years later. For the next ten years he
bore a double load of responsibility in the office, for from 1895
to 1906 the editor represented a Lancashire constituency in the
House of Commons and had to spend much of his time in

London. In his absence Montague was in effect acting editor as well as leader writer. In later years " C.E.M." was to be better known to the world outside the office; first as a dramatic critic whose identity was given away by more than his initials and some of whose best criticism was republished in 1911 in *Dramatic Values*; and after the first World War as the author of *Disenchantment*, as the essayist of *The Right Place* and for the short stories of his *Fiery Particles*. But these were the products of such spare time as his exacting work for the paper left over. He had been at that for twenty years before his first book, *A Hind Let Loose,* appeared and it was as the anonymous leader writer that the bulk of his work was done.

Montague came, like Arnold and like his editor before him, to a Manchester to which he was a stranger and like them he took the city to his heart. But it was as a little-known journalist working through his paper and not in any sense a public figure. His great period was that of Chamberlain's new Imperialism and the South African War, of the Tariff controversy and the struggles for Irish freedom and, at home, for Women's Suffrage. It was with these larger national issues that he was chiefly concerned and, after 1906, with the constitutional issues raised by the House of Lords. In these great polemics Montague brought to the art and practice of leader writing new gifts which have been the inspiration of successors but too often the despair of imitators. His published work sometimes seems to reveal an intensive pre-occupation with the niceties of style, but in all his work for the paper the plain man was his target. Public appeal is the essence of the " Leader " and there was a directness of attack about Montague's leaders that could not be ignored. In controversy, sure of his facts, he was never afraid of provocation, and when out for battle with the shoddy and second-rate, whether in home or foreign affairs, his use of satire and metaphor took one back to the days of Swift. What he wrote on political issues must be put first, since it was here that he carried the heaviest load, but during his thirty-five years on the paper the range of interests with which journalism concerns itself was always growing and Montague was not the man to neglect any of its new opportunities. He would write with his own pungent persuasiveness on anything on which he had qualified himself to do so, and his scope was not narrow. From the beginning he had a passion for the theatre, and the school of criticism which the *Guardian* built up, largely round Miss Horniman's Gaiety, owed more than an inspired leadership to "C.E.M." Some of his work on the theatre, produced not in the leisure of the study but straight from the theatre and in the last late hour before going to press, has been rescued from its first ephemeral setting and has already an assured survival.

Montague was forty-seven when the Kaiser invaded Belgium, and as his hair was completely white his age was hard to disguise. But he dyed the hair and joined the Royal Fusiliers as a private. He reached the front line with his battalion, but it is not surprising that he was soon invalided back. Employment at the base had never formed part of his ambitions but authority obstructed all his attempts to get back to his unit, and after a Provost Marshal period at Etaples he found himself a captain in the Intelligence Department at Haig's G.H.Q.. With a fortunate nicety of selection, perhaps unusual in the last war but one, he was employed for the rest of the war as a conducting officer, shepherding distinguished visitors and fathering war correspondents at the front. This gave him so full and balanced a view of the western war as a whole that he came back full of the material of which he made use not only in *Disenchantment* and other books but in his last years' work for the paper. This continued until 1925 when he retired to the Thames valley which he had left for Manchester thirty-five years before. The war years had left their mark on him, and three years later on a visit to Manchester for some university celebrations, he took a chill and from that pneumonia, from which he did not recover.

L. T. HOBHOUSE

L. T. Hobhouse was a regular member of the editorial staff for five years between 1897 and 1902. After he left he was an intermittent contributor. For a few years he was a director of the firm and towards the end of his life he would come back to Manchester occasionally to do a month's "duty" as a leader writer. But he was not, as was Montague or as Arnold had been, a *Guardian* man in the sense that the paper was his life's interest and his life the paper's. He left Oxford to come to Manchester not as a new graduate but at the age of thirty-three, as an ex-Fellow of Corpus with a reputation already won as a teacher and thinker. His important book, *The Theory of Knowledge*, had been published in 1896. The purely academic life never satisfied Hobhouse, whose more than hereditary Liberalism was allied with a passion for social reform. After he left the *Guardian* he was for a time the secretary of the Free Trade Union. As a chairman of Trade and Conciliation Boards he was an active assistant in the social evolution of the pre-war period, and in the chair of Sociology in London University, which he held from 1907 to the time of his death, he helped to create the international reputation of the London School of Economics. Leonard Hobhouse is remembered for his work as a philosopher and a sociologist. His *Mind in Evolution* ranked him with Russell and Alexander among the original thinkers of his generation, and his great volume of work on social theory as the most eminent of contemporary social philosophers. It was in the interval which lay between his ten years as an Oxford don and his great period of creative activity in London that he turned to the *Manchester Guardian* as giving him an opportunity of applying theory to the practice or criticism of public affairs. (Later the same motive led him to accept the political editorship of the ill-fated *Tribune*.) In the dying years of the last century a great part of Liberal thought was directed to the problems posed by the new fashion in Imperialism, particularly as they were illustrated in South Africa. Perhaps its finest summing-up was to be found in Hobhouse's *Democracy and Reaction*. The book was published in 1904, but the ideas that Hobhouse presented in its pages as a considered criticism had been defended in detail in articles he had written in the *Manchester Guardian* on social and industrial questions and on the South African issue. His gift of trenchant argument and his remarkable power of grasping and judging all the details of a complicated controversy were seen to great advantage in his handling of the South African war and the Chamberlain-Milner policy.

HERBERT SIDEBOTHAM

Two years before the comparatively mature Hobhouse joined the staff there arrived from Balliol a younger man of the same university who, under Scott's tutelage was to exercise as great an influence on the paper and on its staff as Montague. Unlike his seniors, Herbert Sidebotham was a Mancunian and an intensely loyal one. (Manchester in his case must be taken to embrace Salford, for it was in Salford that he had been bred and in Broughton that he continued to live.) The Manchester Grammar School had set him on the road to scholarship, and at Oxford he had been one of its noted successes. In later years when London knew him as a leading figure in Fleet Street, first on *The Times* and afterward as " Scrutator ", Sidebotham never forgot the Lancashire to which he belonged or the school or the editorial corridor in which the first twenty-three years of his journalistic life had been spent. His contribution to the paper was more than that of a writer, and there were few members of its staff from leader-writing colleagues to the junior members of the reporting staff who did not feel and profit from his influence. It was not a process into which self-consciousness entered, but " Sider " (as everyone from " C.P.S." downwards knew him) had a genius for fellowship and a broad humanity which drew the younger men to him as by an irresistible attraction.

In later years Sidebotham came to be known more than for anything else for his work as a military critic, which chimed in oddly enough with the passionate conviction with which he would devote himself to the cause of peace. Scholarship sat lightly on him, he had the imagination of the creative historian and would fit current events into a wide perspective. His first studies of the principles of war in the light of present application were made during the Boer War on which he made a daily commentary. Fourteen years later he was to take up a similar task in the World War when his " Student of War " articles attracted wide attention. (Foch put it on record that he found them the only thing of the kind in the Press worth reading.) It was in this capacity as a critic of military affairs that Sidebotham afterwards served *The Times*, but in the political writing on which he concentrated after the war he was, if anything, even more at home and not less effective. It was as a political writer that he had served and passed his apprenticeship in the early years of the century. He set little limit to his interests and he would write with equal force and penetration on a wide range of subjects in domestic or foreign policy. His emphasis on personality and individuality, his complete freedom from snobbery and humbug and his constant search for principles in the conduct of public affairs derived from a Radical ancestry. To study either his manner or his method was a journalistic education. His political journalism was rooted in the art of persuasion; himself always a " student " in his attitude to anything he was called upon to handle, he sought to convince only by informing and reasoning and, because he paid his readers the compliment of assuming that they were rational men who would desire to know and understand, the influence he exercised was wide and enduring.

1825
A MUSIC SHOP ADVERTISEMENT

4

THE *GUARDIAN* UNDER SCOTT

THE " LONDON END "

By Harry Boardman

IN the beginning, that is in the early sixties of last century and for some time afterwards, the " London End " was embodied in a single person. He was the provider of a London Letter, at first two or three times a week, and then, beginning in 1870, daily. To-day, eighty-six years later, the " London End " is not one individual but many. The single star has become the centre of a constellation. Or, lest it be thought there is a touch of conceit about the celestial simile, let us say he has become the leader of an orchestra. This evolution has been gradual. It represents a continuous response to the enlarging functions of the modern newspaper. Around the London Editor to-day revolve reporters and sub-editors; the Political Correspondent and the Parliamentary sketch writer; the Diplomatic Correspondent and the Labour Correspondent; the Financial Editor, the dramatic, art and film critics. And then, sitting more loosely to the office, are the outside contributors each at command on his special subject. The Political Correspondent and the Parliamentary sketch writer sprang into being, not only on the *Manchester Guardian* but on all the chief newspapers, towards the end of the last century. The Diplomatic and Labour Correspondents arrived on the heels of the 1914–18 war. After the first World War, foreign policy passed for ever out of the exclusive hands of the diplomats and became the concern of the ordinary citizen. That transformation, together with the birth of the League of Nations, called for expert interpretation of the day's foreign news as well as for more and more space for the foreign news itself. So emerged the Diplomatic Correspondent. At home, the great growth in the power and influence of the trade unions, much accentuated by the war, demanded a specialist's treatment of news in this field also. Since the 1914–18 war the London office has become the great relay post for the *Manchester Guardian's* correspondents abroad. All their messages, cabled or telephoned, pour in nightly to be transmitted over private wire and telephone to Manchester. Two of the world's notable newspapers take the *Manchester Guardian's* service, and are lodged with us—the *Baltimore Sun* and the *Winnipeg Free Press*. The *Baltimore Sun's* association with the *Manchester Guardian* began in 1923, and the *Winnipeg Free Press* in 1936. The South African Argus Company, the Associated Press of Australia, the *Amrita Bazar Patrika* (Calcutta) and others also take the service.

This, then, is where we have arrived after eighty-six years. And it all began in the early sixties with Tom Taylor, the playwright. He was the first London Editor. Not surprisingly the author of the *Ticket of Leave Man* chose to write chiefly about the London theatres and art. A Liberal member of Parliament, McCullagh Torrens, followed Taylor. He produced a London Letter three times a week. It was mainly political. Torrens felt he ought to be in Gladstone's Government. Gladstone thought less highly of Torrens than Torrens did of himself, and Torrens let some of his consequent displeasure with Gladstone escape into the Letter. He had to go. Tom Hughes, the author of *Tom Brown's School Days*, next had an innings, but he had too many other interests to remain long in Fleet Street. In 1870 an excellent professional journalist was given charge of the Letter—T. S. Townend. It was under Townend that it began to be a daily feature. Townend carried on for ten years and considerably helped the *Manchester Guardian* on its first stages towards becoming a modern newspaper. To Townend succeeded Sir Arthur Arnold. He was brother of " The Light of Asia " Arnold and M.P. for Salford. His connection with the paper lasted just a year. He gave place to A. J. Mundella (1893–1899), another distinguished Liberal politician. For a year—1900—H. W. Massingham devoted his fine pen to the work; and then came one who set a new stamp on the Letter and made it a model for most other Letters going out of London to papers in the country. This was J. B. Atkins. Like several other notable servants of the *Manchester Guardian*, J. B. Atkins began as its war correspondent, first in Cuba, then in the Graeco-Turkish war and finally in South Africa. Atkins' most marked influence on the Letter was to humanise it. He diluted its strong political bent and gave more space to the kaleidoscopic life of the capital. He found a place for the dustman's point of view as well as the Cabinet minister's. He also pointed the way to spare writing in a period when news-paper writing was apt to be lush. During Atkins' time the staff and contributors multiplied. He left the *Manchester Guardian* in 1905 and continued his distinguished journalistic career, first, in Paris and Madrid as correspondent of the *Standard*, as assistant editor and editor of the *Spectator*, and, later as editor of the Church *Guardian*. We still receive signs, in his retirement, of his interest in the London office.

G. W. E. Russell began his long association with the paper at this time. " It was a curious fate," wrote James Bone of Russell in 1921, the occasion of the *Manchester Guardian's* centenary, " that made G. W. E. Russell a Liberal and a writer in a Liberal paper. For over twenty years he presented his patrician world of the well-born and the powerful . . . He made the great world almost credible to democratic readers." That world and Russell have gone, but much of his writing survives to interest a still more democratic age in that widely-read volume, *Collections and Recollections*, which ran through several popular editions. Atkins was followed by R. H. Gretton, the historian and author, among other works, of that remarkable study, the *Records of Burford*. His London editorship (1905–12) spanned almost the whole of the Liberal renaissance. Under him the Letter caught the tone of the scholar, and yet it did not fail to be also lively and enterprising. For example, it was Gretton who arranged the first interview ever given to a newspaper by George Meredith. The interview quickly circled the world, for it was largely Meredith's political confession of faith.

In 1912 there stepped into the chair James Bone, who had served under both Atkins and Gretton. This was the beginning of the long and shining reign that only ended last Christmas— thirty-three years on. When James Bone retired at Christmas he received such homage as has rarely fallen to a journalist in his own life-time. It came not only from his colleagues on the *Manchester Guardian*, but from the brotherhood of Fleet Street, for " J.B." is much more than the sum of his qualities as a journalist, pre-eminent as those are: he is a rare spirit. Strength and sensibility do not often combine in such a degree as in him. The Letter was his first thought and his pride. Nothing but the best was good enough for it. He despised the trite and the derivative. A good illustration of it is the title of his enduring book, *The London Perambulator*. How gloriously far is that removed from the reach-me-down in titles! But the Letter could not exhaust his superabundant energy. The influence of his tirelessly observant mind, his strong feeling for beauty, his subtle sense of humour flowed into many other parts of the paper. His yearly " Londoner's Retrospect " was one of the joys of the New Year to the reader of the *Manchester Guardian*, while his commentaries on London's new buildings provided sharp evaluations of London's architectural acquisitions. These had gone on since 1903 and broke new ground in journalism. During " J. B.'s " thirty-odd years the Letter consciously followed the convention of a letter from a Londoner to his Manchester friends giving what he could gather of the inner side of affairs in politics and diplomacy; of the capital's social life and patterns; and of developments in the arts. Nor were the humours and curiosities of the great city to be overlooked. The Letter was also to find room for miniatures of public figures. That was the Letter as James Bone conceived it. It was that it became thirty years ago. It is the Letter we inherit from him to-day.

ART IN THE *GUARDIAN*

By James Bone

SUCCEEDING his cousin, John Edward Taylor, proprietor and editor, C. P. Scott began his editorship under the eye of a great art collector. Taylor's art collection with its richness in late Italian masters, medieval stained glass and Turner watercolours, when sold at Christie's, was one of the biggest art dispersals in Edwardian times. Scott himself rarely went to art exhibitions and knew few artists or collectors but he thought art important to the civilised life.

In the earlier years the urgent political issues of the times and his new problems of control occupied his mind, but in the 'eighties the *Manchester Guardian* began to give the same independent and distinguished attention to contemporary art as it was giving to the theatre and had always given to literature. Walter Armstrong, the vigorous and enlightened writer who became Director of the Dublin Art Gallery, was the London art critic from 1885 to 1887, and also contributed in later years. Claud Phillips, author of many notable art books, was the London art critic from 1889 to 1893, and the redoubtable D. S. MacColl contributed from 1894 to 1898, followed by R. A. M. Stevenson, whose book on Velasquez was one of the marking revaluations of the time. Laurence Housman, artist, playwright and poet, succeeded him and held the post till 1910, handling with force and wit the many art controversies of the period, including the Chantrey Bequest Inquiry (which MacColl evoked), the completion of Alfred Stevens' memorial to Wellington in St. Paul's (again MacColl), the Epstein statues on the British Medical Building in the Strand and a lively little engagement with Holman Hunt over Hunt's " Lady of Shalot " picture.

It was characteristic of Scott that he thoroughly backed the

Manchester Guardian critics even when, as in the Holman Hunt case, it must have gone against the grain for his own pictures were mainly pre-Raphaelite. When the attacks on Epstein were strongest, as against the Strand sculptures and the Hudson Memorial, Scott gave space and editorial support. He sat to Epstein for his own bust, and he helped, too, in getting his friend, Admiral Fisher, to be sculptured by him. Laurence Housman was succeeded by the present writer who, as a second string, had been writing in the paper for some time on architecture and the pictorial arts. It may be worth recalling that from 1902, with the exception of the war periods, the *Manchester Guardian* has attempted to give its readers in a yearly article a critical description of the notable buildings erected in London, while Professor Sir Charles Reilly has allowed few buildings of character to go up in the north without critical attention in the paper from his brilliant and learned pen.

A newspaper not published in the capital is more strenuously placed than its London contemporaries for it has to provide responsible critics of the theatre, music and art in its own city and also in London. Recognising the responsibility, the *Manchester Guardian* has always had in Manchester a strong home team—in the theatre its strongest team. The quality of its Manchester art criticism can only be gauged until forty years ago by reading its files as names and initials were not given till then, but in later years, O. M. Hueffer, E. G. Hawke, Laurence Scott, Bernard Taylor, F. W. Halliday and Lawrence Haward indicated its sterling character. Eric Newton, who had been Manchester art critic, took over the London art criticism in 1935, and his penetrating and entertaining writings continue to be a feature of the paper.

Besides the regular art critics, Scott from time to time commissioned authorities on special subjects to throw expert light on particular London exhibitions, usually those of the Burlington Fine Art Club, which so many foreign experts attended. One remembers Sir Frederick Cook, Sir Martin Conway, Sir Arthur Evans, William Burton, Lewis Day, and Sturge Moore among those high authorities. As a footnote to this a member of the

London staff recalls an odd experience he had when instructed to seek the assistance of (then) Mr. Frederick Cook for a highly specialised Giorgione show at the Burlington. He sought him at his great warehouse at St. Paul's Churchyard and after much inquiry he found himself at the end of a queue of young men apparently to be commended or reproved, awaiting admission to the presence. When the *Manchester Guardian* man's turn came the great warehouseman and art collector asked, "Name?" The Pressman, by that time rather daunted by events, gave his name, and Mr. Cook, consulting his book, said, " Not here—what's it about? " " Giorgione," faltered the Pressman. " What, what? " cried Mr. Cook. Then it was all explained and the article was duly written and delivered. Lewis Day was a pioneer in arts and crafts and in art in industry movements, and Sir Arthur Evans a high authority on Greek and Cretan sculpture, and William Burton on pottery. It would be hard to find in the world's Press a newspaper with more distinguished names among its art writers.

Into the art controversies of the time the *Manchester Guardian* threw its weight and wit. If it did not always " greet the unseen with a cheer " its record bears comparison with any contemporary. When the Rembrandt tercentenary exhibitions were being held in Holland, the Editor sent the art critic there and found space for a series of articles, and at the Rome International Exhibition the *Manchester Guardian* was one of the few European newspapers that gave its important art section many articles, one being the first evaluation in the British Press of Ivan Mestrovic's sculptures. Robert Dell (at one time editor of the learned *Burlington Art Magazine*) was for many years Paris Correspondent of the paper, and he contributed many brilliant and intimate articles on French art matters. When the prospect of a new art gallery for Manchester seemed as bright as it now seems faded, the *Manchester Guardian* art critic went round the more modern art galleries of Great Britain to give a critical description of them.

From 1901, when it issued a large illustrated Queen Victoria Memorial Number, the paper has been much concerned with illustrated journalism. In that number and in another ambitious effort, the Coronation Number of 1902, the artists included many of the leading draughtsmen of the time. But it was in the more intimate development of illustration that the paper took a distinctive line. Jack B. Yeats in 1906 visited Manchester and made a delightfully pungent series of drawings with notes of characteristic Manchester scenes, including a gem of the interior of the lamented Old Slip Inn at concert time, and he also illustrated Synge's Irish sketches in the paper. Many years afterwards Karel Capek's " Letters from England," with his own illustrations, appeared in the *Manchester Guardian*, followed by his articles and pictures on his visit to Spain. The great Spanish caricaturist, Bagaria, contributed cartoons, and his mural series of the world's heroes on the walls of *El Sol's* office in Madrid (now destroyed) also appeared in the paper.

Sir Max Beerbohm contributed from time to time many distinguished cartoons, including his series " John Bull's Second Childhood," and his not quite prophetic vision of the First Labour Foreign Minister, and a gallery of the Victorian great after they had been sheared of their whiskers and beards and locks. One experiment was Max's drawing of Lytton Strachey's long figure meandering down the centre of a page with type all round it, so that the reader would exclaim as he opened the paper, " Hello—here's Strachey! " Scott was keenly concerned in the appearance of the illustrations, and introduced " frames " of lines round the pictures and other methods to accentuate their importance. Before technical processes had reached their present excellence in all newspapers the *Manchester Guardian* reproductions had by various devices attained a reputation that brought experts from foreign countries as well as from our London contemporaries to Cross Street to study the methods there which was always open to responsible inspection even though that sometimes meant the loss of the paper's best technicians to these " visiting firemen ".

The number of eminent artists who have contributed of their best to the paper has been a particular pride to it. Sir Muirhead Bone's drawings of the Victory Procession of 1919, and his night

C. E. MONTAGUE, 1867–1928

L. T. HOBHOUSE, 1864–1929

picture of the crowd cheering George the Sixth at Buckingham Palace on Coronation night, and his Spanish series, Sir William Rothenstein's portraits of Rodin, Russell Wallace and other famous men and scenes, and portraits by Francis Dodd, Henry Lamb, Joseph Pennell, F. L. Emanuel and Hanslip Fletcher stand out. Miss Silvia Baker's Zoo studies and Horace Taylor's ingenious cartoons, also deserve honourable mention.

In most of those appointments and commissions instructions came from C. P. Scott, and even when aged he was quick to grasp and accept new points of view, even those which seemed furthest from the pre-Raphaelite conceptions with which he had originally decorated his own characteristic and attractive home, The Firs, at Fallowfield. But one thinks of him there in his brief leisure hours with his mind on his flowers rather than on his pictures. A memory of The Firs that comes back to me is of a birthday dinner with the guests, mainly his sons and his daughter and their families, seated at a long, narrow table like that in Millais's " Isabel and Lorenzo ". The windows to the gardens were slightly open, and a breeze flickered the two long rows of candles and daffodils that he himself had carefully chosen and set in their glasses. An Empire convex mirror on the wall behind gathered and reflected in little in the half light the lit table and the flowers and the animated company and the aged host himself, all at the moment strangely transient and affecting in the flicker of the candles.

BOOKS AND REVIEWERS

By A. S. Wallace

WHEN Scott came to editorship the best in English fiction
still found an outlet in the three-volume novel at 21s.,
and the new trends and discoveries in science, philosophy and
religion reached a limited public mainly through learned
reviews. When he laid down his pen the most brilliant work of
Wells, Bennett or Galsworthy could be had for 6s., and for 6d.
the man in the street could buy a paper-backed explanation
of Einstein's theory of relativity. The reading public had
increased by millions, the annual output of books swollen to
a flood. Between the wars some 7,000 volumes of all sorts
reached the *Guardian* office for review in the course of a normal
year. Scott's working lifetime saw a revolution in the attitude
of the Press to current literature, and in it the *Guardian* played
a distinctive part.

Book reviews were few and anonymous in the paper before
Scott's time, but in his early days in Manchester he took a hand
in what there were. We find him quoting with amused zest the
livelier passages of a new romance by Harrison Ainsworth, or
appraising the latest novel from the pen of " The Author of
John Halifax, Gentleman ". Later, in the 'eighties, his wife took
a share of novel reviewing and Scott began to look for able
outside contributors who could help to meet the growing need
for intelligent handling of books. His lifetime friend Sir A. W.
Ward was notable among these. Before the end of last century
the *Guardian* was steadily carrying its six columns of reviews
a week, and the course was set for the expansion the early years
of this century demanded.

As the tide of books mounted a system for dealing with them
had to be devised, and Scott entrusted the canalisation of the
flood to some member of his staff who, on a paper less jealous

of such titles, would have been called Literary Editor. As it was on the *Guardian*, someone habitually " took the books " in the course of his other duties. But Scott's active interest in the feature was never relaxed. The selection made and the reviewers chosen were referred to him each night. Nor was this an empty formality. Often he would enjoin for a book that specially interested him—usually politics or biography—a greater length of notice than had been suggested. Or he might debar on grounds of incorrigible prolixity or obscurity (seldom of heterodoxy) this or that unquestioned authority to whom a book on a special subject had been consigned.

His mind was predictable. His willingness to listen to reason unfailing. In literature, as in all the arts, he welcomed, even if he did not always approve, new ideas and experimental work, and he sought at once for someone who could explain its basis and intention to his readers.

A serious treatise on any topic from Astronomy to Zionism, a volume on the arts, an essay in English letters would go to the greatest available authority on the subject with the sole provisos —the first not always too strictly enforced—that he should write to the length ordered and that academic eminence should not excuse him for failing to make himself understood by the layman.

Allan Monkhouse who kept keen watch for Scott on the *Guardian's* book columns for over a quarter of a century, and who did so much to strengthen them, wrote zestfully of the contributors in the year of the paper's centenary:

> The reviewers are of many kinds and shades of opinion. There are even Tories, and if we have not a Turk there are certainly Jews, infidels, and heretics. But there are bishops, too, a fine array of professors and dons, poets, playwrights, novelists, artists, politicians, sociologists, historians, men of science and of commerce.

In dealing with fiction, as the output grew, *Guardian* policy held it more important that no first novel of promise should go unregarded than that the latest product of an established " best-seller " should have space. The search for fresh talent, when the spring and autumn tides flowed freely and might cast up three score novels a week, was exacting; but reward came when, as often, a chosen author made good and needed for his second novel a less anxious scrutiny.

Such was the system as it evolved, under Scott, in the hands of Monkhouse and his successors. The aim was to account intelligently for as wide a diversity of worth-while books as possible. The tendency, developed elsewhere in the Press, to entrust a " book of the week " to a single lively writer and give him all the available space for an essay built round it had no reflection in the *Guardian*. It seemed to Scott, and to all who " took the books " for him, to do scant justice to authors, publishers or readers. But for reflections on literary trends and the modes and inspirations of the time room was made in a regular " Books and Bookmen " feature to which Ernest Rhys, among others, contributed, but which, over many years, Allan Monkhouse especially made the medium for essays in which he surveyed the contemporary world of letters with gentle irony and broadly based discretion.

The main plan of book reviewing had of course to be altered and supplemented by occasional quick reviews, for day of publication, of books of outstanding importance or news interest. These adventures fell usually on an inside reviewer and demanded quick reading and writing. One recalls as particularly strenuous the task of accounting, with an eye on the clock, for Shaw's *Back to Methuselah* and Lytton Strachey's *Queen Victoria*. Sometimes, too, routine was varied by the enthusiasm of a reviewer, and who more likely to upset routine than Shaw? When the authentic *Life of Samuel Butler* was published the *Guardian*, recalling Shaw's confessed debt to Butler, asked him to notice it. Back came a characteristically gay note in the familiar green ink remarking that no editor of a daily paper could afford the space that he would need to do justice to Butler. It was equally characteristic of Scott to reply promptly that the space was his, and Butler was duly honoured with a review that took the major portion of a *Guardian* page, with an excellent portrait to embellish a brilliant article.

"Taking the books," was one of the most inspiriting jobs in a journalist's life on the *Guardian*. The sense of community with able minds that came from daily contact with so strong a team of reviewers gave constant interest to the task. Monkhouse put it well: "We owe much to our reviewers," he wrote, "and they owe something to us. We have given chances to fine minds . . ." May it not be long before such contacts can be fully renewed.

1825
AN ENTERTAINMENT ADVERTISEMENT

THE *GUARDIAN* AND THE
NEW DRAMA

By A. S. Wallace

WHEN Scott took charge of the *Manchester Guardian* in 1871, the first faint stirrings were already felt throughout Europe of the renaissance of drama that was to mark the end of the 19th century. Ibsen had written *Brand* and *Peer Gynt,* though he was scarcely known outside Norway. In France, Zola was busy on plays that dealt realistically with the fast-changing world. The vision of man as the sport of inexorable fate that had inspired the greatest playwrights through the ages was giving place to a conception of humanity's struggle for freedom from outworn customs, unjust laws and economic barriers.

In Britain the new drama gained ground slowly. Matthew Arnold could write in 1879: " In England we have no modern drama at all. Our vast society is not homogeneous enough, not sufficiently united, even any large portion of it, in a common view of life, a common ideal serving as a basis for a modern English drama." But in the 1880's the supply of artificial French plays on which the English stage had largely relied began to fail. In 1887 the Théâtre Libre was founded and the French playwrights got to grips with the realities of the age. In England, at the same time, Pinero and Henry Arthur Jones came to the rescue of the theatre. In 1889 Ibsen's *A Doll's House* was produced in London, and two years later the Independent Theatre was founded with Shaw as one of its first playwrights.

Scott from the first was fully alive to the theatre's importance. His paper had from its earliest days given generous space to drama. The succession of famous actor-managers from Kean and Macready onwards who visited the old Theatre Royal in Manchester, had been fully, sometimes trenchantly, dealt with. But Scott was not satisfied. In a letter to his sister in 1871 he mentioned his half-formed thought of becoming dramatic critic. Had he found time for such an extension of his work he would have found himself dealing with drama that increasingly treated the social problems nearest to his heart.

He contented himself with entrusting dramatic criticism to the ablest team he could muster. In Manchester, Sir Adolphus Ward, then a Professor at Owens College, was the first of his appointments, but Ward was soon followed by W. T. Arnold, Oliver Elton, C. E. Montague and Allan Monkhouse. In London, as the new movement gathered strength, it was appraised by, among others, William Archer, who had done so much to pioneer it, and Philip Carr, who later was to keep the *Guardian's* readers in touch with the contemporary French stage.

Manchester, under this cultivation, soon became a city where the intelligent author and actor were assured of informed appreciation. In the last decades of the century the chief fare was still largely Shakespeare and the classics, but soon Montague was writing zestfully of Coquelin in Rostand's *Cyrano*, Elton soberly analysing Ibsen amid the " howling of the dervishes " who found that master's work intolerable, and Arnold remarking of Pinero's *The Second Mrs. Tanqueray* that " at last a living Englishman has written a play of which it is possible to be proud ".

Scott's promotion of dramatic criticism to a foremost place among the paper's features greatly helped to prepare Manchester for becoming, as she soon did, the foremost city in England outside London for the presentation of the new drama. Miss Horniman acquired the Gaiety Theatre in 1908. She had already established the Irish National Players in their home in the Abbey Theatre, Dublin. When they visited London with plays by Yeats and Synge, the comment of the *Guardian* was that " these Irish actors have contrived to reach back past most of the futilities that have grown upon the ordinary theatre of commerce and get a fresh, clean hold on their craft in its elements."

In Manchester Miss Horniman collected a company that did justice with a similar sincerity to the stream of exciting new plays that marked the early years of this century, and in Liverpool, Birmingham and Glasgow, the Gaiety's success proved the inspiration of resident companies who brought distinction to their cities by their presentation of the work of Barrie, Shaw, Galsworthy, Masefield, Bennett, Granville Barker, St. John Hankin and others. The time had come again when an English author with something worth-while to say could turn to the theatre as his medium. In the famous Vedrenne-Barker tenure of the Court Theatre in London, and in the chief cities throughout the country, with Manchester leading them, he could be sure of thoughtful criticism and of audiences attuned to playgoing in which every week offered fresh intellectual adventure.

Scott, with Montague's guidance, strengthened his team to meet the welcome flood of new authorship and memorable first nights. James Agate, Stanley Houghton, Harold Brighouse, with Monkhouse and Montague himself were among those who made the Manchester school of criticism as notable as its stage. Some of the critics were to be memorable contributors to what came to be called the "repertory movement"—though Miss Horniman disliked that misuse of the word. Houghton's *Hindle Wakes*, Brighouse's *Hobson's Choice*, and *The Conquering Hero* and *Mary Broome* by Monkhouse were among the unconventional but successful plays that Miss Horniman's reign at the Gaiety provoked from Lancashire authors.

The movement that the *Guardian* did so much to aid in its beginnings seemed likely to revolutionise British play-going. Enforced contentment with the often shoddy fare offered by the touring "West-end success" was at an end, and large areas throughout the country were given direct contact with the newest and ablest dramatic work of the time. Actors and audiences alike benefited by the stimulus. Many of the Gaiety company's members who later became more widely famous, like Sybil Thorndike, Lewis Casson, Irene Rooke and Milton

Rosmer, have recalled how rare and helpful in their art was the combination then available of worth-while drama, informed criticism and intelligent audience.

Like much else, the repertory movement was hard hit by the first World War. The Gaiety went down, and with it Alfred Wareing's Glasgow Repertory. Sir Barry Jackson at Birmingham, and William Armstrong with the Liverpool Playhouse, survived to carry the torch. But with Montague home from the front and again in charge of drama, the *Guardian* still found much in the theatre to discover and praise. " C.E.M.'s " enthusiasm was infectious to all who worked with him. They learned to set more store by an adventurous and sincere production in one of the little theatres that even the all-conquering cinema could not kill than by the visits of famous actor-managers in the well-tried cloak-and-sword dramas of tradition. If there was no Gaiety, the more reason to seek the survival of its spirit wherever it might be found.

Now the quest might lead one to the first performance of Shakespeare in modern dress—*Cymbeline*— at the Birmingham Repertory, now to Drinkwater's *Abraham Lincoln* or the first night of a new St. John Ervine, or Brighouse, at Liverpool, with the obligation to get thoughts on to paper in a last train that bounced embarrassingly eastward over the springy bed of Chat Moss. Perhaps the Stockport Garrick would daringly attempt Stephen Phillips's *Paolo and Francesca*, or the Unnamed Society of Manchester, tackling its own costumes, scenery and lighting, put on an uncommon play by one of its own members or a gem from world drama that mere box-office vision would never have chanced upon. The files of the paper in the 1920's abound in discovery of new ideas, new treatment, and sincere and often able work by the progressive amateurs and semi-amateur theatres of the north-west.

The great outburst of English playwriting that had marked the beginning of the century had lost its force. The period was not wholly barren. Shaw, for instance, with his *St. Joan* in 1924, became at last a popular dramatist. But it was in Central Europe, in Russia, in Germany, and in Italy, that new conceptions of drama's purpose were to be found. It fell to Ivor Brown, whose appointment to the " London end " as dramatic critic had greatly strengthened the paper's staff, to explain the inter-war modes of the Continental stage as he experienced them on his travels. From his lucid and forceful articles *Guardian* readers learned of the progress of Stanislavsky's Moscow Art Theatre and its revolutionary rivals, of Georg Kaiser, the Capek brothers and the " expressionist school " who, abandoning as their protagonist Ibsen's " alone upstanding man " conceived the individual as a cypher among a mass, or in more fanciful moments, as an insect or a robot. To him also it fell to make clear the meaning and value of those dramatic inquiries into the nature of reality that distinguished Pirandello's work, to relate all this experiment to the main course of drama's history, and to estimate (with a healthy scepticism) its chances of permanence. The Continental work found little echo in the English drama or the English theatre, though Mr. Priestley would probably not deny some debt to Pirandello for those experiments with time which he has conducted so engagingly, and in America Eugene O'Neill and Elmer Rice were conceiving in terms that owed much to the Continental modes.

In Manchester a theatre determined to take account of the new press of ideas came to birth in a suburb. In the 1920's and for some years after a journey to Rusholme gave the Manchester playgoer contact with the contemporary drama of the world, competently performed. A glance at the *Guardian's* files in a year when that theatre was doing its best work shows that Montague's enthusiastic team of writers could measure their love of theatre against work that ranged from the sentimentalism of Barrie to the stark misery of Strindberg, from the mass attack of Elmer Rice to the exuberant individualism of Sean O'Casey. I recall in particular a winter season that yielded in quick succession Susan Glaspell's delicate and haunting play *Alison's House*, Eugene O'Neill's psychological fantasy *The Great God Brown*, Elmer Rice's expressionist adventure *The Adding Machine*, Shaw's *Major Barbara*, and much else that showed the modern theatre in its wide variety of moods.

When Montague retired in 1925, and when Edward Scott, four years later, succeeded his father as editor, it seemed as though the courageous work of this outlying theatre might well be merely marking time for the founding of a centrally sited civic theatre that would put Manchester firmly back again in the place the *Guardian* had so notably helped to make for her as a principal home for the drama of ideas. The second World War deferred that hope, but in a city with Manchester's traditions it can never be abandoned.

MUSICAL CRITICISM

By Granville Hill

During the earliest years of the nineteenth century British music sank to such a low level that no newspaper writer of any importance could have been expected to take more than a passing glance at the subject. Yet the public was keenly interested in concerts as well as in performances of native ballad opera—that legacy from the previous century—and in a few towns fairly big choral societies and small instrumental ones were already established, queerly but firmly. Journalists, however, seldom mentioned these institutions. The *Manchester Guardian* in its first year contains few references to musical events of any kind. Even when on October 20th, 1821, the celebrated soprano Catherine Stephens sang in Manchester in Bickerstaff's opera *Love in a Wood*, no notice followed in the paper. (That singer was the Miss Stephens to whose powers Hazlitt in one of his essays paid a glowing tribute after hearing her in Bickerstaff's work.) There are some half-dozen lines of warm praise for Franz Liszt when as a child he visited Manchester in 1824. His wonderful gift for improvisation is specially noted. But Master Liszt, when thirteen years old, was probably considered to be stricken in years when compared with the concert promoter's other prodigy—the "Infant Lyra", a girl harpist aged three years and nine months. In those days the demand for musical prodigies was strong and steady. Sixteen years later Liszt again visited Manchester—this time in his full brilliancy as the most famous pianist in Europe—yet his two recitals, though mentioned by the paper as being by far the most important occurrences in the city's musical history, drew only a short paragraph—a highly eulogistic one, of course—the reason for such brevity being the rather strange one that " we have neither time nor space for more than a few words about this distinguished event."

It was the music of the Manchester Festivals of 1828 and 1836 that stirred the paper to its first lengthy and detailed criticism of concert performances. The writers were obviously amateurs and perhaps had no deep knowledge of musical technique, but on the whole they showed fine taste and often a judgment that for its time was surprisingly advanced and independent. Great singers who had probably considered themselves as lifted high above all criticism were reminded that they were not always free from serious faults. The splendid singing of Braham when at his best is praised enthusiastically, but he was sometimes far from his best and the critic has a roguish little way of ending an adverse account with a dubious compliment that probes the wound. Referring to Braham's treatment of the tenor solos in the festival performance of Handel's *Messiah* the writer says:

> In " The voice of him that cried " he again gave himself up to his besetting sin; he bawled in a most ruthless manner, and his voice when at its full stretch was miserably out of tune. " Ev'ry Valley " was not sung very well in tune any more than the recitative itself—but with all its defects was a great treat to the lovers of Handel.

The same writer has the courage to protest against the absurd forms of cadenza that were still favoured by singers:

> In both his cadences in the air " Waft her Angels " Braham introduced passages so inappropriate and so trashy in themselves as to revolt the feelings. . . . The shade of Handel forbid that we should ever be so horrified again!

There is surely a touch of sarcasm in the remark about the orchestra's playing of a Beethoven symphony:

> In the first chords there was a little wavering; a circumstance not to be wondered at when it is considered that the symphony had never been rehearsed.

But this critic found most of the playing during the festivals extremely fine both in execution and expression. Here and there his eulogies include words which, employed in their strict and original sense, now look rather quaint—as when he says:

> Mme. Catalani sang Luther's Hymn, and Mr. Harper's trumpet obbligato lent additional grandeur, which nothing could well exceed. The effect was overpowering; it was awful.

It is evident that the two festivals had widened the Manchester public's musical horizon and that the city, though still cut off from the main stream of European music, was ready for a more adventurous artistic policy than had hitherto prevailed. Progressive influences triumphed when in 1847 Mendelssohn was invited there to conduct his oratorio " Elijah ", the new work which had been produced the previous year at the Birmingham Festival. Judging from the *Guardian's* notice the Manchester performance was in the main successful, though the writer is careful to point out that the composer's method of marking the expression rather than the tempo " must be slightly embarrassing to an orchestra at first ". One or two slips resulted from occasional misunderstanding of this novel method. The art of conducting as distinct from mere " time beating " was then in its infancy.

The year after Mendelssohn's visit Chopin came to play in a Manchester concert. The famous Polish musician was weakened by illness—death was not far away—yet in a discriminating notice the *Guardian* critic wrote of the extraordinary subtleties of tone and feeling which probably set Chopin's playing of romantic music still far above that of all other pianists then known.

As time went on music-making grew to be a stronger and more consistent feature of Manchester's activities. Charles Hallé and his orchestra settled there in 1858, the city becoming one of the most prominent musical centres in England. From the fifties to the eighties of last century criticism in the *Manchester Guardian* was very modest in expression but thoughtful and assured, and while rejoicing over many recent improvements in musical performance the writers occasionally showed that they were by no means complacent about the general feebleness of our native art of composition. There was, however, one British composer who came in for high praise, and the critic, writing on a Hallé concert in 1886, admitted that he preferred Sterndale Bennett's *Water Nymphs* Overture to Wagner's *Meistersinger* Overture. Evidently the approach to Wagner's later works was still found difficult. In the eighties and a little while afterwards George Fremantle, a well-known business man and a cultured musical amateur, was writing the *Guardian's* music notices. His style was vigorous and he was able to draw on an unusually large experience of musical conditions in this country and abroad. He was among the first people to recognise that Parry and Stanford were bringing back to British musical composition the vital qualities which had surrendered to Handel and later to Mendelssohn. The only pity was that Fremantle inherited a rather deep-rooted prejudice against one or two of the more modern composers who were also bringing to the concert world a much needed freshness of outlook. He rarely had a good word for Liszt. He apparently refused to admit that even if Liszt's music itself could not be acquitted of certain banalities its vividness and its imaginative power would have a beneficial influence on our native styles of composition and performance.

It was Arthur Johnstone, Fremantle's successor on the paper, who led the way to a more generous view of music's new aspects. Johnstone was a professional writer on music and soon after his coming in 1896 to Manchester, it became clear that a very searching kind of criticism, æsthetic and technical, was being applied to the city's concerts. Johnstone's knowledge was comprehensive, and his ability in analysing orchestral scores and in drawing attention to their finest features was shown in his reviews of new works. He prepared the way in Manchester for Elgar and Richard Strauss. He was, too, an early advocate of the few eminent conductors who specialised in their art as against the musicians who merely included conducting among their other duties; thus his firm support of Hans Richter, whose appointment as director of the Hallé Orchestra was not unopposed. The force of Johnstone's writing gained him wide influence; yet, after his death in 1905, the Manchester public might have settled again into a comfortable tolerance of dowdiness in its music-making had not that brilliant disturber of the peace, Ernest Newman, arrived and preached rebellion against acceptance of any but the highest and most vital artistic principles. Newman was already in the front rank of living writers on music. His profundity of thought was as remarkable as his wit and the vivacity of his literary style. In his contributions to the *Manchester Guardian* he upheld certain standards of performance so uncompromisingly and wrote so frankly about people who failed to reach those standards that his notices sometimes caused strong resentment among concert-givers. Yet though Newman often hit hard he praised with the utmost fullness and generosity that which was fine in achieve-ment or even in attempt, and the city's music profited in no small degree from his short stay before he left in 1906 to take up appointments in Birmingham.

The post vacated was filled by Samuel Langford, a Manchester man. It can truly be said that if ever a critic won not only respect but affection Langford did so. His literary and musical culture was acquired in a haphazard way, but it went deep and ranged far. Easy-going, not to say careless, though he appeared to be in his daily life, he had a capacity for hard and continuous mental work which amazed the people who did not know him well. And nobody who did not know him well could guess at the liveliness of his conversation, for though his writing reflected the mellow wisdom and the broad humanity of his nature, it disclosed little of his humour or of the epigrammatic wit that often sparkled in his talk. His writing showed how eagerly and with what depth of insight his mind ranged over a vast field of musical art and how cleverly he related music to his general philosophy of life. It was richly rewarding to read Langford, for he seldom failed to quicken the imagination by the ever-widening visions of beauty that music opened to him. His criticism of performances was penetrating, but even when he was displeased the wording of his notices was not ungentle. He died in 1927, and Neville Cardus became the music critic of the *Guardian*.

HERBERT SIDEBOTHAM, 1872–1940

E. T. SCOTT, 1883–1932

Editor of the " Manchester Guardian " 1929–32
From the drawing by Francis Dodd, R.A.

Perhaps no other expert on musical subjects has written with such beauty of literary expression as Cardus has. He held that criticism of music should afford the reader as much æsthetic pleasure and as much intellectual interest as we find in the best literature on the other arts, and he proved that the high level of attainment implied was reached in his own writing. His diction and imagery were superb and always appropriate to the matter in hand. He was not one of those writers who, as Coleridge said of a brother poet, " spread out domes of thought over insufficient supports of fact." Cardus got his facts and made sure of his foundations. In his articles for the paper he revealed the individuality of mind that made his judgment authoritative, though it might be entirely opposed to the views commonly held by other critics and by performers. He was suspicious, for instance, of the almost unanimous and surprisingly sudden " movement " away from Richard Strauss and of an equally sudden " movement " towards Sibelius. Whether they agreed or disagreed with his opinions we imagine that few readers could resist the fascination of Cardus's unique literary craft or could object if at times the literary mind seemed to sway unduly the purely musical thinking.

Several other famous writers on music have added lustre to the columns of the *Manchester Guardian*. Ferrucio Bonavia, formerly in Manchester, and Cecil Gray, Eric Blom and Dr. McNaught, successively the paper's musical correspondents in London, have given further evidence of the splendid scholarship and the masterly gifts for criticism that had long ago placed these writers among the high priests of their art.

SPECIAL CORRESPONDENCE

By A. P. Wadsworth

THOUGH Scott expressed himself mainly through the leader columns, the paper's influence was exerted hardly less through its special correspondence, home and foreign. No part of the *Guardian* gave it greater distinction. The secret of it was the freedom given to the writer. To send a man out to a foreign country, to Ireland, or to the British coalfields with a free hand to describe what he saw and leisure to write carefully and well might sometimes produce slightly academic results, but it was a policy that gave a man great encouragement to do his best. Scott was rarely disappointed in his choice of men. Thos. Vaughan Nash was sent to India in 1900 and J. T. Gwynn a quarter of a century later; L. S. Amery covered the Balkans in the 'nineties; Spenser Wilkinson, C. E. Montague, J. M. Synge, and later G. E. Leach and Ivor Brown, described Irish conditions; G. Lowes Dickinson wrote on his Far Eastern tour; T. M. Young investigated the American cotton industry; Arthur Ransome and Morgan Philips Price followed the Bolshevik Revolution. The list is endless and the books made out of those commissions fill a large shelf. Scott was always ready (often to the sub-editors' distress) to throw open his columns to a series of serious informative articles, applying only the test that they should be well written and liberal and should add to knowledge. The *Guardian's* ordinary news service might be no better than that of most papers; its special service of what is now called " background " news had qualities quite its own. In the same way Scott chose his war correspondents and correspondents for great occasions. One has only to mention, for instance, J. B. Atkins and H. N. Brailsford in the wars of the 'nineties; H. W. Nevinson in many fields, warlike and pacific; and J. L. Hammond at the Paris Peace Conference.

The regular foreign correspondents of the paper—men like

J. G. Hamilton and Robert Dell (and later Alexander Werth) in Paris; Cecil Sprigge in Rome; F. A. Voigt in Berlin—and the humblest reporters on home jobs had the same freedom. Scott never attempted to dictate what they should say, to provide them with "angles" or fetter and bewilder them with instructions. An intemperate word here and there might be softened, a verbosity pruned, but their messages usually appeared intact. No journalist can ask fairer than that. The *Guardian* correspondent or reporter was often envied by his colleagues in the field, because he at least was pretty certain of seeing his stuff in print without distortion or manipulation or heavy cutting. There was no suppression, however disturbing the facts. No daily paper, perhaps, ever gave greater freedom to the individual play of the minds of its staff or permitted them more idiosyncrasy in the handling of their material; it is a precious tradition which the *Guardian* has always valued. It implied trust in a man to do his work honestly. It compensated—if these things matter—for the preservation of anonymity; it led to equality because there were no "by-lines" for the "stars"; it strengthened the corporate spirit of the team. By some modern standards of sub-editing (with its "re-write" men) the technique might seem old-fashioned. It is almost a journalistic axiom, the cynical might say, that the bright newseditor or sub-editor in his chair knows better what happened and how it should be described than the reporter on the job; but it had not reached the *Guardian* in Scott's day, nor has it since. The *Guardian* under Scott was therefore fortunate in its reporters; to mention E. W. Record, Francis Perrot, William Haslam Mills, George E. Leach, Harry Boardman, Howard Spring, A. V. Cookman, is to leave out as many again who were trained in Scott's school.

PICTURES AND FEATURES

By M. A. Linford and M. Crozier

Forty years ago there were virtually no illustrations in serious newspapers. Photographs were regarded as frivolous—a moral attitude usefully bolstered by the rawness of the new process of half-tone reproduction—and the few pictures admitted to mark special occasions were line drawings composed in dignity and leisure. The supplement published by the *Manchester Guardian* on the death of Queen Victoria in 1901 contained thirty drawings, most of them large. Four years later a half-tone block appeared at rare intervals, but for the obituary supplement of Edward VII in 1910 it was evidently felt that the camera was not quite good enough, and again drawings provided the only illustrations. In the body of the paper containing the supplement are photographs of the new King and Queen, stretching across five columns' width and handsomely printed. From that time onwards half-tone pictures were used nearly every day, though the work of such artists Hedley Fitton, Henry Lamb, F. L. Emanuel, J. B. Yeats and William Rothenstein were still the chief pride of the paper. In recent years Sir Muirhead Bone's beautiful drawings have carried on this tradition.

By the beginning of the Great War the paper had its own staff photographer and the recently-formed agencies maintained a flow of pictures from places touched by the news. On August 3rd, 1914, the principal illustration showed Manchester, undisturbed by the international outlook, thronging the Blackpool platform at Victoria Station. The next day brought a more awakened crowd in Whitehall, and Keir Hardie addressing a peace meeting in Trafalgar Square. By the end of the month there was a group of pictures taken on a cross-Channel boat, with the wounded from Mons being succoured by women wearing ankle-length skirts and, surprisingly, solar topees.

During those early years of the half-tone process, size was apparently more or less synonymous with quality. The files of the paper between the accession of King George V and the clamping-down on space in 1916, show almost every illustration cast in a heroic mould—a gallery of Titans. Photographs may have been admitted unwillingly and with doubts as to their seemliness in responsible journalism, but at least they were boldly displayed when they got there.

In the last few years of his life, C. P. Scott's interest in pictures was sharpened by the fear that they might trip up the dignity of the paper. Their news value did not, in his mind, justify any deviation from traditional rules of taste and decorum. He liked country scenes, well-ordered processions or parades and, curiously, racing. A photograph of the Derby was submitted to him with the suggestion that perhaps he might not want it published. "Of course I want it," he said, "it's not the racing I dislike; it's the betting." Pictures of disasters never pleased him and for a long time he refused to sanction any illustration of railway accidents. Later he yielded, but he preferred the photographs to be so "cut" that very little wreckage and no victims were left in sight. A few years before his death all hunting scenes were banned, in sympathy with the paper's opposition to blood sports. In profound contrast with modern popular journalism, Scott expected a high standard of worth and achievement from those whose personal portraits were admitted. A man might be both dead and famous, but unless his fame was unspotted by sensationalism his obituary notice did not include a photograph. To "get into the news" was a long way from getting into the *Manchester Guardian* illustrations. Over a photograph of the infant Princess Elizabeth being driven in a car with her nurse, he pondered for some time. The Princess was certainly admissible, but he knew nothing about the nurse, and it seemed too much prominence for a woman who had made no mark on his consciousness. A few hastily remembered facts about the nurse's long service with the Bowes-Lyon family were laid before him, together with the impossibility of blotting her out of the picture and leaving her charge unblemished, and he finally agreed that a modestly-sized reproduction should be given. Among his pictorial interests were cricket, golf, lawn tennis and University athletics, but football matches he thought looked ugly.

Under the editorship of W. P. Crozier the illustrations side was widely expanded. Crozier had his own prejudices—including a fondness for architecture and archaeology and a dislike of performing animals in circuses—but apart from these he liked to have as many pictures as space would allow. He regarded them as embellishments to news pages and broadened their scope to cover nearly every part of the paper. Only the Leader Page was left without its illustration, for pictures of unusual importance occasionally appeared on the page opposite —an innovation rather painfully revolutionary to diehards both within the office and outside it—and single-column portraits were used to brighten the uncompromising stretches of company meeting reports.

A great part of the modern newspaper consists of "features" —miscellaneous reading, grave and gay. It has always been so, though a century ago the scissors and paste were most in evidence and newspapers unashamedly borrowed from each other (and from the reviews and magazines). The *Guardian* of Scott's early years had not developed many regular " features ", but they began to appear in the 'eighties. James Long's " Farm Notes " ran for many years. " Cycling Notes " came with the craze in the 'nineties and reached as much as two and a half columns, to be followed later by a column on " Automobiles ". But where the *Guardian* showed most growth was in literary "features" which came in a flood with the turn of the century. The " backpager " —in the first column of the back page—began irregularly as a general article, an art notice, or a long review; it was slow to evolve into its present form of a sketch or short story. It attracted many well-known literary names; Synge and Mr. Dooley belong to the early years. " Miscellany " came unheralded on October 16, 1903. (Its first title was "A Miscellany", but Scott struck out the article.) It began as a pretty solid, informative column without a touch of the personality that later editors, like "Lucio" (Gordon Phillips), have given it. John Masefield had a hand in its early stages. "A Country Diary" began in the spring of 1904; T. A. Coward and Mrs. H. M. Swanwick were among its earlier pillars. The Churches, Established and Free, have long had their weekly column. For the first "Quartus" Canon Hicks (later Bishop of Lincoln) was succeeded by Canon Peter Green in 1912; for Nonconformity Dr. George Jackson wrote for many years until his recent death. The most famous of all the regular contributors was perhaps George W. E. Russell with his Saturday article; between 1898 and 1910 nine books by "The Author of 'Collections and Recollections'" were made up wholly or in part from these essays. Arthur Ransome, Arthur Ponsonby and Ivor Brown were among his successors.

Before Scott died the *Guardian* had added in 1929 a daily crossword puzzle and a weekly competition, and other "features" were soon to come.

THE SPORTS PAGE

By H. D. Nichols

THE history of the sports side of the paper scarcely begins in its first fifty years; it is a story of modern developments, many of them dating from no earlier than the end of the Kaiser's war, and few of them from earlier than the 'nineties of the last century. This was not in any way peculiar to the *Manchester Guardian*, for the idea of the news interest of organised games is surprisingly modern. When C. P. Scott came to Manchester the idea that a daily paper should make a regular feature of reports even of cricket and football was unknown. Racing, and particularly the news of the racing " market ", had secured a firm foothold—which it was afterwards to lose—but in no other sense was sporting journalism recognised.

Cricket had broken into the news just before the middle of the century when the famous All-England touring eleven was popularising the game in Lancashire and Yorkshire as well as elsewhere. Its matches against enlarged local teams were well reported, and they left behind them a new interest in cricket news. But the systematic reporting of the game was still well in the future. In the 'seventies cricket would be represented by an occasional paragraph and the score sheet of a representative match—say North *v*. South, with the usual big score by " W.G." (who must have been hard to keep out of the news), and by two or three inches, on a Monday, of local club games. By the early 'eighties the more important county matches had staked a claim on space and were getting score sheets with a summary paragraph; and by now the clubs around Manchester were getting two or three columns of detailed scores—a feature which had come to stay and was steadily improved. Before the end of the century the Lancashire matches were commanding full-column treatment and there was already evidence that a new editorial interest was being taken in the treatment of at least one branch of sport. It was being recognised that the literary standards of the rest of the paper were not out of place in the sports columns. By the turn of the century Monday's paper was producing an organised Sports Page, starting with a long comprehensive article, " The Cricket Field "—or, in winter, " The Football Field ". The steady improvement kept up for the next fourteen years must have meant an uphill battle in the office, for the organisation of the handling of sport lagged sadly behind the needs. It was to be almost a generation before a Sports Editor was recognised, and for years the one solitary sports " sub " was only loosely detached from the general work of the sub-editors' room. The presentable cricket page for which the paper was noted in the years before the first world war was largely the creation of F. E. Hamer, who graduated to the sports room in this way. In the years between the wars, when the sports department was put on an altogether new footing, first under A. L. Lee and then with the addition of E. A. Montague as the first sports editor, the first-class cricket reports were to become its special pride. For with the revival of the game in 1919 a young reporter whose role on the paper was undetermined and his future unsuspected, was rather casually sent to cover a county match. Within a week Neville Cardus had found his place on the paper, and before the next season was out its " Cricketer " had won appreciation throughout the cricket world.

It seems to be in the tradition of most newspaper offices that when football began to get into print no one should have been responsible for ordering it. It came in well ahead of any plans for its reception, and in the *Guardian* as elsewhere it probably got most of its " subbing " in the composing room. By 1880 something like two columns of local reports were getting into the Monday paper, mostly of rugby matches with a few paragraphs of " soccer " and already an occasional reference to Lacrosse. In another ten years football must have been putting great pressure on its unspecialised sub-editors, but though there were now football notes as well as the reports the page was little organised and it must have taken a keen reader to find his way through the jumble. There was a gradual improvement in make-up towards the end of the century. A " Football Field " special and notes on the chief local matches were now clearly being done from the office, but probably as a week-end sideline by members of the staff who were better regarded for their more solid activities during the rest of the week.

The methodical development of the sports pages from 1919 onwards owed everything to the news-editorship of W. P. Crozier. Though C. P. Scott had been a fine oar at Oxford and played tennis till well past 70, he had taken little interest in sport as news. Crozier added to his own interest in sport (particularly both forms of football) a complete understanding of its news interest to the majority of readers. It was his influence that began to give the sports page new system and coherence. The effect of Cardus's articles came as a powerful reinforcement to the suggestion that more use might be made of special correspondents both on the staff and from outside it. This gradually affected the treatment of all forms of sport, and almost for the first time football began to be treated as a subject which might be written of with something more than mere technical competence. The sports special began to take the place of the casual contribution, and an interest in the popularities of League football and of the professional rugby game found a new place in columns hitherto dominated by amateur " rugger ".

The new policy had been anticipated, twenty years before its time, in the case of golf. The paper had always been strong on golf from the time when the game first began to be reported. It had perhaps a special appeal to the suburban circulation. Even in the 'nineties, when Vardon, Braid and Taylor dominated the game, with two or three amateurs of almost equal fame, space was found for full-column reports of the championships. Early in the new century A. N. Monkhouse, who was to be better known later for his share in the paper's literary and dramatic criticism, began to write regular golf notes with a special appeal to the northern amateur, and they remained a leading sports feature until the first world war. About the same time more attention was being paid to such local tournaments as the Balfour and Houldsworth cup competitions. From 1919, with the general development of the idea of special correspondence on national sporting events, all the championships were specially covered. A. L. Lee, under whom the sports sub-editing had at last become fully specialised, was an all-round athlete as well as an experienced reporter, and his sound knowledge of golf found scope in a long series of such special reports.

Lawn tennis from quite early days was covered by men well-known in the game, including Liddell Hart (better known as a military writer) and Wallis Myers, and from after the first war it had its regular specialist allotted, the tennis reports becoming a more regular and permanent feature of the paper. With C. P. Scott's arrival the paper had begun to take a new interest in rowing, particularly University rowing, which was usually entrusted to an old Oxford Blue. Athletics were slower than most sports to get into the news columns, but a slow start was more than compensated for in the 'twenties when first F. A. M. Webster and then E. A. Montague became responsible for them. An earlier specialism of the *Guardian's*, arising from the peculiar local popularity of the game, had been Lacrosse, on which Norman Melland, one of the game's greatest players, used to write.

Most of the new departures of the 'twenties were piecemeal and the full organisation of the sports page, under a sports editor with an assistant, was still to come. The fruits of attention to good make-up and adequate planning ahead were to be seen in the sports pages of the last few years before the second world war. It was again the result of the continuing influence of W. P. Crozier, whose plans for the department were realised when E. T. Scott appointed E. A. Montague to take charge of it. The immediate changes were not a matter of innovation so much as organisation, the filling up of gaps and the systematisation of make-up. New specialist correspondents were added to the roll and many gaps were filled, new attention being paid to professional rugby, to local hockey and probably in all to a greater variety of sports than were then being covered by any other but the purely sporting papers. And all with the proviso that, whatever was written about, there should be as much attention paid to

the writing as on any other side of the paper. A post-war generation may look back enviously on the generous allotment of space
then given to sport but will recognise the artistry which went to
its arrangement. The contrast with earlier years was all in favour
of the reader whatever his limited sporting interests might be.
The sports pages of the *Guardian* in the 'thirties are likely to
remain a model to which many references will be made when
the reporting of sport is again able to command such advantages.

1825
ADVERTISING THE " THEATRE OF ARTS "

COMMERCE AND FINANCE

By R. H. Fry

MANCHESTER, in 1821, was inspired by cotton. It was a trade to open the eye and broaden the mind. Its raw material came from across the sea and its products were sold in every continent. As the business expanded, the interests of the Manchester business community outgrew their local bonds and became identified with world-wide trading principles: free trade and rising standards of life. If in the early decades the commercial section of the *Guardian* was principally the organ and the market guide of the cotton industry, that function covered an amazingly wide range of subjects. Even in its first issue the paper carried, next to reports of produce and share markets, an article on " Money Prices " which explained learnedly " the great difference in the value of money in different nations ". By the middle of the century the cotton trade was spreading its attention from one end of the faculty of economics to the other. It was raising capital on the Stock Exchanges (London and local). It was using the acceptance credit of Lombard Street to finance its customers and the advances of the joint-stock banks to finance its stocks. It was using the freight markets of Liverpool and the Baltic and the marine insurance of Lloyds. It must be told by the fastest means existing that rain had fallen in Carolina or that the Nile had risen in flood, for cotton prices move with the growing crops. From New York and New Orleans, from Alexandria and Bombay news must be obtained to show how prices and commodity stocks were moving. The Budgets, tariffs, and political trends of every country affected the prospect of exports. The successful cotton merchant or manufacturer must, in fact, be master of the whole complicated machinery of international trade and finance which was taking shape during the second half of the last century. The *Guardian* served his needs with news, comment and advice. No other industry demanded such a wide-ranging service; no other newspaper provided it.

In presenting to the cotton trade every day a composite picture of the world's markets the paper came to present in turn the cotton trade to the outside world. As a chronicle of events and views in the industry, the commercial pages were read by business people all over Britain and abroad who could have kept themselves informed in no other way except by going to Manchester in person. Many other interests were added to cotton as time went on. Steel and engineering had established themselves early in Lancashire to serve the cotton mills. Shipping and shipbuilding were at home close by on Merseyside. Synthetic dyestuffs brought the chemical industry prominently to the north-west. The great industrial population which had settled in the area developed new needs, and new trades arose to supply them. The *Guardian* watched and chronicled the changes as they occurred. With the growth of investment in public companies a new element was added to the section. Stock Exchange reports and prices began to occupy several columns in the 'forties, though for some time they were mainly concerned with the Funds, cotton shares and railway stocks, and prominence was given to the provincial exchanges. By 1880, almost half of the eight and a half columns of commercial matter was taken up by messages from London, including a full stock exchange report with " prices after business hours ". Ten years later the commercial section had fourteen and a half columns, of which the Stock Exchange took nearly six and American markets (cotton, stocks, produce) almost three. Prosperity was spilling over; the British people were saving furiously and searching the earth for paying propositions to invest in. Moreover, the country's population was rapidly increasing, and to supply it with enough food and raw materials, " new " countries overseas had to be opened up and developed. The *Guardian*, in the early days of this century, reflects this constant widening of interests. By 1910 the commercial pages had grown to twenty-two columns, besides advertisements. Manchester was still the heart of a great export and import trade, but London had become the hub of a world-wide financial mechanism on which Britain's prosperity depended.

The pull of London became irresistible after the 1914–18 war A " Financial Editor " was appointed to report and interpret the activities of " the City ". On April 1st, 1920, Oscar Hobson began to wire from the new City Office a running commentary on financial affairs, which was soon read and quoted all over the world.

The period of C. P. Scott's editorship thus witnessed a great enlargement of the scope and content of the " City " pages. The detailed market reports and news of the seventies had broadened out into a section of the paper which, hardly less than the leader pages, included comment on and interpretation of the whole field of economic progress. Trade and finance had become an aspect of politics or of international affairs, and a newspaper's task in explaining them to the non-technical reader had become infinitely more complex. With the mixture of public and private enterprise we seem now to have ahead of us, it is a task that is at once more difficult and more vital to the national health.

<h1 style="text-align:center">5</h1>

SOME WRITINGS OF C. P. SCOTT

C. P. Scott wrote hardly anything under his own name or outside the columns of his paper. Almost all his work is buried in newspaper files; and leading articles, like political speeches, rarely survive their hour. The controversies on which Scott wrote, the political situations in which he gave guidance, are already half-forgotten. It may be fitting, however, in illustration of Scott's style and habit of thought, to select a few of his articles on some subjects that have not wholly lost their interest.

ON JOURNALISM
THE *MANCHESTER GUARDIAN'S* FIRST HUNDRED YEARS
(May 5th, 1921)

A HUNDRED years is a long time; it is a long time even in the life of a newspaper, and to look back on it is to take in not only a vast development in the thing itself, but a great slice in the life of the nation, in the progress and adjustment of the world. In the general development the newspaper, as an institution, has played its part, and no small part, and the particular newspaper with which I personally am concerned has also played its part, it is to be hoped, not without some usefulness. I have had my share in it for a little more than fifty years; I have been its responsible editor for only a few months short of its last half century; I remember vividly its fiftieth birthday; I now have the happiness to share in the celebration of its hundredth. I can therefore speak of it with a certain intimacy of acquaintance. I have myself been part of it and entered into its inner courts.

W. P. CROZIER, 1879–1944
Editor of the " Manchester Guardian " 1932–1944

THE SCOTT TRUST
July 26th, 1946

PAUL PATTERSON, OF THE " BALTIMORE SUN ", HANDING OVER THE TRUST
DEED WHICH WAS KEPT FOR SAFETY IN AMERICA DURING THE WAR

Left to right: A. P. Wadsworth, editor of the " Manchester Guardian ";
Sir William Haley, a trustee; L.P. Scott, assistant managing director; Paul
Patterson; J. R. Scott, chairman of the Scott Trust; James Bone, director;
and J. C. Beavan, editor of the " Manchester Evening News "

That is perhaps a reason why, on this occasion, I should write in my own name, as in some sort a spectator, rather than in the name of the paper as a member of its working staff.

In all living things there must be a certain unity, a principle of vitality and growth. It is so with a newspaper, and the more complete and clear this unity the more vigorous and fruitful the growth. I ask myself what the paper stood for when first I knew it, what it has stood for since and stands for now. A newspaper has two sides to it. It is a business, like any other, and has to pay in the material sense in order to live. But it is much more than a business; it is an institution; it reflects and it influences the life of a whole community; it may affect even wider destinies. It is, in its way, an instrument of government. It plays on the minds and consciences of men. It may educate, stimulate, assist, or it may do the opposite. It has, therefore, a moral as well as a material existence, and its character and influence are in the main determined by the balance of these two forces. It may make profit or power its first object, or it may conceive itself as fulfilling a higher and more exacting function.

I think I may honestly say that, from the day of its foundation, there has not been much doubt as to which way the balance tipped so far as regards the conduct of the paper whose fine tradition I inherited and which I have had the honour to serve through all my working life. Had it not been so, personally, I could not have served it. Character is a subtle affair, and has many shades and sides to it. It is not a thing to be much talked about, but rather to be felt. It is the slow deposit of past actions and ideals. It is for each man his most precious possession, and so it is for that latest growth of time the newspaper. Fundamentally it implies honesty, cleanness, courage, fairness, a sense of duty to the reader and the community. A newspaper is of necessity something of a monopoly, and its first duty is to shun the temptations of monopoly. Its primary office is the gathering of news. At the peril of its soul it must see that the supply is not tainted. Neither in what it gives, nor in what it does not give, nor in the mode of presentation must the unclouded face of truth suffer wrong. Comment is free, but facts are sacred.

" Propaganda ", so called, by this means is hateful. The voice of opponents no less than that of friends has a right to be heard. Comment also is justly subject to a self-imposed restraint. It is well to be frank; it is even better to be fair. This is an ideal. Achievement in such matters is hardly given to man. Perhaps none of us can attain to it in the desirable measure. We can but try, ask pardon for shortcomings, and there leave the matter.

But, granted a sufficiency of grace, to what further conquests may we look, what purpose serve, what task envisage? It is a large question, and cannot be fully answered. We are faced with a new and enormous power and a growing one. Whither is the young giant tending? What gifts does he bring? How will he exercise his privilege and powers? What influence will he exercise on the minds of men and on our public life? It cannot be pretended that an assured and entirely satisfactory answer can be given to such questions. Experience is in some respects disquieting. The development has not been all in the direction which we should most desire. One of the virtues, perhaps almost the chief virtue, of a newspaper is its independence. Whatever its position or character, at least it should have a soul of its own. But the tendency of newspapers, as of other businesses, in these days is towards amalgamation. In proportion, as the function of a newspaper has developed and its organisation expanded, so have its costs increased. The smaller newspapers have had a hard struggle; many of them have disappeared. In their place we have great organisations controlling a whole series of publications of various kinds and even of differing or opposing politics. The process may be inevitable, but clearly there are drawbacks. As organisation grows personality may tend to disappear. It is much to control one newspaper well; it is perhaps beyond the reach of any man, or any body of men, to control half a dozen with equal success. It is possible to exaggerate the danger, for the public is not undiscerning. It recognises the authentic voices of conscience and conviction when it finds them, and it has a shrewd intuition of what to accept and what to discount.

This is a matter which in the end must settle itself, and those who cherish the older ideal of a newspaper need not be dismayed.

They have only to make their papers good enough in order to win, as well as to merit, success, and the resources of a newspaper are not wholly measured in pounds, shillings and pence. Of course the thing can only be done by competence all round, and by that spirit of co-operation right through the working staff which only a common ideal can inspire. There are people who think you can run a newspaper about as easily as you can poke a fire, and that knowledge, training, and aptitude are superfluous endowments. There have even been experiments on this assumption, and they have not met with success. There must be competence, to start with, on the business side, just as there must be in any large undertaking, but it is a mistake to suppose that the business side of a paper should dominate, as sometimes happens, not without distressing consequences. A newspaper, to be of value, should be a unity, and every part of it should equally understand and respond to the purposes and ideals which animate it. Between its two sides there should be a happy marriage, and editor and business manager should march hand in hand, the first, be it well understood, just an inch or two in advance. Of the staff much the same thing may be said. They should be a friendly company. They need not, of course, agree on every point, but they should share in the general purpose and inheritance. A paper is built up upon their common and successive labours, and their work should never be task work, never merely dictated. They should be like a racing boat's crew, pulling well together, each man doing his best because he likes it, and with a common and glorious goal.

That is the path of self-respect and pleasure; it is also the path of success. And what a work it is! How multiform, how responsive to every need and every incident of life! What illimitable possibilities of achievement and of excellence! People talk of "journalese" as though a journalist were of necessity a pretentious and sloppy writer; he may be, on the contrary, and very often is, one of the best in the world. At least he should not be content to be much less. And then the developments. Every year, almost every day, may see growth and fresh accomplishment, and with a paper that is really alive, it not only may, but does. Let anyone take a file of this paper, or for that matter any one of half a dozen other papers, and compare its whole make-up and leading features to-day with what they were five years ago, ten years ago, twenty years ago, and he will realise how large has been the growth, how considerable the achievement. And this is what makes the work of a newspaper worthy and interesting. It has so many sides, it touches life at so many points, at every one there is such possibility of improvement and excellence. To the man, whatever his place on the paper, whether on the editorial or business, or even what may be regarded as the mechanical side—this also vitally important in its place—nothing should satisfy short of the best, and the best must always seem a little ahead of the actual. It is here that ability counts and that character counts, and it is on these that a newspaper, like every great undertaking, if it is to be worthy of its power and duty, must rely.

THE FUNCTION OF THE PRESS
(*Political Quarterly*, January–March, 1931)

THE first function of a newspaper is indicated plainly in its name; it is an instrument for the collection and dissemination of news. But what news? That is a material question. All sorts of things happen in the world every day and every hour of the day. It is all a question of selection, whether of the serious or the frivolous, of the clean or the unclean, of fact or of fiction. Some people like one sort and some another, and the newspaper can usually be found to respond to each demand. Here, in the favourite phrase of President Wilson, is the acid test of quality. It is a wonderful function and, with the progress of invention, has been carried far. It ministers to knowledge, to curiosity, to education; in a real sense it makes the whole world one. To know is not always to value, and intimacy may breed repulsion, even hate. But, on the whole, it is not so, and knowledge not only opens the way to sympathy but mitigates instinctive dislike. For men are extraordinarily interesting and every society has its own character and its own attraction. Perhaps we do not sufficiently realise this. We study with ardour and minuteness the dead civilisations of Greece and Rome and we forget that India and China may have just as much to teach us which is a good deal nearer to hand. The newspaper cannot throw its net too wide. Its folly is to affect omniscience, but its function is to supply all the material needful for those that know.

It may go further; it may, and it ought so far as it is able to, supply some guidance in the maze of things, to act in some degree, not merely as purveyor, but also as interpreter. That, no doubt, is a delicate operation and lends itself all too easily to abuse. But there are cases in which nothing is so misleading as the bald fact. To be understood it must be seen in its whole connection, as part of a process, not merely as an incident. That is a work of interpretation and makes all sorts of demands, not only on knowledge, but on the impartial temper. Nor does impartiality imply indifference; indifference is an atrophy of the sympathies, impartiality a poise of the mind. The first condition of a real understanding is perhaps a sympathetic approach. And how vital this all is history shows. The worst crimes which it records are perhaps the crimes of ignorance. War, modern war at least, is its child. We are past the stage of sheer aggression; we know too well that in war both sides lose; that there is no such thing as victor and vanquished, but that war is a defeat for both. In this sense all war is madness; its beginning and its end. To each side the other is the aggressor and, in fact, that is the truth. For to be the first to attack is a clear advantage, and when trouble is brewing, each side, knowing this, imputes the intention to the other and in that belief itself determines to be first. How easily this may happen was seen in a crucial and terrible instance that none can forget, yet the spirit of aggression for its own sake was, perhaps, equally absent from both sides. If only each had known, and in its heart believed, that this was so, how easy would understanding have been, how sure the road to safety. Here, surely, is the precious opportunity of all who can form, or influence opinion. And yet how rarely it is fully used? How often do not newspapers in their assumed vocation of watch-dogs for the nation, ready to bark at every footstep as though it must needs be that of an enemy, serve rather to scent danger where none is and to howl denunciation where, if they but knew, there is not the slightest need for alarm. Not that the error need be intentional. Nothing is easier than to persuade oneself that danger is in the air. Both sides may be equally to blame, and sheer ignorance is usually the vice of each. The mischief is easily done. There may be no actual perversion of the facts; a judicious selection may equally suffice, and this apart from any real malice. That is why the sources of information are so important and the responsibility of the purveyors of news is so great. That of those who handle and display it is, perhaps, no less. For the important may be shown as unimportant, and the unimportant as important, by devices so simple and innocent as type, headlines, or position on the page. It is all a matter of discretion and good faith.

Not that the task is easy. What, in fact, can be more difficult than really to enter into the mind of a man of another nation, still more to grasp the conditions which go to make him what he is—his education, the atmosphere of his home, the traditions of his people. Yet it is all these things which, when the test comes, go to determine his outlook and his action. It is for the Press, so far as it may, to act as interpreter, and one of its first duties is to qualify for the task.

But, after all, men are not necessarily enemies because they are strangers to each other, though that is apt to be the assumption among primitive peoples, and nothing can be more foolish than to regard a neighbour primarily as a possible enemy. Every nation has something in race, in temperament, in history and development which marks it off from other nations and makes it rich in interest and instruction. And the further off nations may be from each other in these respects the more interesting they become and the more knowing. Sometimes where a very long development has taken place in complete, or almost complete isolation, a real understanding, a spiritual intimacy, becomes very difficult, or actually impossible. And this is a misfortune. It is the price we pay for the emergence of a type. And the type may be so strong that it must forever remain apart, self-sufficient, impenetrable. Such types exist. They have their special gifts for the world. But we do not love them. They do not invite love. Such differences may cut very deep, or they may be quite subtle. What is it that divides us from our own past, from the builders, say, of the Middle Age? What is it they had which we have lost? And why, and at what point, did we lose it? It is in art and, above all, in architecture that the difference tells. Perhaps it is because beauty is so subtle a thing. Yet these men were bone of our bone and flesh of our flesh as we are of theirs. Differences in time, differences in space, each of these has gone to make up that wonderful complex which we call humanity. The newspaper has at times to adjust itself to both. It must overleap all barriers. It cannot possess omniscience and need not pretend to it. But its interests should be as wide as the field that invites them, and it need not be without allies, or scorn the expert, though it may be wise to observe him carefully.

The newspaper is a vast machine. What matters is the spirit that lies behind it. The world is its province, but that is an empty boast unless it implies a real fellowship. Europe already begins to think and speak of itself as a unity. America was born one. India, but yesterday an aggregate of disparate peoples, to-day is finding its soul. The world does move, and every day it moves faster. The newspaper stands by to interpret and, where it can, help. What a spectacle! What an opportunity!

AN INDEPENDENT PRESS
(April 5th, 1928)

A FREE and independent Press, a Press, that is, which is free to say what it chooses, subject only to the restraints of decency and the law of libel, and which at the same time is representative of the full variety of opinion and of interest throughout the country, has come to be an indispensable instrument of popular education and of popular government. How far does the increasing concentration of newspaper ownership in a few hands tend to weaken or destroy this instrument, and thus to impair the security we at present possess for the free play of public opinion and the wise control of public affairs? A perfectly simple answer cannot, perhaps, be given. The newspaper as we know it to-day serves a variety of purposes. It is primarily and before all else a mechanism for the collection and distributions of news, and in this capacity its duty is to suppress nothing that matters and to corrupt nothing. Coloured or doctored news may be more misleading than no news at all. On the other hand, the suppression of news in whole or in part may amount no less to a fraud upon the reader. Apart from its function as a vehicle of news the Press as a whole is regarded, and as a rule rightly regarded, as an index of the opinion which it seeks both to represent and to guide, but clearly if the index is not to be deceptive it must represent a real variety, and the voice of the Press must not be the voice of a megaphone. A free Press, again, has ever been and ever will remain alike the bulwark and the sure sign of public liberty. It is not merely that it is in the modern State the necessary means of political propaganda and political agitation, without which no active and healthy political life can exist at all, but only through it can the individual obtain the effectual expression of his thought and make his due and perhaps essential contribution to the life and energy of the nation.

These are lofty and indispensable functions. To sap or weaken them is to help to destroy not the least of our guarantees for the safe working of popular institutions and for personal and public liberty. It is not to be pretended that the Press discharges its duties perfectly, but at least in this country it has created a great and, on the whole, responsible organisation on which the public has learnt to rely. Clearly it is not a thing to be lightly invaded or changed in its essential character. Like most other big things it has a body and a soul. Its body is its goodwill and its property, its soul its responsible use of them. The syndicated Press is primarily an accumulation of newspaper property. That is a tangible thing. As to the intangible part it is not possible to speak so surely. It is in truth a matter of much uncertainty, and the thing itself is perhaps a hazard. Obviously unity spells sameness. The same man or corporation cannot honestly express a variety of opinions, and if he leaves others to express opinions for him what becomes of responsibility? Thus the variety, the local colour, the sense of individual responsibility which are the very life of a healthy Press must, it is to be feared, tend to fade, perhaps ultimately to disappear. Nor is that all. Even for a single newspaper it is not always easy to secure the continuity of purpose and ideas which the public have learnt to look for from it. But tradition and family connections often help. Where these are absent, and property, bought and sold on the market, is the basis on which everything rests, what security is there against changes of policy with a change of hands? The movement towards aggregation and the concentration of power is young at present, and any dangers that may be involved in it are as yet largely undeclared. But it is growing and may yet attain to vastly greater dimensions. And what then?

PRESS AND GOVERNMENT
(March 12th, 1918)

THERE appear to us to be very strong reasons indeed why great newspaper proprietors should not also become members of Governments. To begin with, they are quite powerful enough already because of the extraordinary influence which they can exert over the minds of millions of men. But there are other objections. First, if to own a great newspaper is the sure road, or even a possible road, to political advancement, of course that road will be used by the less scrupulous and therefore the more undesirable as a means to that end, and we shall never know whether a furious Press campaign is directed to legitimate political objects in which the newspaper magnate believes, or is designed to put pressure on the Government—after the familiar House of Commons method—to cause the critic to be absorbed into the body criticised, because otherwise he will continue to make himself unpleasant or dangerous. That is one objection, and no one who knows anything about the inner working of politics and the grounds for some political appointments will dispute its validity. Another is the very great probability that the person appointed for such reasons would not be the best person, perhaps not even a tolerably suitable person, for the post to which he has raised himself. A third is that the stock-in-trade of a newspaper is news, and that a member of a Government or the holder of a great administrative post is bound to have access to confidential information of the most important kind. It is sheer nonsense, as Mr. Austen Chamberlain yesterday remarked, to suppose that he can divest his mind of it. Nor can he by merely for the time being relinquishing the direct management of his newspaper divest himself also of his responsibility. Unless he parts with the property he retains the control. The analogy of the director of a limited company who on accepting office is called upon to resign his directorship is in this case wholly misleading. The proprietor is the company.

And this further question arises: If the proprietor does not guide his paper, who does guide it? And has he any right, so long as the power is his, to disclaim responsibility? Upon this earth there can be no much greater responsibility than that involved in the control of a great newspaper. All a man's days and all his powers, all the conscience that is in him, and all the application he can give are surely not too much fitly to discharge so great a task. No malefactor he, indeed, if he rightly regards himself and his duty, but a public servant in a post as honourable and as taxing as that of any Minister. Intercourse with Ministers he may well have. If they can trust him, the more the better. Intercourse, too, with all sorts and all conditions of men, and with the affairs, so far as strength will carry him, of many countries. Surely here is labour enough and distinction enough for any man, even though his name should not be known. That is his proper place if he knows his vocation. But he has no business in a Government, and the precedent now set should never be followed.

ON PEACEMAKING

THE GREAT DAY
(November 12th, 1918)

THIS is the great day—the great day of Peace, hoped for, longed for, at times appearing remote, almost unattainable, yet never despaired of, resolutely pursued, at last conquered. Now it is ours, and not ours only; it is the world's, it is for our enemies no less than for ourselves; it is like the rain from Heaven, it is a gift to all. In name it is not peace but only the cessation of arms, but the arms, once laid down, will not be taken up again; the fighting is over, the slaughter is over; the armies may still stand on guard, and some of them must continue so to stand till the peace itself is signed, but their work is done. Recruiting has stopped. The vast machine of military munitioning may continue to work for a little, as it were by force of habit, but with fast-diminishing energy and with no serious purpose before it except that of bringing itself, as soon as possible and with as little injury as possible to the interests of the millions of men and women it has absorbed, to a complete standstill. Soon—as soon as possible—the men of the armies will begin to return, not for the present in masses, but rather by industries in prearranged order, with preference, no doubt, at the same time for the war-worn men, for those who for three years or four years have borne the heat and burden of the day, who have been wounded and returned to the fighting line, who at length have earned, if any men have earned, relief from the burden and the weariness of the long-drawn strife. Thus will hope come to many homes, and one by one at first and in ever-growing stream the men who have saved England, who have saved the world, will return to the land which owes them so deep a debt, which they have ennobled by their valour and their steadfastness, which will ever honour them but can never adequately repay.

It is a great hour, a wonderful victory which we celebrate to-day —hard won, bitterly fought for, dearly paid. Yet if we are true to ourselves, worthy of an heroic destiny, it should yet be worth, and well worth, the price. It was by a fine inspiration that Mr. Lloyd George, after his brief statement in the House of Commons, called upon the House to adjourn for a service of thanksgiving at St. Margaret's Church, hard by. In so doing he struck at once the note of seriousness, of deep responsibility, of appeal to what is best in the mind and purpose of the nation. It was well and fitly done, and marks, we may believe, the temper in which the Prime Minister desired that the nation should approach, and in which he himself intends to approach, the great task of the resettlement of Europe and the permanent terms of peace. Events within the last few days have moved with breathless rapidity, and the whole conditions of the problem as regards the Central Powers are changed. We have no longer to deal with two great and highly organised military autocracies, but with a whole series of States not merely democratic in form but in which the democratic forces have definitely assumed the upper hand. The process of change was as rapid as it was sudden, and even to the most careful observers unexpected. It has given us an Austria resolved into its elements of diverse nationality, each now claiming complete independence of the rest, and all, including even the German districts, having renounced allegiance to the ancient ruling house; a Hungary freed from its powerful ruling caste and no longer claiming itself to exercise rule over the subject nationalities so long held down by force within the body of the State; a Germany—most wonderful of all—freed from Prussian dominance no less than from the personal rule of the Imperial house which Prussia had imposed on the other German States, founded as it was on military victory, now ruined and discarded through military defeat. Even the most sceptical, the most wooden-minded, must at length see in this mighty evolution something more than the German cunning, the Teutonic tricks, for which they are ever on the watch and have hitherto never failed to discover. Facts are spectators of great and transforming events, and Germany stands disclosed before us not merely as a great democratic State—or rather, we should say, as resolved or resolving itself into a series of such States, destined, we may believe, to form the United States of the Germany of the future—but as one which may easily pass to a position far more extreme. The inborn and acquired sense of discipline so strong in the German people will, we may well hope, save them from the excess, the disorder, and the bitter internal strife of which Russia has shown the world an example, but Bolshevism had its root in the mind of a German doctrinaire, and it remains yet to be seen whether Germany, in her deep humiliation and staggering under the load which is the legacy of four years of war, will resist the contagion. We have yet to see what her returning legions, suffering and bitterly disappointed, may have to say. Certainly if they should go back to find themselves workless and foodless the result is not likely to be happy for the German State. . . . In the interests of order, in the interests of humanity, we must see to it that the German people, whose fate is now largely in our hands, shall not starve. That is a first duty which we owe to a conquered enemy. Let it be handsomely performed.

THE DUTIES OF PEACE
(November 19th, 1918)

I T is too soon, incomparably too soon, to see the events of the
... past four years in their true perspective or to estimate their
effect on the future of our own nation or of the family of nations.
The ideas and the events of the French Revolution have not
even yet, after more than a hundred years, begun to exhaust
their influence on the course of European history, and those of
the war now reaching its close in such catastrophic developments
may well prove no less potent and disintegrating. We cannot
probe the future; it is hard enough to take even an approximate
measure of the present as it passes in its fated course before our
eyes with all its majestic development. We are parties to it,
actors in it, and yet it seems all to move with a life and purpose
of its own apart from our will, surpassing our intelligence, and
the thought most insistent through it all is the littleness of man
measured by the greatness of events. Yet if this is a sobering
reflection it must not lead us too far. For in the midst of the
greatest events, and in proportion to their greatness, is the duty
laid on us to play our part, each man, each nation, in the tasks
which the day presents and which no future day can repeat or
recall. It is this moral sense, this consciousness of an immense
opportunity and of a duty no less great, which has guided the
policy and informed every utterance of the most powerful and
reflective mind which the war has produced among those who
stand at the head of affairs. It is well that it is so, and it is doubly
well that the same man who has thought hardest of duty and of
policy is also the man who stands at the head of the greatest
potential power in the world, that youthful Hercules, the United
States. We have no need to follow blindfold any man or any
statesman, and President Wilson has made his mistakes, but he
can perhaps help us more than any other to retrieve our own

and to extort from the tangle of contending interests and ambitions—these are not yet extinct in the world or in the Foreign Offices—a result which, broadly at least, shall conform to justice, which shall, as the King in his speech divines, substitute order for violence and co-operation for enmity and release the nations from the stupendous burdens of armaments and the obsession of fear which have weighed them down and corrupted and impoverished them. It is well that the Sovereign should hold out this hope to us and designate this goal. For only so can we achieve the real victory, the victory over our own folly and hate and greed.

It is not to be achieved by words or by pious aspirations. It is an immensely difficult task, from the theoretic point of view no less than from the moral and practical. It is easy to talk about a League of Nations, even to draw up quite clear and specious schemes that would work beautifully if the nations were nations of angels. The real difficulty is to devise and elaborate a scheme which men will consent to work, and to which, when the pinch comes, they will submit; a scheme not so ambitious as to involve an entirely new world order, yet adequate for its primary and dominant purpose of preventing war, and with force behind sufficient to that end. In a word, we have to build up what has been variously described as a supra-national authority or a world-State. The task has been enormously eased and simplified by the disappearance or transformation of several existing States. There could have been no real union or co-operation of free nations with a militarist and autocratic Germany; only a most imperfect one with an autocratic Russia; none, again, with an Austria-Hungary of which the smaller half held in bondage the larger half of its total population. All three have disappeared, disappeared for ever, and in their place we have a new Europe, with new States springing into life, and old ones yielding to new and revolutionary forces. This vast upheaval, as yet carrying with it no complete order or stability, may indeed in itself present fresh difficulties, but at least they are far less than the old, for freedom, the essential base of real co-operation, has been won. Our task is twofold: on the one hand, to recognise and satisfy the sense of nationality, to give it everywhere concrete expression, within if need be, new territorial limits; on the other hand, to prevent this sense of nationality from breaking bounds, to forbid the trespass of nation upon nation. It is a mighty and a difficult task to which the King calls us and for which the world is now making ready. Happily it has the full and resolute support of our greatest ally, the ally who shares our political tradition and our speech; and no less, we may trust, that of all that is best in our own people, as we know it has that of our own Prime Minister. With such backers it should win through.

THE SLUMP IN IDEALISM
(December 3rd, 1918)

WHATEVER else the election may have brought, it has not brought any better spirit into our politics, any raising of the tone of public discussion, any better prospect for a good peace. An election is usually something of a scrimmage, but no election within memory was such a poor sort of scrimmage as this. It is supposed—so Mr. Lloyd George has told us—to have for its objects, first, the strengthening of the hands of the Government for the negotiation of a just peace, and, secondly, the laying down of the lines of what is called, in the cant phrase, Reconstruction—the repair of the damage of war, the restoring of the old privileges of peace, including, we must hope, some modicum at least of our ancient liberties; the building up and strengthening of the whole national life, and especially our economic life, so that we may the better bear the terrific burden of the war losses. Excellent objects no doubt, but how far are they being attained? And first as to peace and its negotiation. It is a difficult business. Under pressure of a common danger the great nations who stood against the German assault have held pretty well together—extraordinarily well, if we look to past precedents and the inevitable difficulties of such a combination. Outwardly they have presented a singularly united front, and any differences—of course there have been differences—have been discreetly suppressed and as far as possible genuinely compromised. But they are there, and the moment of victory—that is, the moment when the controlling influence is withdrawn—is naturally the moment for their revival and emergence. Thus Italy, our very good friend, whose gallantry, chivalry, and idealism evoke in all forward-looking men so quick and fervent a response, has also her strictly materialistic or Imperialistic side, which at the present moment is actively demonstrating itself in a manner which may well cause uneasiness. Or take France, again a country for which those of us who know her best have the deepest admiration and affection. Her civilisation is the brightest, the most attractive in the world. It has in these last years stood in deadly conflict with the stolid if massive equipment of the German mind, the German conception of man and of the German man, wholly lacking, unhappily, in humour, and it has conquered. It shines forth henceforward unhampered at last by the sense of defeat, by the oppression of a great danger and a great fear. Yet Chauvinistic France is not dead, the France which in 1870 shouted its " à Berlin ", and which aspired and plotted even in the course of the present war for the annexation of purely German territory and extension to the Rhine. There are Chauvinists yet among its leading men —even the chief of them, the Prime Minister, now justly acclaimed in his own country as " the man of victory ", has almost frankly professed his fidelity to that ancient faith in which as a public man he was reared and to which by temperament he belongs. Or take America—after all, we have got to face facts in this great business—America (though the telegrams are careful not to inform us) is at present seething with an orgy of ill-instructed passion, provoked by the realisation of the crimes (which have lost nothing in the telling) of German troops and German rulers of all grades from the Kaiser downwards. This feeling, quite strong enough and natural enough in itself, has been stimulated and played upon to the utmost for party purposes by the political opponents of the present administration and of the President, and they have been so far successful as to carry the recent elections for the Senate and the House of Representatives against him, and thus most seriously to embarrass him in the execution of his declared policy—a policy the wisdom and the justice of which have been recognised the world over, and on the execution of which in its main outlines our whole hope for the future resides.

It is in this state of the world and of our alliances that Mr. George has chosen to embark on a general election. The time was a time for coolness, for restraint, for dignity in the hour of victory, so that, if possible, we might achieve that most difficult of all conquests, the conquest of ourselves, and win that final success, the success of moderation and of statesmanship, rather than that of violence and self-assertion and the letting loose of passion. Already we begin to see the results. As for anything constructive, for any mandate on policy such as we were bidden to look for, there is no such thing. An outline of reforms was laid down in the joint manifesto of the Government at the beginning of the contest, but it receives a merely perfunctory assent from their followers. All the real ardour of the Coalition goes into execration of the enemy—who doubtless deserves curses deep and long, but is already paying a penalty which might satisfy even those whose mind cannot travel beyond the ethics of commination—and the demand for vengeance on him, high and low, and his utter exclusion for all the time to come from our land and our commerce. It is all as natural here as it was in America, and may prove no less effective as a political weapon. But in any larger view it is not helpful. It will not assist us to get rid of Chauvinism among ourselves or others; it will not strengthen the hands of those who wish to play the part of states-men at the Peace Conference; it will not advance by a hair's-breadth the cause of a just and enduring peace. It will, on the contrary, make all these things more difficult. Perhaps Mr. George, with his quick perception of the working of popular emotions, foresaw this and was prepared to pay the price. At any rate he is doing nothing to restrain the forces he has let loose. He is, on the contrary, actively playing up to them, and that is perhaps the most serious result of all. He may think that the ferment, after all, is but a passing one, that when the election is over and he has got his majority he can drop the electioneer and revert to the statesman. He may hope that then he can play the part which we honestly believe he would desire and on which his mind was at one time set, of evoking the permanent victory of peace from the passing victory of war, of turning to its true account perhaps the greatest opportunity that ever came to an English statesman for winning lasting credit and a great future for his country and salvation for the world. Why has he risked it all and made it all more difficult? Truly it is hard to look into the heart of any man, hardest of all perhaps for himself.

And what for us is the moral? The election is on us, and we have to make what we can of it. The first necessity is to send to Parliament at least a strong body of stable and independent men, friends of international order, not mere screamers against Germany, but who can see even in Germany the possibility of far better things, not partisans wedded to the game of party—surely in our ranks there are none such now left—but resolute for principle, which so many easy-going and invertebrate politicians are eager to scrap because they cannot understand; and as to the great figure of the election, the conquering hero of the hour, friends not of the charlatan but of the statesman in Mr. Lloyd George. For in the time to come nothing is more certain than that he will need such discriminating support. The duty is a common one; it attaches to all honest and independent men, whether they march under the flag of Liberalism or under that of Labour. The two bodies are but wings of the same army, the army of social and political progress. Hard times are ahead of us, taxing and perhaps dangerous times. Men of goodwill should stand together.

THE CONSTITUTION OF THE
LEAGUE OF NATIONS
(February 15th, 1919)

W E publish to-day the momentous document in which the constitution, powers, and obligations of the future League of Nations are defined. The terms of this great international treaty, as when adopted it will become, have been agreed to by all the Great Powers. It is not necessarily a final draft, and may, we hope, be in some respects amended after it has been subjected to the full public discussion which clearly is needed in regard to a matter of so much intricacy and such far-reaching importance. The scheme is in the main based on the admirable proposals put forward for the consideration of the Peace Conference by General Smuts and reproduces most of its salient features. Only in one material particular does it depart from the main lines of General Smuts's proposals, but that, unfortunately, is a point of very great importance. The first thing which we have to ask ourselves in the constitution of such a body is where is its mainspring, where is the force to which we can look to give it power and vitality? General Smuts found this in what he called a " General Conference ", which was to be the Parliament, as it were, of the League. True, this Parliament of the League was not to be a legislature in the full sense. It could make proposals but could not pass laws. Still it was to be no mere debating society. Its proposals would have to be considered by the Council, or Executive, of the League, and if approved by it would take effect. But the great advantage of the General Conference was that it was to be a thoroughly popular body, and one, in General Smuts's conception, evidently of considerable size. All the Powers, members of the League, were to be represented on it, and its members were to be elected partly by the governments of the several Powers, partly by the Parliaments. The small Powers were here to be on a level with the great, and as the Conference had no power of enactment but only of advice, voting was to be by majority. It was to be a genuinely popular body which would possess an equal interest for all concerned, and might serve to kindle and sustain interest in the League and, as General Smuts put it, to spread the atmosphere of peace. It was a wise and far-reaching proposal, marked by the true democratic feeling of its author—for is not the small State just as important to itself as the great State?—and his penetrating imagination. Unfortunately it finds no place in the draft scheme as now published. Instead, we have a body of "Delegates", small in number and of meagre and ill-defined functions. In place of the wide franchise proposed by General Smuts, it is to be restricted to three representatives of each of the four Great Powers among the present Allies, voting not as individuals but as States. There is no provision, as in General Smuts's scheme, for publicity, and there will consequently be little public interest and no educational effect. The executive body is the Council, but as it is only provided that it should meet once a year and as a vast mass of business will have to be constantly transacted, it is obvious that the real power, the mainspring of the whole business, must be sought elsewhere.

The permanent body which is to transact this business is to be the Secretariat, a purely official body, with a Secretary General who will nominate the members of the Secretariat, subject, of course, to the approval of the Council, and who will act as secretary to the other bodies at their somewhat occasional meetings. In other words, we stand a good chance of getting a League of Nations run not by the peoples but by the officials. It would be a poor exchange and one which we trust may yet be avoided. But the defect is one which cannot be overlooked, and when the President comes back from America we trust that the constitution of the League may be subject to somewhat searching revision. Apart from this, it corresponds with all the hopes that have been founded on it. Its primary object is the prevention of war, and this it proposes to achieve, first, by providing for the submission of all disputes to the arbitral machinery provided by the League and insisting on a considerable period of delay before hostilities can be begun, partly by elaborate provisions for the reduction of armaments, partly by putting a check on the private manufacture of munitions, and therefore on the sinister working of private interests bound up with it. There is no provision for an international armed force, but each signatory nation is bound in certain circumstances to put its armed forces at the disposal of the League. The chief weapons of the League, however, will be economic. There will be a rigorous boycott of recalcitrant or pledge-breaking members amounting to a complete refusal of intercourse. As against almost any State this would be a deadly weapon indeed. Nor can the moral forces brought into play be regarded as of small account. After all, the organised opinion of the world, taking effect with full publicity and on an impartial statement of the facts of any dispute, is a tremendous weapon. It may well prove also to a be a growing one. Where is the Power which dare in the long run expose itself to universal obloquy?

These matters are largely for the future. The most immediate task of the League is to determine the fate of the vast regions which, through the operations of the war, have become derelict. They are two kinds, the barbarous and the semi-civilised, and the treatment to be accorded to each will correspond with this fundamental difference. In all cases they are to escheat in the first instance to the League of Nations, which will appoint " mandatory " or trustee powers. In the case of the barbarous countries in Africa and the Pacific Islands certain definite and invaluable restrictions are placed on the rights of the mandatory. There is to be no forced labour, no forced military service except for police or purely defensive purposes, no corruption by alcohol, no exploitation of their natural resources for the sole benefit of the occupying Power, no use of them as military bases. It is to be a real trust, and there is to be the open door of trade for all nations. In the case of the other class of territories, those, that is, that once formed part of the Turkish Empire, quite different conditions will apply, and there will be protection for religion and customs and a measure of local autonomy, passing later into self-government. In all cases there is to be an annual report of the administration to the League of Nations. This part of the scheme will need very careful examination. We miss, too, any provision for the assertion of the necessary powers of the League in regard to the new nations now in process of formation in Central Europe out of the wreck of two great empires. These owe their existence to the Great Powers who have won the war and are establishing the League. It is not merely the question of boundaries which will have to be determined. This will be done in the Treaty of Peace or the arrangements consequential on it, but there are religious liberties and local autonomies which need assertion and protection here no less than in the remains of the Turkish Empire. This is a matter which cannot be neglected, and it comes naturally within the province of the League.

IS IT TO BE A REAL PEACE?
(February 25th, 1919)

W E are no longer waging war, but most certainly we are not yet enjoying peace. We are in a kind of limbo, with the hell of war, it is true, well escaped, but the haven of an assured peace, of the kind of peace which alone could compensate for the immeasurable calamities of war, still remote, difficult, present to the eye of faith, but demanding a robust faith in order to inspire belief and a moral effort greater even than the effort of war before it can be translated into reality. Paris presents us with one series of problems, Germany and Russia mock us with others still more unmanageable. In Paris there is for the moment something of a pause. The dominating figures are withdrawn. President Wilson has landed in America to grapple with his own difficulties there, which are sufficiently formidable; Mr. Lloyd George, with a spirit happily ever buoyant, is engaged on a similar task in his own country; M. Clemenceau, wonderfully recovering and triumphing over age and wounds, is still not able to take up the full burden of his great responsibilities. Yet the need for haste was never greater. Germany is seething with disruptive forces, and, until she knows her fate and recovers so much of liberty as is essential to economic life, cannot attain political stability. Russia is in the throes of a social and political upheaval perhaps unexampled in history for its intensity and destructiveness. Even peace when it comes will not bring us much of ease, unless conditions in these two great nations, numbering between them some two hundred and fifty million people, can be so far improved and stabilised as to make free intercourse possible and to give some measure of unity once more to the family of nations.

What hope, what prospect, is there that things may work out to this end, and what can we do to help them forward? First of all, undoubtedly, by hastening the actual conclusion of peace. Until that is done nothing will have been done, and even then little will have been done unless the peace is a right peace, a peace not of vengeance but of principle, resting not on any delusive "material" guarantees, but dictated by a statesmanship which takes account above all of the moral factors in the affairs of men, which will have the courage and the wisdom to base itself on these, and will refuse to repeat the error of the last great so-called peace, dictated in Versailles, which has proved but the breeding-ground of war and of a world-cataclysm. Yet there are signs in abundance that it is precisely this error towards which powerful forces are seeking to urge us, and that the wisdom of moderation may once more be ignored. In these matters, matters touching the most intimate concerns of the great nations by whose side we have fought and whose welfare we earnestly desire to protect and sustain, it is difficult to speak quite frankly without running the risk of appearing to be unfriendly; yet surely frankness is the truest friendship, since it is not our own interests in particular for which we are concerned, but the interests of us all. It all comes back to this: Are we to find security, in particular are France and Italy to find security, in territorial annexations and similar limited and material guarantees, or are we to look for them in a new direction? In other words, is the general conception of a League of Nations, of an alliance, or combination, of all the great and most of the small nations of the world for the preservation of the world's peace, to prevail and be made effective, or is it to be treated as secondary and any real security to be sought, as hitherto it always has been sought, in frontiers, alliances, armaments? It is a great choice; it is perhaps a perilous one; but it has got to be made, and there can be no half-way house, no merging of the two in the hope of gaining the advantages of both. In that view President Wilson is, to our mind, absolutely right, and we hope he will hold fast to his position and refuse to make a peace other than the "peace of justice" for which he stands, and to which, in truth, the whole of the Allies are in terms committed.

Let us look at the matter in the concrete. France (or shall we say the French Foreign Office and the more articulate French opinion, which is not quite the same thing?) is known to desire one small annexation of undoubted German territory—that of the Saar Valley with its coalfield; and one much larger semi-annexation—the political separation from Germany, which would also imply economic dependence on France, of the whole of the German territories west of the Rhine, which at present constitute Rhenish Prussia. The first desire can only be gratified at the cost of a clear infraction of the basis in principle of the League of Nations, which is that populations, small and great, shall not be transferred " like cattle ", as the President expressed it, from one Power to another. It may be said that the population is small, and that, being largely a mining population, it is more or less migratory, but the whole question of principle is involved, and that is not small. As to Rhenish Prussia, that is in scale a much greater matter. It is a great and prosperous manufacturing area, and contains such famous cities as Cologne, Aix-la-Chapelle, Trèves, Coblenz, Bonn, Düsseldorf, and Crefeld, to say nothing of Essen. To cut it off forcibly or by any merely colourable device from Germany would be to invoke in Germany precisely the same feelings that have existed in France for nearly half a century in regard to Alsace-Lorraine, with results probably not dissimilar. The same considerations apply to the desire of a powerful party in Italy, though not, we are glad to think, of the best Italian opinion, for extensive annexations of Jugo-Slav districts on the east side of the Adriatic. Such gains may be tempting, they may even have a delusive appearance of protective value, but at bottom they are a source of profound weakness, first because they create bitter and prolonged enmity, and secondly because they alienate friends. It is impossible that this country, as a member of the League of Nations, should consent to guarantee the permanence of such acquisitions; it is even more impossible that America, with her traditional reluctance to engage herself in European troubles, should guarantee them. There would, in consequence, be no League of Nations, or only a sham one. What France had taken from Germany, what Italy had taken from her neighbour, they would have themselves to defend, and to defend by the old means of power. What, then, would be their security? It would have vanished. They would have sacrificed the substance for the shadow. All loyal friends of both in this country must desire that they should avoid so fatal an error.

1830
ADVERTISING PERFORMING ANIMALS

THE TREATY OF PEACE
(May 3rd, 1919)

THE vast work of the conclusion of a world-peace yesterday reached its most formal and dramatic stage. In the presence of the representatives of all the great Allied Powers and of nearly a score of lesser ones, the document containing the terms was presented at Versailles to the plenipotentiaries from Germany. These terms are of course primarily terms of peace with Germany. They define her future frontiers east and west and north and south; they demand from her, besides the surrender of territory, the payment of a vast indemnity; they define the conditions, military and other, to which she is called upon to submit as security for the fulfilment of these obligations and for the maintenance of peace; they demand the surrender for trial and punishment of specific offenders against the laws and customs of war. But they do more than this; they include proposals which are of far wider scope and which are not punitive but constructive. In the very forefront of the proposed treaty stands the whole scheme of the League of Nations, in which at present Germany is not invited to become a member, but of which in its application to the general settlement her acceptance is required. There is besides the great International Labour Convention, for which also her concurrence is needed, though it is not in the same measure obligatory. And, besides the terms having special application to herself, her acceptance is required in advance to those which may hereafter be imposed upon her former allies— upon Austria-Hungary, or so much as remains of it, upon Bulgaria, upon the Turkish Empire. It is an immense programme, and it is not wonderful that it should be embodied in a document of unexampled complexity and length. It has taken five months to draw up; Germany is to be allowed a fortnight for its consideration. M. Clemenceau yesterday promised all needful explanations. The time is not likely to prove too long.

The question which most deeply concerns us in regard to it is: How far does it supply a just basis for an enduring peace? That again mainly depends upon how far the territorial changes it proposes can be justified on grounds of equity apart from the passions of war and national ambitions. There are some tremendous historical reparations. What would the Liberal England—for there was a Liberal England—of the 'thirties not have felt had it been told that the great wrong of the partition of Poland would within a hundred years have been utterly undone? What would the older men still living not have felt if they had known that the rape of Slesvig would be atoned in little more than fifty years? What would we all not have given any time this last forty years to have known that to-day France would recover her lost provinces and the crime and folly of 1871 be a thing of the past? And there is an even older account to be squared, though less present to men's minds to-day—the successful raid of the Great Frederick in Silesia, the prototype and model for all those later raids by his successors. It is all over now, the wrongs are to be undone, the peoples to be liberated, justice and liberty to claim their own, and the Peace Treaty will declare and secure it. But is there nothing on the other side, no overleaping of the line of wisdom and of moderation, no fresh wrong which the years may be called upon to undo? Something, we fear, there is to be set on this wrong side of the account. It is hard to pretend that the arrangement proposed for the Saar Valley is an ideal one. It bears on its face every mark of a compromise, and of a pretty bad compromise. No one will deny to France her right to all possible reparation, and, having been despoiled for a good many years to come of great part of the produce of her ruined northern mines, she may justly claim compensation in kind from the German coalfield on her southern border. But the complicated arrangement by which she acquires the mines in absolute possession, instead of merely their produce for a fixed term, with a sort of contingent claim to the whole or part of the territory, is thoroughly unsatisfactory and disturbing, and can only tend to keep open a sore which it was as much in the interest of France as of the general peace to heal. All that can be said for it is that it is better than the sheer annexation which French Chauvinism—a different thing from France—would have demanded. So, again, of the Danzig arrangement on the eastern front. It is better than the worst with which we were threatened, but falls pretty heavily short of what might have been desired. It may be admitted that the problem was not a simple one, and that it was not easy to reconcile the need of Poland for a port on the Baltic—her only access to the sea—with German historic and territorial rights. Yet it might have been done, and it has not been done. Happily, here also the original proposal to transfer a million or two Germans to Polish sovereignty has been severely cut down, and this we owe mainly to the good sense and courage of the British Prime Minister. But none the less a wedge is driven clean through German territory. East Prussia, the historic seat of the Prussian power, is cut off from the rest of Germany, and a source of deep and, we fear, permanent unrest is created in the heart of Europe. It is something that Danzig and its immediate district is to be a free city with some sort of municipal self-government under the Polish flag, but it is idle to suppose that this will permanently satisfy either Germany or the Danzigers. You cannot with impunity violate national self-consciousness or place people of a higher civilisation under those of a lower, the implacable adherents of one religion under the fanatical professors of another. This source of permanent unrest has now been only partially avoided, and incidentally Poland is assured of the permanent hostility of her mighty neighbour.

So much cause we have for rejoicing, so much for foreboding and regret. Of the other main provisions of the Draft Treaty by far the most important is that relating to the payment of the indemnity, because it governs so much else. The great interest of Europe, and of ourselves as sharing its destinies, is to revert as soon as possible to normal conditions of intercourse and national relations. For that reason it is in the highest degree undesirable to embody in the treaty what are virtually war conditions extending over a long period of time. It is not perfectly clear what is really designed in the matter of indemnities, but one clause of the Draft Treaty actually contemplates the establishment, by a Commission with authority for the purpose, of " a schedule of payments " to discharge the obligations of Germany extending over thirty years. Well, we are not going to worry about Germany for all that space of time, nor, it is safe to say, is she going to worry about us. What might be called a provisional estimate for war damages of various kinds has been put, so far as appears from a perhaps purposely obscure provision, at some five thousand millions, of which a thousand millions are to be payable within two years by means of the issue of a loan of 20,000 million marks (gold), but payments are to be " subject to postponement in certain contingencies ". As security for payment the occupation of German territory is contemplated for a period of fifteen years, with the right of re-entry in case the instalments are not duly paid. Such a period would certainly much more than exhaust British patience. Would it not be better to fix a sum which Germany may fairly hope to pay within a shorter period, and thus to do what we can to help her to pay it? At present her industries are ruined, her people enfeebled, her government in total disorder. She is not in a position to resist any terms we may choose to impose. But a wise policy will treat her no longer as an enemy to be feared and destroyed, but as part of the Europe of which we ourselves form an integral part, and which for many a long year will need all our help and all our care to save it from ruin.

THE GERMAN PROTESTS
(May 10th, 1919)

For us the fundamental question is whether we desire a
. . . peace of appeasement or a peace of violence. Nothing
is easier in the hour of uncontested victory than for the victor to
overreach himself. It happened to Germany in 1871, as Bismarck
only too truly augured at the time; nothing is easier than that it
should happen to us now. Does our true interest lie in a Germany
so crushed that she will despair of herself and fall a victim first
to anarchy and then, as would inevitably happen in a people with
so strong an instinct for discipline and order, to reaction? If
not, then we must not seek wholly to deprive her sense of
national pride and self-respect. That may be called weakness; it
is, on the contrary, the most elementary prudence and common
sense. When Germany overthrew her military autocracy it was
undoubtedly in the hope and belief that, as a democratic State
in line with the other democratic States of Europe, she might
escape from her past and be regarded as having in some degree
at least atoned for its errors. So she was told, and so we ourselves
at one time honestly believed. Who does not remember the
declarations that to a democratic Germany much might be conceded which to a Germany still militarist, still autocratic, could
not be allowed? So Germany parted with her militarism, parted
with her autocracy, only then to discover that she was still
regarded in precisely the same light as before. Such discoveries
breed disillusionment and are apt to be followed by reaction. If
the worst has happened to her in her democratic state, might she
not perhaps have fared as well, or better, had she not overthrown
her traditions and her Emperor overboard? Who shall say that
similar developments may not take place in Russia, and that, out
of the civil broils we are industriously engaged in there, foment-
ing reaction may not shortly raise its head and a Koltchak come

forward as the destined saviour of society? And what of the League of Nations? If for fifteen, perhaps thirty years, Germany is to be an occupied territory, clearly she cannot at the same time desire to enter a League which for her will represent nothing more than the force behind the occupation. It all comes back to this: our task in Europe is not to destroy but to rebuild. Even a diminished Germany will still be the greatest State in Europe. She will have to be rebuilt with the rest, and we shall have to help her.

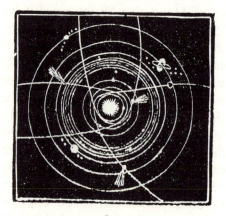

1830
ADVERTISEMENT OF ASTRONOMICAL LECTURES

AUSTRIA
(June 4th, 1919)

THE treaty with Austria excites far less interest than that with Germany, partly because, in point of fact, there is no Austria. What was Austria has ceased to exist. Part of it has become Italy, part Jugo-Slavia, part Czecho-Slovakia. Austria was in essence a composite empire, and if it had recognised its true function as a composite empire it might yet have remained. The recognition of Hungarian liberty saved it for a time; the recognition of Slavonic and Bohemian liberty might have saved it now. Something of this truth had dawned on the murdered Archduke Francis Ferdinand, but it was too late. His death was the signal for war, and the penalty of war has proved to be dissolution. Austria is to-day Austria in name only, and when the translator of the Draft Treaty, at its ceremonial presentation, spoke of her by a slip as " German Austria ", he spoke the truth, or a little less than the truth, since parts even of German Austria have gone elsewhere, and the country now bearing this historic name is a little State of some six million inhabitants, one among a series of little States carved out of the body of the ancient empire, and by no means the greatest of them. No parallel to such a disruption of a great European State is to be found since the dissolution of the Roman Empire. It is vain now to speculate whether on the whole it is likely to prove a gain or a loss to the political life of Central Europe, and whether some loose form of federation, recognising the economic and political interdependence of this extraordinarily mixed and varied body of men of many races, might not have been better. The thing is done and cannot be undone, and any reversal of the purely separatist movement can only come with time and the recognition of common interests, together with the growth of the great democratic movement on which in the end the reconciliation of the peoples and the establishment of a stable order in Europe must depend.

Meanwhile the German fragment of what was Austria stands alone and forlorn. She pleads, and pleads justly, that she must not be called upon to bear the whole burden of the sins of the old Empire, for which she is no more directly responsible than her neighbours. The terms of reparation are not yet published, but no doubt they will take account of Austria's vastly diminished area and resources. The natural course for German Austria would be to throw in her lot with Germany as part of a future federal German Republic. The country, as it stands, is not self-sufficing or organised as a separate community. What is a very small people to do with a very great capital? What is it to do with a poor soil, without coal, without ships, and cut off from the sea? As a part of Germany it might hope to recover something of its position as a member of a great State. Union with Germany is not at the moment a particularly inviting prospect, but that, after all, is a matter for the German Austrians to consider. Clearly, on every principle by which we have professed to be guided in the resettlement of Europe, on the principle of nationality, on the principle that a people has a right to determine its own allegiance, the German districts of Austria may claim liberty to link their fate with that of the Germans across the borders. By one of the strangest and least defensible provisions of the treaty with Germany they are prohibited from doing so, unless with the consent of the Council of the League of Nations. But as the decisions of the Council are valid only when unanimous, this means that any single nation represented on the Council can prohibit union. France, in fact, is left as absolute arbiter. It is only of a piece with this that, by the proposed treaty with Austria, the German-speaking districts of the Tyrol are annexed to Italy, and that we are presented with an *Austria irredenta* in place of the old *Italia irredenta*, and this, as in other cases, without any pretence of consulting the population concerned. And yet a few months ago we were told that populations were no longer to be transferred from one allegiance to another " like cattle " and we really believed it.

These are things which it is hard indeed to defend, still more to applaud. Yet there are features in the Austrian treaty which suggest hope. The reduced Austria is a purely inland State and, as such, presumably as much entitled to access to the sea as Poland or Czecho-Slovakia. This is provided for. Austria, it is laid down, " is to have free access to the Adriatic, with rights to freedom of transit over territories and in ports severed from the former Austria-Hungary ". If this free commercial access to the sea suffices for Austria, may it not also suffice for Poland? May it not even suggest a line of compromise for the thorny question of Fiume? But there is a much more important clause than this in the Austrian treaty, which we also welcome as a precedent. Austria is to undertake " to bring her institutions into conformity with the principles of liberty and justice ", and she is " to acknowledge that the obligations for the protection of minorities are matters of international concern over which the League of Nations has jurisdiction ". Specific mention is made of the protection of the distinctive language, religion, and education of the minorities, and all Austrian subjects are to be " equal before the law ". It is required that this charter of liberties or Bill of Rights shall form part of the fundamental law of the land, guaranteed by the League of Nations. This is the first clear indication we have had that the protection of racial minorities will form part of the charter of independence of the new States and will be insisted upon by the Peace Conference as a condition of recognition. Obviously it must apply all round —in Poland, in the new Rumania, in the liberated States of the old Austria no less than in the diminished Austria itself. Apart from this, we should simply be substituting a new tyranny for the old tyranny. Already the aspiring new States are protesting in advance. Their protests must be absolutely overruled. It is the vital condition of any approach to peace in Europe.

THE END OF THE WAR
(June 24th, 1919)

THE Great War is over. The terms of peace as finally drawn
up by the Allies have been accepted by the new German
Government constituted for that special purpose, and the actual
document will be signed by the new German plenipotentiaries
almost immediately. Thus is the curtain rung down on the
Titanic struggle, and within a few days of the fifth anniversary
of the Sarajevo murder—it was on June 28th, 1914—the mighty
Empire which made it the excuse for a mad aggression lies
humbled in the dust. That at least, apart from all other considerations, is matter for profound thankfulness and for some
legitimate pride. No nation which was not tough in fibre and
strong of soul could have gone through such an ordeal without
blenching, sustained by a faith which nothing could shake in
the justice of its cause. Immense issues were at stake. The
triumph of Germany, of the old Germany of autocracy and
militarism and of the ideal of power, would have meant such a
set-back to all the democratic forces of the world, to the whole
conception of a peaceful civilisation, as it might have taken
generations to undo. It would have meant the supremacy of one
great military State in Europe and the greater part of Asia, the
crushing of France with all that France and the French spirit
stand for, the military occupation of England, a menace to all
free peoples in every part of the world. And such a domination
would have been a soulless, mechanical thing, spelling degenera-
tion to the conqueror no less than ruin to the conquered. From
such things at least the world has been saved by the victory on
which this week will place the seal.

It would be well if, in the hour of defeat and bitter suffering,
the German people themselves could remember something of
these things, and could recognise in the fate that has befallen
them something more than the malice of enemies and the cruelty
of fortune. For us no less is there occasion for searching of heart.
What use have we made, what use are we making, of an un-

paralleled victory, an unequalled opportunity? Apart from the negative gain of dire disaster escaped, what fruit are we drawing from success, what permanent gain are we securing for the world? And it is here that rejoicing must be qualified and heavy doubts recur. We started on the waging of the war with high ideals, we entered with ideals yet higher and clearer on the making of the peace. And then—what happened? It would be hard, perhaps, fully to explain, still more to justify, but in the six or seven months of discussions and of bargaining among the victors the best fruits of victory have somehow disappeared, and the peace which emerges is not the peace we had promised ourselves or, as the enemy bitterly urges, which we had promised them. The peace we had hoped for would have been one which so far as possible presented elements of finality, which had careful regard, therefore, to the deeper forces by which nations are swayed, and would enlist these on the side of peace and of permanence. It would above all have refrained from outraging the sense of nationality, that potent emotion which holds masses of men of like tradition and sentiment together and renders them capable of unlimited endurance and unlimited sacrifice. We have not done this. We have, indeed, freed more than one oppressed nationality and created new States, but at more than one point we have needlessly and flagrantly violated the national sense of existing States, and above all of Germany, the greatest of them. It is a capital error which not only violates the principle on which we professed to act but introduces an element of instability into the whole structure of the peace which goes far to destroy its value. Again, the peace was to have marked and established the triumph of democracy, but what is democracy apart from the democratic spirit? And that spirit implies the sense of common interest and of mutual goodwill. How much of these has gone to the making of the peace, how much of them will remain to cement it? How much thought has been bestowed on the future of the German people in the imposition of an unlimited indemnity, in the complicated system of economic restraint and isolation by which at the same time their commerce is to be ruined and their industries forbidden to expand? It may be said that to ask for any such consideration, even though the common interest of the world demanded it, from peoples who have suffered as the French and to a less extent we ourselves have suffered, is to ask too much from human nature. We do not believe it. The real democratic forces in all the countries, here, in France, in Italy, have in this matter gone far in advance of their rulers. Had they had the making of the peace it would have been far and away a better, a juster, a more stable.

None the less must we all be profoundly thankful that there is a peace at all. Had our terms not been accepted war would have begun once more to-day at one minute past the fated hour of seven. And what kind of a war? A war of starvation telling chiefly on the children, the women, and the aged, and a war of arms from which all the glory and the adventure would have departed and only the cruelty would have remained. Well may we give thanks to have escaped so intolerable a necessity. Nor can it be doubted that the German Government has been wise. Nothing could have been gained by delay and only added misfortune could have come from resistance. No one supposes that the terms accepted now are eternal and immutable, and the day may not be distant when they will be sensibly modified. The entry of Germany into the League of Nations cannot be long postponed, and that will carry with it the right to equal rights with other nations in access to raw materials, besides giving a ground from which modifications in the existing settlement may be pressed. In his speech to the National Assembly on Sunday, Herr Bauer, the new Premier, urged as one of the grounds for acceptance of the treaty that the Allies had themselves within the last few days held out such a hope. In their Note of June 19th they pointed out that " the treaty creates the machinery for the peaceful adjustment of all international problems by discussion and consent, and whereby the settlement of 1919 itself can be modified from time to time to suit new facts and new conditions as they arise." That may be vague enough, but at least it opens a door to better things. It will be for the democratic forces of Europe to see to it that it is not closed.

ON LIBERALISM AND LABOUR

LIBERALISM AND LABOUR
(July 8th, 1912)

As a result of the three-cornered contests in the two constituencies it is quite possible that while Liberalism and
Labour are snapping and snarling at each other the Conservative
dog may run away with the bone. That would be lamentable,
but it might have its compensations if it led to a somewhat
deeper consideration of the whole question of the relations of
the two divisions of the party of progress. And first we must
ask whether they are properly described as two divisions of the
same army, or whether they ought rather to be regarded as quite
separate armies pursuing distinct ends which might at any time
bring them into direct and necessary antagonism. Few Liberals
will hesitate as to the answer to be given to this question. They
are in too complete accord with the essential aims of Labour,
with its deep social sympathies, its demand for justice to the
disinherited classes, its advocacy of international co-operation
and a pacific policy in all external relations as the condition of
internal reform, its steady refusal to permit the burden of taxation
to be replaced on the means of subsistence of the poor by any
cajoleries of tariffmongers—they see too clearly in all this the
very life and temper of the only Liberalism worthy of the name
to doubt for a moment that they have here not possible enemies
but real and trustworthy friends. Tories may shriek of con-
fiscation and parade the Socialist bogey, but the working men of
England are not Socialists in any revolutionary sense, and it will
be time enough for Liberals to refuse to co-operate cordially with
those who most directly represent them when, if ever, the danger
arises. For the present most Liberals will agree that, judged by
their action in the House of Commons, the Labour members

have shown themselves so far perhaps the very best Liberals in that assembly. Towards such a party the natural attitude of Liberals would seem to be one not of jealousy or hostility but of frank and intimate co-operation. Their aims are in substance our aims, their strength is our strength. In combination with them we can achieve great things; but any real antagonism would bring disaster to both.

Of course there are difficulties, as the present troubles indicate. The Labour party have a separate organisation, they refuse all party allegiance, they hold themselves free to run Labour candidates for Liberal seats, and in the constituencies which they hold they will not co-operate in party matters with Liberals, even where, as often happens, they depend absolutely upon Liberal support for the election of their candidates. It is a provoking situation, deeply wounding to the pure party man. But even this aspect of it has its compensations. If Labour organisations did not maintain this distinctive character and a real independence they would win no Tory support. It used to be denied that they did win any worth counting, but that can hardly now be maintained, and as the party grows in strength and reputation it is likely to draw increasingly from the ranks of the Tory working men. Liberals can hardly be expected to welcome the loss of seats which they could hold against all comers, even to representatives of another progressive party, but as till recently they held all the seats which were not held by Tories, the Labour Party could never have had any representatives in the House of Commons at all if some transfers of this sort had not taken place. The difficulty is one which arises not from the nature of things but from the defects of our electoral system. It would disappear at once and for ever with any tolerable system of proportional representation which grouped existing constituencies into larger units and gave to the different parties in each of these aggregates representation in exact proportion to the number of its adherents. There would then be no question of Labour men having to vote for Liberals or Liberals for Labour under penalty of handing over the seat to an anti-progressive utterly unacceptable to both of them. Meanwhile, and failing this radical reform, invaluable also for other reasons, there is nothing for it but mutual consideration, a fair regard for each other's numerical claims, respect for the real wishes of the progressive elements in constituencies—in a word, compromise.

1830
A MENAGERIE ADVERTISEMENT
AT KNOTT MILL FAIR

COALITION
(April 24th, 1923)

To pretend that there is no difference worth speaking of
... between the Conservative and the Liberal standpoints
is even more absurd than to pretend that over a vast part of
the field of politics there is no natural affinity between
Liberalism and Labour. Let us each rally to our standards.
There need be no exaggeration of differences and certainly no
mere partisan hostility or pretentiousness. Mr. Fildes [then M.P.
for Stockport] exhorts us to believe that "kindly feeling and
unselfish desires" are not the exclusive appanage of any single
party. Of course they are not. They are the common property
of all decent men and women, the foundation of goodness and
sobriety on which the very structure of the State must rest. But
there are different ways of giving effect to these feelings. Knowledge, tradition, sympathy, all these have their part in moulding
political opinion. Interest, too, plays its part, and, consciously or
unconsciously, an enormous part. It is not enough to have good
intentions; it is needful also to know how best to give effect to
them, and the more vividly and conscientiously men realise this
the more they will tend to separate into the groups which we call
parties and the better and more honest will be the political life
of the nation.

Surely the point we have to come to is this: Is there or is there
not need and a place, a vitally important place, for Liberalism
rightly understood in the life of the country? There can be few
men who have studied political history and in whom the spirit
of all that Liberalism stands for lives who could do anything but
shout an affirmative reply. Liberalism is not, as some would
have us believe, the shibboleth of a party, or, as Mr. Fildes
would appear to hold, a doctrine, a programme which, its main
objectives having now been achieved, may be dismissed as of

small account. It is a spirit and a principle capable in itself of growth and of ever fresh application. Historically it is the mother, in all countries, of free institutions. It is the foe of all tyranny, of the tyranny of opinion no less than of the tyranny of institutions and of administration; it is the friend of the oppressed and of the common man. It hates privilege, it seeks no advantage for a class which it would not share with all. Within the limits of what is possible it makes for equality. It hates war, as the destroyer, though it is willing to wage war in defence of things more precious than life or property—in defence of justice and of the higher interests of civilisation. In much of this, it may be said, it has no exclusive property, and it is true that its spirit is pervasive. So much the better; let all share who will. But will it be pretended that there is any party which on the whole has so persistently held before itself these ideals, or on the whole so faithfully followed them? The Labour Party will claim that it also holds by them. The Labour Party is the child of Liberalism and, should the Liberal Party ever prove unfaithful to its traditions, might claim to supplant it. But it has as yet no tradition and scant experience. It is a party of social experiment, untried and, in the minds of some of its advocates, subversive. It has yet to create a body of doctrine on which it is even itself agreed. Between Liberalism and Labour there are deep natural affinities, but for many a long day each is likely to pursue its separate path. If and when there is question of political co-operation the best elements in Liberalism will find it easiest to join hands with Labour. Mr. Fildes and his friends, it seems, would prefer to turn in another direction.

LORD OXFORD'S FAREWELL

(October 16th, 1926)

THERE is little in Lord Oxford's powerful and restrained speech at Greenock last night with which Liberals generally will not agree, though they might state a little differently the position which he states with great force but a certain limitation of outlook. The speech may be regarded as in some sort a political testament, summing up the essentials of the political faith of a lifetime and looking forward to the future to justify it. There is no Liberal worthy of the name who will not share Lord Oxford's deep faith in the permanence of Liberalism as an indestructible part of the life of the nation. And the reason for this is that it contributes certain elements of truth and conviction which are vital to our welfare and which are by both the other great parties denied or neglected. Lord Oxford finds the essentials of Liberalism in two things—in the supreme value it places on liberty and in its insistence that in all things the interest of the nation shall come before that of any section or class. Both claims are just, though they need perhaps to be qualified or supplemented. Historically the Liberal Party has, beyond doubt, been the party of liberty. It has fought for the enfranchisement of the people, for the freedom of trade, for equality before the law which is vital to freedom, for the opening of the schools and the universities, without which the freedom of the spirit is impossible and the avenues of advancement are closed. For all this it has fought, but no principle is absolute, and let it not be disguised that there was a time when the principle of liberty was misinterpreted and misapplied and when it took on the grotesquely perverted form of every man for himself and the Devil take the hindmost. Let it also not be denied that some good Tories were found to dispute these perverted maxims and that the first Factory Acts were carried by their aid.

The second great principle which Lord Oxford invoked as of the essence of Liberalism has been subject to no such partial perversion. It is true, and it is gloriously true, that Liberalism stood and stands for the supreme interest of the State, of the whole community as against the partial claims of any and every section. It is not true of any other party. The Conservative Party is, and always has been, the party of interests, of powerful sections of the community whose interests might or might not coincide with the public advantage, but which had in either case to be protected. Property is its fetish, and where the interests, real or imaginary, of property are involved the dice are apt to be heavily loaded against the common good. And in a very real sense the same thing is true of Labour. The Labour Party is based on the trade union, and the trade union, invaluable as are the services which it renders, and has rendered, is, after all, a sectional organisation with sectional interests and, as at present organised, tends naturally and almost inevitably in the wars it carries on to forget that to every such war there is a third party—the public —which pays most of the costs. Liberalism is under no such temptation. It is bound neither to the sectional interests of class or property nor to the sectional interests of the great Labour organisations; it is bound only to serve the State. But do these two great principles of freedom and disinterestedness really exhaust the vital meaning and purpose of Liberalism? Is there not something more and even deeper in which it no longer differs from Labour but is at one with it and with the elect—alas! none too many—of Conservatism? What is it that has given its true strength and driving force to Labour? Is it not the sense, deep and strong, of the sorrow, the disabilities, the miseries, the wrongs of the great masses of the poor, and does this not supply its moral impulse and its community of purpose and ideal? And does not the Liberal Party, all that is best in it, share these feelings, sympathise in the pity and the indignation, draw something of inspiration itself from the closer experience and perhaps deeper feeling of men who have themselves struggled and suffered and seen others go down? And is it not in this roused social sense and the resolve that goes with it to think and to plan and to labour for better things that the spirit and the power of Liberalism are being fed? Here at least it is not at odds with Labour; it is wholly at one with it.

Lord Oxford, we cannot doubt, is conscious of this need, and prepared to join in the search for remedies. But is he fully alive to it, and does he draw the needful moral? The moral surely is that for all these pressing and vital services the natural and necessary ally of Liberalism is Labour. Lord Oxford would seem to deprecate and fear any such partnership. He dwells not on co-operation but on independence. Independence by all means, if by that is meant the independent search for truth, the shunning of the quack remedy, the discovery with labour and searching of the true. In this again Liberalism can render essential and unique service. It is bound by no preconceptions and shibboleths wearisomely repeated and never understood such as those which hamper and distract the counsels of Labour, and it is free from the disabling prejudices and shackles, the commitments to this interest and to that, which hamper and futilise every effort even of the more well-meaning Conservatives, to evolve remedial policies of any force or value. If the general strike is the final condemnation of Labour sectionalism, the utterly futile and nerveless handling by the Conservative Government of the problem of the mines, which even a little political courage could long ago have solved, is no less the condemnation and exposure of the fatal disabilities of a Government resting on no solid basis of principle and public advantage in the conduct of even the most elementary duties of State. Truly there is room and to spare for a revived and aggressive Liberalism. . . .

ON IRELAND

LAWLESSNESS AS A POLICY
(October 11th, 1920)

SOMETHING is happening in Ireland which is new in our
... history—unexampled, at least, for more than a hundred
years—but the Ireland of to-day is not the Ireland of 1798 and
the listening world is not the same world. What was tolerated
then in the way of lawless violence by the forces of the Crown,
though even then not without strong protest from responsible
British statesmen, will not be tolerated now. It is not for nothing
that we have seen and reprobated German methods of frightful-
ness to terrorise a helpless enemy. We are not going to emulate
them in our dealings with even the most rebellious of our fellow-
countrymen. Nor are we going to accept this as the last word
of statesmanship in dealing with by far the most important and
urgent of our internal problems, a problem exceeding in importance and urgency any question of foreign policy whatever.
Englishmen are at bottom resolved to do justice to Ireland. Still
more are they resolved in the process to keep their hands decently
clean and their reputation in the world unsullied. That is where
Mr. George is failing us. Let us take the simplest test—the test
of fact as to murder and outrage by the forces of the Government, unchecked so far and unpunished by the Government, and
by no single word reprobated by the Prime Minister. The fact
is, as is known to all the world, including the Prime Minister,
that, not once or twice, but in a score of quite recent cases, the
murders of policemen—cowardly and brutal murders which
every decent man must utterly condemn—have been followed
by acts of wholesale and indiscriminate incendiarism and
violence and by quite a definite number of cases in which men
were deliberately seized, dragged from their beds or homes, and

shot. Nobody has been punished for these things. It is only within the last few days that (except for one abortive general order to the troops who are not chiefly involved) they have been even officially censured, and they are still going on, exactly as though such censure were not serious and might be quite safely ignored. What has Mr. George to say to this? Just nothing. Instead he pretends that what is really involved is the right of the police to defend themselves, to shoot when they are shot at, and to call on persons suspected of an intention to shoot to hold up their hands for examination of their pockets. He knows it is not so. He knows—nobody better—that these are not the things to which objection is taken. He knows that this is not what is called murder; he knows that real murder by the forces of the Government has been committed, and that no one high or low has even been censured. Yet he puts us off with this barefaced evasion. It will not avail. He is of all the members of the Government most responsible for these scandalous outrages, because he is by far the most powerful member of the Government. Why cannot he tell us honestly what he thinks of them? His silence is his condemnation and that of his Government. He often talks of the greatness and glory of the country. Is its honour nothing to him?

THE IRISH TREATY
(December 8th, 1921)

I T is only by degrees that we shall realise the great change
which has come over British politics by the settlement—we
venture on the unqualified term—of the Irish question. It has
been with us so long, it has entered so deeply into the very
structure of our politics and even into the character of our
national life, that its removal is like a change in the climate.
Nothing henceforth can be as it was before. It may take some
time for the change to make itself fully felt, but there it is, and
more and more it will declare itself. To take a small thing first.
There can henceforth no longer be a Unionist Party. The name
has ceased to have a meaning since the thing which gave it birth
has disappeared. When we think of what the great split of 1886
has meant to the Liberal Party, of the long years during which
it wandered in the wilderness, and of the bitter struggle through
which it sought at long last but in vain to achieve its aim of
Irish liberty, we must realise that it is a new political world indeed
which sees this aim achieved, and achieved in fullest measure
at the very moment of the party's own defeat and weakness.
The old party boundaries, largely submerged by the war, are now
more than ever dislocated and overlaid by events. When we
see Mr. Chamberlain, as leader of the Conservative Party, appealing with earnestness and eloquence to Sir James Craig to
bring his followers in Ulster into their place in the new Irish
Free State; when we see also Lord Birkenhead utterly disavow-
ing the traditional policy of his party and declaring that " he
would rather fail in translating the dream " of a reconciled
Ireland " into reality than succeed in a policy discredited by 300
years' trial, the policy of complete coercion ", which would " still
leave behind a bitter, estranged and hostile Ireland "—when

we see all this we must indeed feel that the old boundaries have crumbled.

These things are important not merely in their purely party aspect. They are even more important in their wider implications. What has happened is that a tremendous and far-reaching Liberal reform, a supreme act of Liberal statesmanship, has been carried through with the active support of men who hitherto have worked in the Conservative tradition. Does anyone suppose that Mr. Chamberlain and Lord Birkenhead, the " galloper " F. E. Smith of the old days, can be the same men after they have done this great thing as they were before they had done it? That would be strange indeed, and would go to show that the mind of man can be divided into such hard-and-fast compartments as have not hitherto been thought possible. For, be it observed, this is no case of merely conventional assent to a new policy from motives of political convenience. No one can read the speeches delivered by the two men at Birmingham on Tuesday without recognising the authentic note of sincerity. There is no honester man in politics than Mr. Chamberlain, and Lord Birkenhead spoke with all the fire and force of genuine conviction. It can hardly be but that their outlook on affairs is changed and the current of their sympathies altered. And the same thing is perhaps true of Mr. Lloyd George. The Irish peace is the crowning achievement of his career. It is the fulfilment of the earliest efforts and aspirations of his political life. It can hardly be but that it should recall him somewhat to that earlier tradition from which in these last days he has at times conspicuously departed, and that we may yet regain much of the fighter for all good Liberal causes. And what is true of the leaders is bound to react on the followers. It is hard to say how far the change may go with either, and no doubt plenty of the old Adam will survive. Yet there must be a change, a quickening, and surely much will be possible now which was not possible before. It is not for nothing that a moral and political miracle happens.

Then there is the case of Ireland herself. The remarkable article by Mr. Michael Collins which we published yesterday must not, of course, be taken as necessarily typical, because obviously Mr. Michael Collins is an exceptional man. He is a great fighter, but he is a bad hater, and he has, what the professional soldier rarely has, the steady outlook of the statesman. His article was not written after the settlement; it was written in the very thick of the debate, when the whole issue was uncertain. Yet his mind travelled right forward beyond the conflict of the moment, and the more terrible conflict which might yet follow it, to a vision of world peace, in which Ireland and Britain and the British—and Irish—daughter States and the United States itself, where Ireland counts for so much, should form a new confederation of friendly States, making a solid foundation for a yet larger unity. It is a fine vision, worthy of young Ireland entering on her inheritance, and showing what gifts for others she may bring in her hand. It is significant, too, of the new atmosphere of appeasement which may come from the healing of this old sore. It will not make for peace between this country and Ireland only; it will make itself felt far more widely. It will be felt in Washington, and there is not one of our Dominions where it will not bring a sense of relief. On our own policy also it must surely react. The problem of Egypt, the problem of India, cannot look quite the same in the light of the Irish example, and it has its lessons also for our whole policy in Europe. Ireland has her own problem of appeasement, which may test all her new-found statesmanship and strength. But there also there is hope. The quarrel between North and South in Ireland is not so old as that between Ireland and ourselves, and it should not prove more intractable.

ON MEN AND MOVEMENTS

WOODROW WILSON

(February 4th, 1924)

THE death of ex-President Wilson completes quietly, as nearly all great tragedy is completed, the most famous personal tragedy of our time. We use the word tragedy in its strict sense of the wreck of something very noble, the breaking of a column really stately and the quenching of a veritable beacon light in dampness and smoke; and all this not wholly by malign accident or the defection of weak friends or the cunning of enemies, but partly, too, through flaws in the fine steel of the victim's own character, faults venial now in any generous eyes but fatal in the time of trial as the indecision that futilised Hamlet or the mystic self-assurance that led Caesar to extinction. At the time of the Armistice in 1918 President Wilson was the leader of the world which was crying out to be led. By bringing America into the war he had ensured its ultimate result, and he had done wonders of political wisdom in timing her entry so well that virtually the whole of her entered. He seemed slow to many passionate friends of ours like Page, the great ambassador of the United States in London, whose friendship in our time of danger ought to be remembered in England as long as the war. But probably Wilson knew that the war could not have been a truly national one for Americans if they had joined in it sooner than they did. And then, when the Allied victories of the autumn of 1918 had made Germany's early collapse certain, it was Wilson whose famous Fourteen Points opened to the conquerors and the conquered the prospect of a peace honourable to both and not ruinous to what was left of the civilisation of Europe. The population of Germany believed that the Fourteen Points were an honest offer of terms morally binding on the

Allies. In their relief from fear of a peace of savage vengeance they threw off their militarist rulers, conveyed their own will-to-peace to their men in the field, and asked the Allies for an armistice. No words can describe the thrill of enthusiastic delight that passed through our own armies, too, when the Fourteen Points became known to them. Here was peace, it seemed, about to come in the inspiring form at first proclaimed by all as our object and then almost lost to sight during the souring years of indecisive warfare soiled with foul weapons and unknightly spites.

When Wilson came to Europe for the Conference, his place in popular imagination and hope throughout Europe was beyond all precedent. If by any miracle he could then have dealt, face to face, with the masses of decent, friendly, and simple people who form the bulk of every nation, a new era of peace and well-being might have opened for the world. But at Versailles he had not peoples to deal with but a few politicians fatally barred by their own past from acceptance of the rule of being just and fearing not. Some had already bound their countries over, by furtive treaties, to carry out bargains that would not square with the Fourteen Points, or indeed with any honourable rules of international conduct. French politicians had, on their country's behalf, gambled so heavily on the wild hope of wringing fantastic sums out of a Germany already half-starved that now the alternatives seemed to be French national bankruptcy or the repudiation of the Fourteen Points by which Germany had been persuaded to abridge her resistance. The Prime Minister of England had just won his commission to make the peace by a demagogic appeal to faith in his power of "making Germany pay". In the cool, quiet rooms of Versailles, with all the generous relentments and chivalrous or Christian impulses that were then stirring in Europe safely outside the shut doors, Wilson had to deal alone with that entangled, sophisticated, and materialist diplomatic world which so many Americans believe to be Europe, the whole of Europe, and nothing but Europe. It beat him. But what could he have done? Thrown up his hand and walked out when first the honourable undertakings of the

Fourteen Points were repudiated by the others? But that would have been to throw away the last hopes of his dearest project of all, the League of Nations; the others only paid it lip homage; they did not ardently wish or intend its success; still, they might agree to its formal creation as an equivalent to his acquiescence in the wrongs that they specially desired to commit; and then, the League once established, with America a leader in it and infusing her free and uninfected spirit into it, the world might at last be well on the way to a true democracy of free nations. Wilson gave in. To gain, as he hoped, something splendid for the world, he first agreed to let the peace-making go on in the dark. And then in that darkness he accepted, with the same lofty motive, complicity in the ignoble peace of revenge which has given us the Europe that we see to-day.

It was only after the bitter sacrifice had been consummated and Wilson had signed a peace abhorrent to the principles of right for which he had stood up that the smashing blow came. Out of the wreck of his generous leadership among the Allies nothing was left but the Covenant of the League of Nations. Still, in it were boundless possibilities for beneficent American predominance in the world's councils. And then all of Wilsonism that Europe had not destroyed America threw over when the Senate rejected the Covenant. Perhaps the two most tragically closed of modern political careers before Wilson's were Parnell's and Joseph Chamberlain's. Both presented in full measure the essential tragic spectacle of a powerful personality wholly given to a greater object than personal ambition, and wholly wrecked by a casual passion or a faulty calculation. But in no case has the Lucifer-like fall from great power and brilliant distinction to impotence and decay been set off with so many intensifying circumstances as in the tragedy of Wilson. For his stage was not a country, but the world; his opportunity was such as, perhaps, the world never before gave to a man, and the completeness of his collapse was made surpassingly poignant by the circumstance that in his eagerness to achieve at least one half of his ideal he had let himself desert the other half, and then lost all. We do not know enough to try to define here the failings in Wilson's equipment which contributed to his calamity. That he was incompletely endowed for his almost superhuman task seems to be the general opinion of those who knew him. But in a terribly soiled political world he was a most honest and high-minded leader; at a crisis in human civilisation he was the man who told mankind most truly and clearly the right way and the wrong; and already most of those, at any rate in Europe, who pushed him aside can see now that he knew better than they and was a better man.

LORD COURTNEY
(May 13th, 1918)

With the death of Lord Courtney there passes from us as noble and austere a figure as the public life of the past century has produced. In intellect, in political judgment, in unshakable adhesion to what he deemed the right, in the search for truth and reverence for justice—in all these things he stood out a hero among men and politicians. Personalities so strong, so individual, and so uncompromising are not apt to be popular, and, though no man could in private life be more kindly or more lovable, it was his fate as a public man to be the mentor rather than the idol of his age. Such men are extraordinarily valuable in any State, but above all in a democratic State and in one governed by public opinion. He never hesitated to confront opinion, and he never failed, in support of his own view, to produce reasons and facts which, whether accepted or not, could not be ignored. Thus, when he became a Unionist he remained to the marrow of his bones in essence a Liberal, and, while sitting on the Tory benches, he was perhaps the most effective critic in the House of Toryism, far more feared, and for that reason perhaps more disliked, by his company than anyone whose assaults could be ascribed to party motives. He ought by every title of character and capacity to have been elected Speaker of the House, but he had rolled Mr. Chamberlain in the argumentative dust, and it was not forgiven him. The causes he had most deeply at heart were unpopular causes, the sort of causes which are apt to earn for their professors the name and the odium of " crank ". He was an upholder of the rights of a small people when almost everybody else imagined they could be safely ignored; he was an upholder of peace when the people desired war; he advocated with earnestness the political rights of women through a whole generation of mockery; he was the convinced and persistent exponent of a system of representation which Mr. Lloyd George professes himself unable to understand. Events at long last have justified him in all but the last of his eccentricities, and who shall say that here, too, he will not be justified? Truly a very wise and strong and far-seeing man. When shall we look upon his like again?

1830
A DRAPERY ADVERTISEMENT

PALESTINE AND THE JEWS.
THE BALFOUR DECLARATION
(November 9th, 1917)

IT is an accident, but a happy accident, that the important declaration of the Government on the subject of the future of Palestine should appear on the morrow of the British military successes in that profoundly interesting and important country. We speak of Palestine as a country, but it is not a country; it is at present little more than a small district of the vast Ottoman tyranny. But it will be a country; it will be the country of the Jews. That is the meaning of the letter which we publish to-day, written by Mr. Balfour to Lord Rothschild for communication to the Zionist Federation. It is at once the fulfilment of an aspiration, the signpost of a destiny. Never since the days of the Dispersion has the extraordinary people scattered over the earth in every country of modern European and of the old Arabic civilisation surrendered the hope of an ultimate return to the historic seat of its national existence. This has formed part of its ideal life, and is the ever-recurring note of its religious ritual. And if, like other aspirations and religious ideals which time has perhaps worn thin and history has debarred from the vitalising contact of reality, it has grown to be something of a convention, something which you may pray for and dream about, but not a thing which belongs to the efforts and energies of this everyday world; that is only what was to be expected, and in no degree detracts from the critical importance of its entry to that world and the translation of its religious faith into the beginnings at least of achievement. For that is what the formal and considered declaration of policy by the British Government means. For fifty years the Jews have been slowly and painfully returning to their ancestral home, and even under the Ottoman yoke and amid the disorder of that effete and crumbling dominion they have succeeded in establishing the beginnings of a real civilisation. Scattered and few, they have still brought with them schools and industry and scientific knowledge, and here and there have in truth made the waste places blossom as the rose. But for all this there was no security, and the progress, supported as it was financially by only a small section of the Jewish people and by a few generous and wealthy persons, was necessarily as slow as it was precarious. The example of Armenia and the wiping out of a population fifty-fold that of the Jewish colonies in Palestine was a terrible warning of what might at any time be in store for these. The Great War has brought a turning-point. The return of the Turk in victorious power would spell ruin; the rescue of this and the neighbouring lands from Turkish misrule was the first condition of security and hope. The British victories in Palestine and in the more distant eastern bounds of the ancient Arab empire are the presage of the downfall of Turkish power; the declaration of policy by the British Government to-day is the security for a new, perhaps a very wonderful, future for Zionism and for the Jewish race.

Not that it is to be supposed that progress in such a movement can be other than slow. Nor does the British Government take any responsibility for it beyond the endeavour to render it possible. In declaring that " the British Government view with favour the establishment in Palestine of a national home for the Jewish people, and will use its best endeavours to facilitate the achievement of this object ", the Government have indeed laid down a policy of great and far-reaching importance, but it is one which can bear its full fruit only by the united efforts of Jews all over the world. What it means is that, assuming our military successes to be continued and the whole of Palestine to be brought securely under our control, then on the conclusion of peace our deliberate policy will be to encourage in every way in our power Jewish immigration, to give full security, and no doubt a large measure of local autonomy, to the Jewish immigrants, with a view to the ultimate establishment of a Jewish

State. Nothing is said, for nothing can at present be said, as to the precise form of control during the period of transition, which may be a long one. Doubtless the form of government, or ultimate authority, would be similar to that which may be set up in other and neighbouring regions from which the authority of the Ottoman Government may be removed. Palestine has a special importance for Great Britain, because in the hands of a hostile Power it can be made, as our experience in this war has shown, a secure base from which a land attack on Egypt can be organised. The attack in this war has been feeble because the preparations were wholly inadequate and the force ill-organised. But with a European Power in possession it might easily be made infinitely more formidable, and might even make our position in Egypt untenable. Our interest, and practically our sole particular interest, in Palestine is that this danger should be effectually guarded against, and that no Power should be seated in Palestine which is or under any circumstances is likely to be hostile to this country. That condition would be fulfilled by a protectorate exercised by this country alone or in conjunction with, say the United States, or by the United States alone, or by an international body designating us as its mandatory on conditions to be mutually agreed. Such may be the ultimate development of our policy, but in any case the fundamental principle now laid down will condition it. We recognise, and we shall continue to recognise, the Holy Land as the " national home of the Jewish people ".

Other conditions are involved, and are stated or implied in the present declaration. The existing Arab population of Palestine is small and at a low stage of civilisation. It contains within itself none of the elements of progress, but it has its rights, and these must be carefully respected. This is clearly laid down in the letter, which declares that " nothing shall be done which may prejudice the civil and religious rights of existing communities in Palestine ". There is, again, the question of the custody of the Holy Places, in which Russia and France are alike warmly interested. This is not expressly referred to, but will undoubtedly have to be carefully considered, and, with goodwill, should present no difficulties. The final words of the letter may not, at the first glance, be perfectly intelligible. Not only are the rights of existing communities in Palestine to be protected, but it is also declared that " the political status enjoyed by Jews in any other countries " are in no way to be prejudiced. That may appear a rather far-fetched precaution against an imaginary danger, and so perhaps it is. But if anxiety is anywhere felt on this score, it is well that, so far as we are concerned, it should be allayed. And anxiety, though it may not be widespread, no doubt there is. It is feared that Jews who have made their home in foreign lands and have accepted to the full the new allegiance may suffer in esteem, if not actually in political status, by the creation of a distinctive Jewish State, and may come, in a new sense, to be regarded as aliens. No such danger can possibly arise in this country or any other country which, like the United States, welcomes its Jewish citizens on a footing of absolute equality. In countries where anti-Semitism still prevails it is not likely to be given a fresh edge, but the risk, such as it is, must be run, and it is to be feared the declaration in the letter cannot prevent it, though it constitutes a protest in which, at the Peace Conference, other Powers may be invited to join. But in any case what is this for the Jewish race compared to the hope and the promise of re-entry on their birthright? A small people they must be, for Palestine will hold but perhaps one-fourth of the scattered Jewish race; but they were a very small people when they gave two religions to the world, and, seated in their old land, they may yet become the vital link between East and West, between the old world and the new.

THE GOVERNMENT OF INDIA.
THE MONTAGU REPORT
(July 6th, 1918)

WE publish to-day a full summary of the recommendations of the Montagu Commission's Report on the
Government of India. The Report itself is a long and extremely
able document of nearly two hundred Blue-book pages, dealing
not merely with the changes needed in the structure of Indian
government, but with the history of its development and the
conditions of Indian society in relation to which any changes
now made must be considered. It deals with all the main aspects
of this vast and supremely important subject—with local self-
government in so far as it has already been called into existence,
with the governments of the provinces into which India is
divided, with the central government and its relation to the provincial governments and to the Secretary of State and Parliament, with the reform movement in India and the proposals of
the Indian National Congress, with the governments of the
Native States, with the fundamental principles on which the
development of free institutions in India should proceed, with
the method of advance, and with the possibilities of the future.
But the scale and the complexity of the inquiry must not be
allowed to deter interest or unduly to delay action. This is no
ordinary inquiry and, whatever the fate of some investigations
consigned to oblivion in Blue-books, no such fate can attend this.
The mighty argument once entered upon must be steadily
pursued and courageously concluded. There need be no undue
haste; there must be no sort of unnecessary delay. Any Government which provoked such an issue and then sought to evade it
would sign its own death-warrant. This, we are convinced, is
recognised by all who have any share of responsibility in this

great matter. It will supply the final test of capacity, of courage, and of statesmanship.

It may be thought that a problem so great and so critical cannot properly be dealt with in the midst of the overwhelming preoccupations of war, and that its solution should be postponed to more leisurely times. It cannot be. It is precisely the war and India's part in the war which have given the question its urgency by awakening the pride, and in a real sense the national self-consciousness of India, no less than by the contagion of the very principles of democracy and the political rights of peoples, for which it has been proclaimed far and wide that the war is by us being fought. But the question is no longer open to argument. When, on August 20 last, the momentous declaration was made in the House of Commons that the policy of the Government, with which the Government of India was in full accord, was that of " the gradual development of self-governing institutions with a view to the progressive realisation of responsible government in India as an integral part of the British Empire " the die was cast. No such promise can be made and its fulfilment then indefinitely postponed. The despatch of the Montagu Commission was the immediate result, and the further steps needed for giving effect to our declared policy must follow in due course and with no unnecessary delay. Yet it must be admitted that no more momentous and difficult constructive task was ever undertaken by a governing Power. " Self-government " might have been understood as implying simply the transfer of the control of the machine of government from a British bureaucracy to one mainly or wholly composed of Indians, with the mass of the population taking, as at present, practically no part in the conduct of affairs; in other words, the substitution of one oligarchy for another. " Responsible government " means something much larger and more difficult, but also full of a far greater and more enduring promise. It is the well-understood term for the largest measure of popular and representative government in a colony or Dominion. It is so understood by the Commission, and it is to this and to no less lofty a goal that all its recommendations are directed. The goal is necessarily distant, but its recognition makes all the difference to the scheme of reform now proposed and to all the steps hereafter to be taken in its future development. We are now to lay the foundation on which the whole fabric of Indian government must hereafter rest. It may be said, and no doubt it will be said, that the materials do not exist, that responsible government implies an electorate capable of exercising it, and that such an electorate has in India yet to be created; that, moreover, the whole conception of popular or representative government, or democracy as it is understood in this country and in other Western countries who have in large degree accepted our model, is alien to Eastern ideas and incapable of transplantation and effective growth in Eastern soil. It may be so, but it has yet to be proved that it is so. Some surprising developments have taken place of late years in the Eastern mind and in Eastern institutions, of which Japan furnishes the most striking examples, and the old confident commonplaces of the "East is East and West is West" kind have received some rude shakes. Nevertheless, the magnitude and difficulty of our task are as obvious as its novelty and courage, and progress, as was stated in the August declaration, can only be tentative and gradual.

It is a great experiment. . . . It may not satisfy the more extreme Nationalist demand, but it is far more democratic than the scheme of the Congress, which looks rather to the substitution of an Indian for a British directorate than to the extension of governing powers to new classes of the community. While further inquiry will no doubt suggest improvements, it will, we should hope, be recognised by all the more stable elements of Indian opinion for what it is—one of the boldest and most far-reaching schemes of enfranchisement ever proposed. It will meet with plenty of opposition from those who dislike and dread the whole principle of self-government on which it is based; it ought to receive no less energetic support from those to meet whose hopes and needs it is designed.

6

THE *MANCHESTER GUARDIAN*
SINCE SCOTT

C. P. SCOTT'S SUCCESSORS

For ten years before C. P. Scott's death the editor-designate had been his third son, E. T. Scott. His eldest son, Laurence, had died in 1908, after a short but promising career on the paper. His second son, John, had become its business manager. Edward Scott (born 1883) had joined the staff in 1912 and, after an interval of war service (during which he became a prisoner in Germany), took more and more responsibility in the conduct of the paper. C. P. Scott formally handed over the editorship in July 1929, but E. T. Scott filled it for barely three years. He lost his life in a boating accident on Windermere on April 22, 1932, less than four months after his father's death.

Overshadowed, even cramped, for so long by the prestige and authority of his father, Edward had little chance to display his great qualities of command and leadership. Yet none who knew him could doubt that in him the paper would have had an editor as firm in purpose as C. P. Scott, and fully as independent in judgment. He combined the gifts of a good man of business and a writer and reasoner of strength with a character of singular charm. The thing that stands out most in one's memories of him is his intellectual honesty. He never wrote or thought as a party man or the follower of this or that economic school. He was uninfluenced by authority or expediency. His conclusions were often unexpected, not to say daring, but they were those of a mind remarkably free from prejudice, open to welcome the heretical, and always logical and searching in its processes. The integrity of his intellectual judgment was as great an inspiration to his colleagues in its way as was the nobility of his father's humanism. For twenty years, with the brief interval of the war, he gave himself to the paper; after an apprenticeship under an exacting master he succeeded, as his father's grip slackened, to increasing responsibilities and cares. The issues of the 'twenties had become more economic than political and Edward Scott handled them with a mastery that concealed great pains. His knowledge, for instance, of the intricacies of the reparations controversy was profound, and it was a joy to see him puncture the ingenuities of a Churchillian Budget or chart a conciliatory course of humane principle in the jungle of the great mining disputes. He left his mark on the paper especially in the broadening of its financial services, the extension of its treatment of economic and industrial subjects, and the establishment of its subsidiaries, the *Manchester Guardian Weekly* and the *Manchester Guardian Commercial*, with its well-known Reconstruction and other supplements.

E. T. Scott was succeeded as editor by W. P. Crozier who had then been on the paper for twenty-eight years, and who was to direct it for another twelve. Crozier's influence on its structure, if not on its policy, began long before his editorship, became apparent towards the end of the first world war, and increased steadily throughout the following years. Beginning in the sub-editors' room, he was after a few months given charge of the foreign news, which every year was becoming more and more important and to which the paper had always given greater attention than any of its contemporaries outside London. After making his mark here he was added to the leader-writing staff. While continuing his work as a leader-writer Crozier next accepted the post of news editor, a comparatively new rank in the journalistic hierarchy and one hitherto unknown in the *Guardian* office. From the outset he planned to modernise the paper and it is not too much to say that in the course of the next ten years he transformed it. The responsibility for the innovations was, of course, shared; often it was C. P. Scott or E. T. Scott who suggested their general idea, but it fell in the main to Crozier to carry them out.

Thus foreign correspondents were appointed in the principal countries—full time representatives in Paris, Berlin, Vienna and Rome, and other regular correspondents in the Dominions, the United States, Russia, Poland, Greece, Spain, Belgium, Egypt, China, India. Crozier organised the whole of this service and kept in constant touch with the men who provided it. Letters to the Editor had always been a notable feature of the paper under Scott, but Crozier when he became editor developed it and gave it greater prominence. The principle of catholicity was carefully preserved; the columns were never allowed to be one-sided.

In pictures and maps Crozier again followed the Scott policy, but developed it enormously. The picture pages were particularly notable for their views of rural England. Only the other day an American reader wrote pleading for more of them; he had, he said, come to love the English countryside through *Guardian* photographs, although he had never seen it.

The greatest reform Crozier brought about in the structure of the paper was in classification. To keep the same kind of news or article in the same place every day may seem a simple matter but it is really most difficult under conditions of daily paper production. It is easy enough to fill the pages anyhow by shovelling in the type as it becomes ready until they will hold no more —that was the usual nineteenth-century practice with most newspapers—but it is far harder to classify the material for these pages, to fit it in to comply with a pre-arranged plan, and yet to prevent the " make-up " from having a formal, stereotyped appearance. The task calls for the active co-operation of many hands and firm control at the head.

The *Guardian* had always concerned itself with the interests of women, political and other, but it came only reluctantly to the idea of a " women's " or " home " page. Crozier gave much thought and labour to this new feature. Newspapers as a whole were slow to realise that the public would be as much interested in criticism of the new forms of entertainment provided by the cinema and broadcasting as they had long been in the criticism of plays, music-halls and concerts. Notices of films are universal now, but when Crozier introduced them they were a novelty and it was some time before other papers saw their news-value. Much the same thing can be said about broadcasting in the critical appreciation of which the *Guardian* was almost an innovator. Other ways in which the paper widened its appeal, either on Crozier's initiative or with his encouragement, were a great extension of the space devoted to sport, especially at the schools and universities, weekly articles on motoring and bridge, detailed reports of all important chess tournaments at home and abroad, and a daily crossword puzzle.

It remains to point out wherein Crozier resembled his great predecessor and wherein he differed from him. Both had a deep attachment to Oxford and tended to look to their old university for recruits. Both were convinced Liberals; both were conscious of a mission " to make righteousness readable ", but determined that no appeals to vulgar prejudice or to debased appetites should be used to attract the crowds. Both wrote good plain English and enjoined it on their staff and disliked equally the clichés of journalese and literary preciosity. Almost alone among editors Scott began his wonderful career at the top, whereas Crozier had served for years in the ranks. This gave him the advantage of knowing from personal experience how each department did its work and what its difficulties were. There was no task that fell to the journalist that he could not do himself, and do extremely well—from reporting a football match to devising make-up, from writing a weekly record of the progress of a war to cutting down the contribution of a long-winded correspondent. He had a passion for terseness and a horror of verbiage, and would quote with approval Scott's remark to him : " Depend upon it, Crozier, there is very little written for a newspaper that would not be improved by being made shorter."

Some twenty years ago, in the days of his news-editorship, this estimate of Crozier's influence on the paper was written by a colleague :

He suggests a wheel of immense importance in a highly complicated machine, revolving steadily and remorselessly and causing a multitude of other wheels, great and small, to revolve with it. It is hard for the younger generation to realise that the machine used to work and the light to shine without him; and yet they undoubtedly did. Perhaps the truth is that the extra wheel has made the machine run a little faster, and that the old illuminant glows more brightly through a clearer glass. Perhaps it is rather more than this. Turn up the files of fifteen or twenty years ago and compare them with those of to-day. It is as though a Welsbach mantle had been slipped over a Bunsen burner.

This is a professional judgment which the journalist at least will appreciate. In the twelve years of Crozier's editorship the *Guardian* kept its place as an independent organ of opinion and held its own technically in a period of rapid change in methods of newspaper production. It was the paper's good fortune to have at its head in those years a " working journalist " of something approaching genius.

Crozier died on April 16, 1944, and was succeeded as editor by A. P. Wadsworth, who had been a member of the staff since 1917: first as reporter, then as industrial correspondent, leaderwriter and assistant editor.

LIBERALISM AND LABOUR

THE *Manchester Guardian*, when Scott came to it, had long
been cautiously Whig. It looked on the rising Radicalism
of the late 'sixties and 'seventies with scepticism, even distaste.
It would have none of payment of members (that would
" degrade politics to a trade ") or women's suffrage; it disliked
the secret ballot. But it was reconciled to compulsory education,
more State intervention (in the interests of safety) for mines and
railways, more factory legislation, more stringent laws on public
health. The paper was borne along on the broad current of
developing Liberal feeling, but without enthusiasm. In 1872 it
could rebuke Sir George Trevelyan for making extravagant
promises of social reform—" even Conservatism, if sober, is
better than Liberalism drunk." Yet it had no sympathy with
those who thought it " incredibly shocking " that working men
should seek to enter Parliament; the nation would not be a great
loser if the entry of a few artisans into the House tended to
impair its " clubbable character ". There was, it admitted, the
danger that working men might become delegates, not representatives, and if enough of them were delegated from " trade
societies " there might be class legislation of an intolerable kind.
Still, that seemed remote, and the risks were worth running.
Towards organised labour the *Guardian* was cold and a little
fearful. It remembered the Sheffield " outrages "; " trade
agitators " were a menace, and the demand for shorter hours
futile. It could " confidently be asserted (in 1871) that no law
of the land will ever be able to restrict hours to nine a day "; it
would be " unjust, oppressive and finally inoperative ".

A few months later the finality of economic prophecy was
tempered about nine hours, but still held about eight. Twenty
years later the same columns could approve the eight-hour day
of the New Unionism as a fine ideal and support the miners'
Eight Hour Bill as " a measure for the expansion of industrial

freedom ". The *Guardian* had become positive instead of negative. It had been lukewarm towards Chamberlainite Radicalism, but by 1885 it had come to hold that " Radicals and Moderates are equally necessary to each other . . . the fault of the Radical is that perhaps he has too much faith, that of the modern Liberal that he has too little." And in the next decade it came to range itself ever more deliberately with the men of faith.

The effective beginnings of the modern Labour movement lie in these years and, as has been elsewhere described, the *Guardian* treated the new forces with a sympathy and fairness that were far in advance of the bulk of Liberal opinion. It adopted most of the Radical measures, many of which it had formerly opposed, and (in 1892) could treat the differences between Mr. Sidney Webb and " any ordinary Liberal " as lying " more in the latter's dislike to commit himself to the reasoned Collectivist faith which Mr. Webb finds necessary, than in hostility to his suggestions for legislation ". It saw no inherent conflict and every cause for association between the more vigorous Liberalism and the rising Socialism.

So much recent writing about the history of the modern social movement has been a rather naïve recital of the " inevitability of gradualness " that it is easy to forget that to the Progressive of that day the 'nineties were a time of reaction. The sixteen years between 1886 and 1902 had something in common with our later two decades between the wars. The period, as Hobhouse wrote,

> witnessed an ebb of Liberal ideas, not in this country alone, but throughout the world. It was a time in which the older conceptions of civil, political and religious liberty lost their vital force; when the middle class, frightened by the first murmurings of Socialism from the cause of progress, and satisfied with the rights which they themselves had won, transferred their influence to the side of established order when the dominant social philosophy of the day confronted the plea for justice and equality with the doctrine that progress depends on the survival of the stronger in the struggle for existence. The idealism which is essential to modern nations was diverted from the cause of social reform to that of imperial expansion.

But it was in this disheartening time of "revolt against the Liberal idea", when Liberalism itself was divided and confused, that the *Guardian* found its soul and achieved its influence. It had the satisfaction of having contributed in no small part to the great revival of Liberalism when it came in 1906.

Scott, however, never conceived of Liberalism as a strictly party affair. He, and those who wrote under him, thought always in terms of what he called "the progressive movement". What was important was that those who were agreed on reforming measures should work together to secure them. In the days of Liberal strength this implied toleration for the rising Labour minority. When, in the years just before 1914, Labour began to assume a new aggressiveness, Scott was pleading for "frank and intimate co-operation" between those "two divisions of the same army"; and not least because the Labour members showed themselves "the very best Liberals" in the House. If their interests in the constituencies clashed, the way of accommodation lay through Proportional Representation; "there would then be no question of Labour men having to vote for Liberals or Liberals for Labour men under penalty of handing over the seat to an anti-progressive utterly unacceptable to both of them". But the Liberal Party, when it had the opportunity, did not take Scott's advice—perhaps the cardinal mistake of its history.

The end of the war of 1914–18 broke the Liberal Party, but established the Labour Party as an independent force. Scott now turned, until the end of his life, to preaching the simple practical doctrine of co-operation as the only way of saving the country from Conservative domination. This he saw as the more necessary because the unhappy divisions of Liberalism—first during and after the Coalition, then over the general strike, then over the crisis of 1931—weakened the Liberal wing of the "party of progress".

It is impossible in any broad way to dissociate Liberalism from Labour [he wrote in November 1922]. They have the same root in aspiration and purpose, the same resolve at all cost to place the welfare of the community above that of any class—Labour as representing by far the most numerous class may sometimes tend to forget this, but not for long—the same sense of community with other nations as opposed to a narrow and exclusive nationalism. They may, and often will, differ as to the wisest means, but their aims do not differ. At present they are forced into an unnatural antagonism by the limitations of an antiquated electoral system wholly unsuited to the needs of the day, but the moment that is reformed and proportional representation gives us a true mirror of the nation the truth will emerge. Between them Liberalism and Labour constitute the party of progress in this country. They may never combine, but they should always understand, and in the main support, each other.

The Liberal Party, he argued, must make itself more Radical. There were some who played with the idea of an anti-Socialist Centre party, but "Liberalism, unless it be constructive, is a barren and an impotent thing, and, reunion or no reunion, its destiny is the dust-heap".

The defeat of the Baldwin Government at the end of 1923 brought Scott's prescription to the test. For months he had been preparing the way, and there are grounds for thinking that his influence and his persistent advocacy of Liberal–Labour co-operation were decisive in determining the action of the Liberal Party. Lloyd George, at least, afterwards said that MacDonald owed his office to Scott, and that the Liberal leaders (apart from Lloyd George) first toyed with the idea of taking office themselves with Conservative support. There were some days of uncertainty before Asquith took the line of independence. Scott, of course, wanted much more than that. He tried hard to build a bridge between MacDonald and the Liberals and to establish a working agreement. MacDonald was touchy and suspicious; even then he had a greater affinity for Conservatives than Liberals. Scott rose superior to rebuffs; party was secondary. "For what, after all, does the Liberal Party exist? Is it not in order to carry Liberal measures, and if it can carry them by the aid of the Labour Party, or if the Labour Party can carry them by its aid, why are they to be regarded as in any way the worse?" Throughout the short lifetime of the Labour Government he argued forcefully for this co-operation. "What smallness of spirit is it which would repudiate friends because they may one day become rivals?" The failure of the experiment was a bitter disappointment, all the more keen because the collapse was so unnecessary.

In the years between the first and the second Labour Governments the *Manchester Guardian* kept constantly to its theme of the working alliance, though neither side regarded it with much favour, and Scott was often reproached for his iteration of a doctrine which was not palatable to party men. The general strike did not weaken Scott's insistence on this counsel of reason. He refused to take the ultra-legalist line or to treat the strike as a revolutionary act. As may be seen from his comments on Asquith's political farewell (given elsewhere in this book) and from a speech at the National Liberal Club in the autumn of 1926, he was not stampeded by fear of trade union excesses; a working alliance with Labour was better than Toryism. The paper had given strong support to the Liberal intellectual revival which found expression in the Liberal Yellow Book of 1928, and to Lloyd George's new Radicalism. Scott welcomed this with enthusiasm. The scales, however, were weighted against the Left unless the Left would combine. As the Baldwin Government was drawing to its close, he looked forward with keenness to a new period of progressive alliance. "In making choice of an ally," he wrote in February, 1929, "shall we not be compelled to look rather to those with whom we largely agree than to those whom it is our first object to get rid of?" And when the Labour Government was formed, in the last political leader he wrote, he warned against a repetition of the disaster of 1924: "We have at present in power a Government which on the whole we can trust alike for a sane policy abroad and a progressive policy at home."

Under other hands, but with Scott's approval, the *Manchester Guardian* gave critical support to the Labour Government until the storm of 1931 overwhelmed it. The binding thread held even then. The paper viewed with the gravest misgivings the Liberal Party's continuance in the National Government after the election. At the election it gave its support to those candidates, whether Liberal or Labour, who opposed a Government under Conservative domination. Again, in 1935—and in 1945—

it applied the same pragmatic test of how best to secure a Progressive against a Conservative majority. The *Guardian* welcomed the War Coalition of 1940, as it had welcomed the Coalitions of 1915 and 1917, because it was the best means of winning the war, and gave the Government unstinted, if critical, support. It viewed the break-up of that magnificent partnership with regret, but once the decision had been taken and a " peace election " called (as in 1918) it held that the national fortunes were better entrusted to the parties of the Left than to those of the Right. And when the verdict was given, the paper could not fail to be gratified that, on the whole, the " Progressive movement " had won. The " silent revolution " of the ballot-box which had confounded all the prophets it regarded as " the kind of Progressive opportunity that comes only once in every few generations ".

The *Guardian* has now been politically, for sixty years, a paper of " the Left ". The period has seen many party vicissitudes. The Conservative Party has twice suffered crushing defeat. Labour, the last comer, was almost extinguished in 1931. The Liberals, in eclipse in the 'nineties, had their great day under C.B. and Asquith, and then twenty-five years of schism and electoral decline. They are now much weaker in Parliament than was the new force of Labour when it first emerged as a party group in 1906. But they represent, on any true reflection, a body of opinion immensely larger than their vote, though that is substantial; with proportional representation they would have come out of even the cataclysm of 1945 fifty strong and have held the political balance. It may have to be confessed that the sheer reason of P.R. is now less attractive to the bigger parties than it has ever been. But it is too soon to assert that the Liberal Party has dropped out of the race as an independent party and that the " Progressive movement " of the future has to be sought either in Labour with a faint Liberal fringe or in a liberalised Conservatism. We cannot tell what in these days of world convulsion the British political alchemy may produce. How long will the Labour Party itself remain cohesive? Is it not in danger of outrunning the Left sentiment of the country which, though strong, perhaps expressed itself in exaggerated form in July 1945?

Two things, moreover, make the present Labour Party differ from that of the 'twenties. First, it is no longer dominated in the House by the trade union members; it has ceased to be the party of an " interest " and has become rather more representative of the social classes that make up the nation. Secondly, it has become more definitely Socialistic. The future historian will trace the stages by which the idea of public ownership came to dominate Labour's domestic policy. As late as 1929–31 it was largely academic, and the party leaders had no burning determination to apply it to major industries, whatever lip-service they paid to it as a programme-piece. The Great Depression increased its talismanic value; the Baldwinian and Chamberlainite experiments in State-aided industrial self-government (usually of a restrictive kind) widened the habit of State intervention. The war, with its huge accretion of powers to the State, left a situation in which, whatever party had been returned, the atmosphere must have been strongly collectivist. The question was whether that collectivisation should be diminishing or increasing. Having the majority, and having its programme commitments, the Labour Government has chosen to put its first instalment of Socialist measures through. There are wide misgivings whether it has not forced the pace too rapidly. But, as so often in our political history, the issues are not clear-cut. In every field it has yet chosen there is no plain antithesis between public and private enterprise. In every case some amount of State intervention is inevitable: it is mainly a matter of pace and degree. The consequence of this is a blurring of party lines. The tests are not those of doctrine but of practical efficiency, of what gives fullest scope for the individual's contribution to the common good, of what secures the widest measure of social and economic equality. A progressive paper must hold itself free to support and to oppose, to praise and to criticise, without being tied to the decisions of any party. The politician's line is frequently tactical, if not actually cynical; the newspaper, as a guide of public opinion, has to look rather farther ahead.

But the Liberalism for which the *Manchester Guardian* has stood finds the justification of the "Progressive movement" even more in international than in home affairs. With the lessening of the pressure of poverty and the increase of equality of opportunity, which Liberalism and Labour have held as common aims, has gone a broad identity of view on the great questions of peace and international government, and the place of the British Commonwealth and Empire in the world. This was always present to Scott's mind in the days when the small Labour Party in the House (apart from its pacifist element) took the Radical line, and even more in the years of upheaval after 1918, when Labour was so consistently the asserter of Wilsonian principles. In the inter-war years there were few international issues on which Labour and Liberals found themselves in divergence. In their attitude towards German reparations, disarmament and security, towards the diplomatic recognition of Russia, the rise of Italian Fascism, the authority of the League, the terrorism and predatory aims of Nazism, right down to the great test of Munich, the parties of the Left were at one. A wide gulf separated them from the men in power.

The *Manchester Guardian* can look back on its attitude to international affairs in those years with some pride. It seemed a losing battle; Liberalism was a decaying faith in Europe; British official policy was too often timid and given to appeasement. Scott had been greatly interested in, and disturbed by, the growth of Italian Fascism; the care and fulness with which, in its foreign correspondence, the paper described the stages in the suppression of Italian liberal movements won it the honour of having its circulation prohibited in Mussolini's Italy. When the German counterpart of Fascism began to gather force the *Manchester Guardian*, more fully than perhaps any other English paper, devoted itself to the exposure of the crimes of Nazism. In the field of policy this was, perhaps, W. P. Crozier's greatest contribution to the paper he enriched in so many ways. He showed much courage and risked the displeasure of readers —and of the British Government—by the persistence with which he kept the distasteful subjects of the extermination of the Jews and the cruelties of the concentration camps to the front. The paper was prohibited from circulation in Germany, and the *Manchester Guardian Weekly* which, under the Weimar Republic, had had a large circulation for a Berlin-printed edition, could no longer be distributed there. F. A. Voigt who, as the paper's Berlin correspondent, had studied the pathology of post-war Germany since 1919, organised an underground service of news from inside Germany, messages that came out under the noses of the German authorities. The paper had no illusions as to where Hitlerism was leading or as to the futilities of British Conservative policy in face of Hitler's rising demands. The revelations of the Nazi documents produced at Nuremberg are the historical justification of those who refused to be deceived when to be deceived was the way to popularity and a quiet life.

The " Progressive movement " stood out in two other respects —in its attitude to the new forces let loose by the Russian Revolution and in its attitude towards India and the dependent and colonial peoples. The *Manchester Guardian* welcomed the Russian Revolution with a sympathy that was not dismayed when the Liberal Revolution was submerged in a Communist one. Through its correspondents in Russia during the Revolution, M. Philips Price, Arthur Ransome and Michael Farbman, it treated the young Republic with respect and understanding. It opposed strongly the policy of intervention and later the exclusion which, as we know now, implanted in the Russian mind such deep suspicions of the Western world. If, now, after the second World War, the original democratic impulses of the new Socialist society seem to have been so largely turned into imperialist and expansionist channels the " Progressive movement " has not wholly lost trust in the possibilities of fruitful co-operation for world peace and the extension of social justice.

Nowhere did the quality of Scott's liberalism stand out more than in the continuous attention he gave to the movements for full self-government in India and Egypt, for a Jewish National Home in Palestine, and for an advanced policy of social welfare and the extension of democratic responsibility in the dependent Empire. In this field, often neglected by the bulk of the British

Press, the *Guardian* has tried to be consistent, and in none has it seen causes for which it worked make greater advances and become more commonly accepted.

Now new problems press forward, but in essence they are old. The United Nations is the League with a new face, and the same spirit that was needed to make the League work must be awakened if the United Nations and its complex of organisations are not to fail us too. Peace-making after the war of 1939–45 raises all the difficulties—and more—that faced us after the war of 1914–18. The *Manchester Guardian* then made its contribution, notably in the shape of the series of Reconstruction Numbers (in four languages) edited by John Maynard Keynes, to the understanding of the economic problems of recovery. To-day the international spirit is weaker, the bonds of European civilisation have worn thinner. But the fundamental conditions of peace are unchanged, and the re-establishment of the European community (hinging on the wise treatment of the defeated peoples) and the building of a firm world organisation are ends to work toward in faith, if with tempered hope. At least we know better than did the peace-makers of the last generation what, in this atomic age, are the penalties of failure.

THE CONTROL OF THE *GUARDIAN*

J. L. HAMMOND in his life of C. P. Scott has described his attitude towards the financial side of newspaper ownership, and how the paper, after he became its owner, was "carried on as a public service and not for profit". From the time he acquired the *Manchester Guardian* in 1907 until his death Scott never drew a salary exceeding £2,500, devoting all profits to strengthening and improving the paper.

The profits were never large and the ever increasing capital requirements of newspaper production swallowed most of them. The reserves, however, did prove sufficient to carry out the purchase of the *Manchester Evening News* over the years 1923 to 1930. The two papers had started under common ownership but, although always produced by the same plant, they had drifted apart after the death of J. E. Taylor in 1905. C. P. Scott approved this purchase as a sound business move but he never exercised any editorial influence on the *Manchester Evening News*, the guiding hand of which was Sir William Haley's until he went to the B.B.C. in 1943. The two staffs are distinct and their conduct and direction independent in every way. The purchase proved invaluable, financially, to the *Manchester Guardian*, enabling it to weather successfully a number of difficult years which might otherwise have proved crippling.

There are always people who find it difficult to conceive that a newspaper can be independent, and that if it advocates this or that opinion it is not serving some base pecuniary motive. When the *Guardian* under Scott and John Edward Taylor opposed the Boer War there were the credulous who professed to believe that Kruger must own a block of its shares. And since C. P. Scott's death the removal of his powerful and well-known personality and the constant changes in newspaper control have made rumours recurrent. It may, therefore, be of interest to carry the story of the business side of the paper down to 1946, and to explain the steps that have been taken to establish its editorial and financial independence.

In 1913 C. P. Scott made the first move to ensure, as far as he could, continuity in the conduct of the *Manchester Guardian*. He divided the Ordinary shares, which of course carried the control, equally between himself, his son-in-law, C. E. Montague, and his two sons, Edward and John. An agreement was entered into between them that the share of any one who died or left the paper should be offered to the others.

The first of the four to leave the paper was C. E. Montague who retired in 1925. C. P. Scott waived his right to purchase, so the ownership then became: C. P. Scott, one quarter, E. T. and J. R. Scott three eighths each. On C. P. Scott's death on January 1, 1932, Edward and John became each half owners, and it became evident that some fresh agreement would soon be necessary. Discussion of this was in progress when, on April 22, 1932, Edward lost his life in a boating accident, leaving John the sole owner.

There was no lack of suitable colleagues with whom some new and similar agreement might be made, but grave difficulties in respect of taxation had emerged. In the first place the company had to contest a claim from the Inland Revenue for sur-tax on the undistributed profits. This was successfully met, but a red light had been shown. A greater threat, perhaps, to the desired continuity was the attitude taken by the authorities in valuing E. T. Scott's half-share for Death Duties. The *Manchester Guardian* at that time was running at a considerable loss, the *Manchester Evening News* at a corresponding profit. It was contended that to continue to publish the *Manchester Guardian* was a personal whim, and that almost any newspaper magnate in London would readily pay a very large price for the *Manchester Evening News* alone. As such offers were in fact frequent, and considerable, it was difficult to meet this contention. It was evident from these two happenings that the fiscal system was not adapted to accommodate a business run in such an unbusinesslike manner.

Protracted discussion with lawyers resulted in a scheme which seemed to give the best chance of permanence by ruling out the disturbing element of private profit and by preventing the possibility that a sudden death might force a total or partial sale. In 1936 J. R. Scott permanently divested himself of all beneficial interest and formed a trust to which all the ordinary shares of the Manchester Guardian and Evening News Limited were assigned. Dividends are paid to the trust and must be applied to furthering the interests of the newspapers.

Such a trust cannot be perpetual, so wide powers are given to the trustees to reconstitute the trust from time to time. The intention is that the period of each trust shall not be excessive, so that no considerable change is likely to have occurred in the personality of the trustees. While the trustees thus have vested in them the whole of the Company's Ordinary capital, they do not exercise control over the policy of the papers. Full editorial control is vested in the Editors, A. P. Wadsworth for the *Manchester Guardian* and J. C. Beavan for the *Manchester Evening News*, and business control in the Managing Directors, J. R. Scott and L. P. Scott, ultimate control remaining with J. R. Scott by virtue of his chairmanship of the Company and of the power which he retains to appoint and dismiss trustees. This ultimate control, now divorced from any financial interest, will pass in time into the hands of one or more suitable persons nominated by John Scott or, failing that, by the trustees. By this means it is hoped to continue surely into the future the traditions of independence and integrity established by C. P. Scott. The present trustees are:

J. R. Scott, Chairman and Managing Director.

L. P. Scott, Assistant Managing Director.

A. P. Wadsworth, Director, and Editor of the *Manchester Guardian*.

Sir William Haley, late Managing Director; now Director General of the B.B.C.

Sir Ernest Simon, late Director (1932–1938).

E. A. Montague, Director, and London Editor of the *Manchester Guardian*.

Paul Patterson, President of the *Baltimore Sun*, Maryland, U.S.A.

The presence of Paul Patterson in this body requires explanation lest it form the basis of a fresh rumour that American interests have acquired control! For many years before the war the *Manchester Guardian* had enjoyed the distinction, unique among British daily newspapers, of being forbidden entrance into Germany. In the anxious days of 1940 it was therefore confidently anticipated that if the worst happened all the British trustees would find themselves on Hitler's black list. Since the war this has been amply verified.

It seemed desirable therefore to appoint at least one trustee of higher survival value. For many years the *Manchester Guardian* had enjoyed most cordial relations with the *Baltimore Sun*—a paper kindred in spirit and independence—and with its publisher, Paul Patterson. He undertook to become a trustee in the hope, if need arose, of raising the standard once more after the flood had subsided. The trust deed was thereupon sent across the Atlantic, to be returned on July 26, 1946, when at a little ceremony in Manchester Paul Patterson handed back the document for custody in the *Manchester Guardian* offices.

No trust, however skilfully framed, can guarantee a newspaper's permanence. It must have a sound business foundation. It can be independent only as long as it is commercially successful. But, provided that it can maintain the confidence of its readers, attract a steady flow of new subscribers as old ones pass away, and strengthen its value for the advertiser as a means of contact with the public, there is a sound future for the serious newspaper even in the difficult conditions of modern production. That its circulation is now larger than at any time in its history and twice as large as it was in the early nineteen-thirties is some justification, at least, of the *Manchester Guardian's* efforts to keep its ownership and control independent of any outside interest or combine.

1831

ADVERTISEMENT OF A PATRICROFT SCHOOL

INDEX